Luigi Cossa

Guide to the Study of Political Economy

Luigi Cossa

Guide to the Study of Political Economy

ISBN/EAN: 9783744645478

Printed in Europe, USA, Canada, Australia, Japan

Cover: Foto ©Suzi / pixelio.de

More available books at **www.hansebooks.com**

GUI[DE]

TO

[T]HE STUDY OF POL[ITICAL ECONOMY]

BY

DR. LUIGI CO[SSA]

PROFESSOR OF POLITICAL ECONOMY IN T[HE UNIVERSITY]

TRANSLATED

FROM THE SECOND ITALI[AN]

WITH

A PREFACE BY W. STANLEY [JEVONS]

London:

MACMILLAN AND CO.

1880.

To Mrs. Fawcett

THIS VOLUME

IS WITH HER KIND PERMISSION

RESPECTFULLY DEDICATED

BY THE TRANSLATOR.

PREFACE

THE ENGLISH TRANSLATION.

To a reader fairly acquainted with the English Literature of Political Economy it will be evident why this translation of an Italian text-book has been undertaken. The sufficient reason is that no introduction to the study of Economics at all approaching in character to Professor Cossa's *Guida allo Studio dell' Economia Politica* is to be found in the English tongue. This work presents, in a compendious form, not only a general view of the bounds, divisions, and relations of the science, marked by great impartiality and breadth of treatment, but it also furnishes us with an historical sketch of the science, such as must be wholly new to English readers.

Every economist would grant that we have in English the works of the father of the science, Adam Smith, and of not a few successors or predecessors who have made the science almost an English science. But this fact, joined perhaps with the common want of linguistic power in English students, has led our economic writers to ignore too much the great works of the French and Italian economists, as well as the invaluable recent treatises of German writers. The survey of the foreign literature of the subject given in this *Guide* will enable the English student to fix the bearings of the point of knowledge which he has reached, and to estimate the fraction of the ocean of economic literature which he has been able to traverse.

Of course it is not to be expected, nor even to be desired, that English students of Economics should at once endeavour to master treatises in the French, German, Italian, and other languages. A few may be able thus to extend their studies; and it is believed that they will find in Dr. Cossa a safe pilot to the course of reading they may best pursue for their special purposes. The ordinary student must neces-sarily be contented with a second-hand and superficial acquaintance with the masses of literature here indi-cated. But it would be a mistake to treat such knowledge as worthless. The late Professor De Morgan said, or at least very happily repeated the saying, that "true education consists in knowing everything of something and something of every-thing." Applying this maxim to our science, the judicious student of Economics must necessarily select the works of Adam Smith, of Ricardo, of J. S. Mill, of Cairnes, or of some one or a very few leading

English economists, and must study them, so to say, completely. They will be the something of which he must learn everything. But, when this has been sufficiently accomplished, he cannot do better than learn the something of everything in economic literature, which is admirably given in this *Guide*.

One valuable result which will probably be derived from the reading of Professor Cossa's work is the conviction that the *historical method* must play a large part in economic science. Without for a moment admitting, with some extreme advocates of that method,[1] that there is no such thing as an abstract science of Economics, the student will readily become convinced that in such matters as land tenure, agriculture, the organisation of industry, taxation, &c., theory must be applied with very large allowances for physical and historical circumstances. National character, ancient custom, political condition, and many other conditions, are economic factors of great importance. Although some of our best English economists were fully alive to this fact, there is nevertheless an almost inevitable tendency to regard the complicated industrial organisation of England as if it were the natural and best organisation, to which other nations have failed, in a more or less serious degree, to attain. Wider study

---

[1] See, for instance, Professor Cliffe Leslie's Essay on the "Philosophical Method of Political Economy," in *Hermathena*, No. iv., 1876.

will show that economic as well as political and social development must bear relation to the historical and physical circumstances of the race. It is surely time to abandon the idea, for instance, that the landlord system of land-tenure of England, even supposing that it is the best for English agriculture, is necessarily the best for France, Belgium, Norway, India, Australia, Ireland, and the rest of the habitable world in general. In the fourth chapter of the First Part Dr. Cossa has very clearly refuted some of the prevailing errors on the subject of the historical method.

Now and again we meet opinions and expressions in the *Guide* in which it is impossible to coincide. On page 124 of this translation, for instance, the author speaks of "the notable advantages to industrial organisation and progress," which he thinks have been conferred in its time by the Protective System. Few, or probably no English economist, would now accept this opinion, unless with qualifications and explanations which would really reverse the writer's meaning. Nor is this, as we think, the only scientific or doctrinal blemish of the work. Yet after all exception is taken it must be allowed that the author has performed his difficult task in a most judicious and impartial manner.

As Dr. Cossa has passed over without mention most of his own economic labours, it should be stated that

he has been, since the year 1858, Professor of Political
Economy in the University of Pavia. During nearly
a quarter of a century he has devoted himself entirely
to the promotion and dissemination of economic science,
and not a few of the rising economists of Italy owe
their success to his instructions. Among his principal
works may be mentioned the *Primi Elementi di Economia Politica*, first published at Milan in 1875, of which
a fourth edition, considerably augmented, appeared in
1878. Spanish and German translations were printed
in 1878 and 1879. His second work was the *Primi
Elementi di Scienza delle Finanze* (1875), of which a
third edition is about to appear. Various essays on
economic subjects have been reprinted in a volume
under the title *Saggi di Economia Politica* (Milan,
1878).

The *Guida allo Studio dell' Economia Politica*, of which
the following pages contain an English version, was ori-
ginally published at Milan in 1876 ; a second revised
and enlarged edition being issued in 1878. A Spanish
translation was printed at Valladolid in 1878, and it is
said that a German translation by Dr. Edward Moor-
meister is to appear during the course of the present
year at Freiburg. The considerable use which is thus
evidently being made of Professor Cossa's text-books
will not surprise a reader who can appreciate the extraordinary extent and accuracy of Dr. Cossa's knowledge of the economic literature of almost all nations.

This characteristic of his works may be partly explained by the fact that he was in early life a pupil of that most learned and eminent economist, Professor Wilhelm Roscher. In England we cannot hope to compete with the polyglot learning of a Roscher or a Cossa, but it is to be hoped that not a few English students of economics, who are seldom polyglots, will use this translated *Guide* in order to make themselves a little less insular than they would otherwise be.

The work of translation has been carried out by a former lady student in one of the excellent classes of Political Economy, conducted under the superintendence of the Cambridge Society for the Extension of University Teaching. Acknowledgments are due to Professor Cossa for corrections and additions, which bring up the work to the present year.

W. STANLEY JEVONS.

PREFACE

TO

THE SECOND EDITION.

In publishing the Second Edition of my *Guide*, corrected and enlarged, more particularly in the later chapters, it is with much pleasure that I acknowledge the valuable suggestions and advice which have lightened my labours. Still more grateful am I for the services rendered by my excellent colleague, Professor *Mariano Mariani*, and by my distinguished pupil and friend, Dr. Feruccio Nicolini. The former took upon himself the task of correcting the manuscript and proofs, both of this and other works of mine, and the latter compiled the accurate *Alphabetical Index of Authors*, which makes the book much more useful to those who wish to study, side by side with the *Historical Part*, the original writings and sources of information pointed out in the text.

L. C.

PAVIA, *December 2, 1877.*

CONTENTS.

GENERAL PART.

CHAPTER I.

PAGE

DEFINITION OF POLITICAL ECONOMY 1

CHAPTER II.

DIVISION OF POLITICAL ECONOMY 11

CHAPTER III.

RELATION OF POLITICAL ECONOMY TO OTHER SCIENCES . . 20

PRIVATE ECONOMY 21

MORALS 22

HISTORY 24

STATISTICS 25

LAW 27

POLITICS 31

CHAPTER IV.

METHOD OF POLITICAL ECONOMY 33

CHAPTER V.

IMPORTANCE OF POLITICAL ECONOMY 51

CHAPTER VI.

EXAMINATION OF SOME OBJECTIONS WHICH HAVE BEEN
MADE TO THE STUDY OF POLITICAL ECONOMY 57

HISTORICAL PART.

CHAPTER I.

THE CONCEPTION, DIVISION, METHOD, AND SOURCES OF THE
HISTORY OF POLITICAL ECONOMY 73

CHAPTER II.

POLITICAL ECONOMY IN ANCIENT TIMES AND IN THE MIDDLE
AGES 85

CHAPTER III.

POLITICAL ECONOMY IN MODERN TIMES 108

CHAPTER IV.

THE POLITICAL ECONOMY OF THE PHYSIOCRATIC SCHOOL . . 142

CHAPTER V.

ADAM SMITH AND HIS IMMEDIATE SUCCESSORS 161

CHAPTER VI.

POLITICAL ECONOMY IN THE NINETEENTH CENTURY . . . 174

CHAPTER VII.

CONTEMPORARY ITALIAN ECONOMISTS 210

INDEX 231

GUIDE

TO

THE STUDY OF POLITICAL ECONOMY.

CHAPTER I.

DEFINITION OF POLITICAL ECONOMY.

In common language *economy* sometimes means frugality or thrift, sometimes a well-ordered system of things. This is the case, for instance, in such phrases as the economy of the universe, the economy of the human body. The name as thus used always implies the conception of order, proportion, harmony. On the other hand, the etymological meaning of economy (from οἶκος, house, and νόμος, law) is the law of the house, the government of the family, or else, though in a subjective sense, the science or art that treats of these matters. Again, in a somewhat more restricted sense economy may mean the management of the patrimony or of the wealth of the family. And when the adjective *political* (from πόλις, city or state) is added to the substantive, economy comes to mean the direction of the state,

B

or, here again in a narrower sense, the direction of its *wealth*, and is thus the counterpart of what is called by pleonasm *domestic economy*. Therefore in a subjective sense political economy might be either an equivalent of politics, the science of government, or else of the science of state finance.

Neither the ordinary nor the etymological sense of the word corresponds precisely to the conventional scientific meaning which is now generally attached to the phrase *political economy*. And in truth political economy ought not to be confounded with the doctrine of the state. By an extreme hypothesis it might exist apart from a state. Neither ought it to be confounded with the doctrine of state finance, because it is concerned not only with public but with all social wealth, whether public or private, individual or collective.

Political economy, or, as it is variously called, *public, social, civil, national* economy, the economy of *nations* and of *states*, &c., is *the science of the social ordering of wealth*, that which examines its *general laws* in order to deduce from them *guiding principles* for the wise administration of public and private wealth. In other words, political economy studies the social phenomena to which wealth gives rise, with the double purpose of investigating its causes and considering its relation to public and private well-being.

Political economy has an object in common with other branches of knowledge also called economic, and these form with it a more complex science which might be called simply *economy*, *economics*, or the science of wealth. But they are distinguished from one another by differences in the aspect under which they regard their *common subject-matter*, wealth. And in our days, the special point of view taken with respect to any given class of phenomena is the characteristic that distinguishes one science from another and determines the position of each in the encyclopædia of human knowledge, that indivisible unity which we from mere didactic necessity divide and subdivide, unable by reason of the imperfection of our intellect to grasp as a whole the complex existence of physical and moral facts.

Political economy must then be first distinguished from *domestic economy*, which studies wealth in its relation to the family, seeking for the best method of regulating the patrimony in the interest of the members who compose it.

Political economy must also be distinguished from *technology* in the wider sense of the term, meaning the application of physical and mathematical science to separate industries, enabling producers to carry them on more profitably. And it comprehends *agriculture* (and the branches of knowledge connected with it), *the technology of manufactures, commercial technology,* and *the science of those arts* called *liberal.*

Political economy is also distinguished from *industrial economy,* the science of the administrative organisation of industrial affairs in respect to the interests of individual employers.

Domestic economy and industrial economy, sometimes comprised under the generic term *private economy,* and technology in like manner, are distinguished from political economy in that they consider economic phenomena from a different and narrower point of view than the one proper to that science, which occupies itself with *general laws* and *social relations.* Private economy and technology, on the contrary, treat of *physical laws, technical processes* and *relations* which are merely *individual.*

Political economy, as a science which examines the social relations arising from wealth or from the economic activity of men united in civilised societies, is further connected with another group of sciences called *social sciences* because they investigate the natural laws of the formation and progress of civilised communities in general.

But political economy only studies society in its relation to wealth, and therefore cannot claim to include in itself all the social sciences, which treat of civilised life under its various aspects, having regard not only to economic matters but also to *physical, intellectual,* and *moral* considerations, which must be held of more importance than those purely material.

However, political economy does not differ from the other social sciences simply in having a narrower field of investigation, but also in its particular mode of regarding the object which is in part common to them all, that is, the social ordering of wealth.

Hence it should be distinguished from that part of *social morals* which on account of its subject might be called economic and which treats of the right use of wealth in the highest interests of man, looking at it therefore in relation to the influence it may have over human conduct, either as a means or an obstacle to that exercise of virtue which is the ultimate end of morals.

Equally necessary is it to distinguish political economy from that department of *civil history* which is occupied with economic facts and analogous institutions, studied in their chronological order and in their outward forms.

The narration and even the explanation of concrete manifestations, though always brought into connection with a particular class of phenomena, is a very different thing from the examination of the natural laws by which they are governed. It is, for example, one thing to relate the history of English commerce in the nineteenth century, and quite another thing to investigate the laws that explain in its intimate workings the economic function of commerce at all times and in all places.

Again, political economy must not be confounded with *economic statistics*, a branch of applied statistics which expounds in an orderly manner the facts relating to industries, presenting them in a form which sums up their total result, and stating them where it is possible in the exact language of figures. It treats of phenomena in their external form and in their variable and contingent manifestations, not of natural laws or necessary and constant relations. The statistics of prices during the last ten years in the market of London, or Hamburg, or New York, are a very different thing from the general theory of prices.

Finally, political economy must be clearly distinguished from those legal sciences which deal with economic facts and institutions, and which comprise the whole of *commercial custom* and the greater part of *civil law*. Both these branches of jurisprudence study the rights and obligations springing from economic facts, that is from the relations of debtor and creditor, whether in their correspondence with the immutable laws of justice (*philosophical law*) or as resulting from legisla·tion (*positive law*). Political economy, on the other hand, seeks for the primary causes of these same facts, and deduces from them general laws for the good guidance of public and private administration. It is one thing to examine the legal foundation of *private property* or its conditions in Italian law, another to determine its economic function, to show what are its advantages, its various aspects, and the necessary limits to it in the general interest.

From the definition of political economy already given results, not only its special *mode* of considering its subject, but also its *twofold office*, from which the exact nature of the science may be more clearly inferred. The *office* of political economy, or, as some would say, its *function*, is twofold, because it comprehends two fields of inquiry, each having special characteristics which ought to be accurately observed.

In the first place there is an economic *science*, in the strict sense of the word, which includes the explanation of economic phenomena and the examination of their causes and of their laws. This is the *pure science*, of which the object is to expound that which is, to explain *theorems*, to solve *problems*, and, as we shall see later, to construct theories by a mixed process of *deduction* and *induction*.

There exists also an economic *art*, an *applied* political economy, which from the knowledge of those natural laws which govern economic phenomena deduces *guiding principles* for the good management of public and private wealth, or in other words for the enlightenment of practice.

These two departments of economic *theory*, the *science* and the *art*, the distinction between which may be compared, as Mill says, to that between the *indicative* and the *imperative* moods, are yet strictly connected, the first being the foundation of the second, while the second in its turn increases the importance of the first, converting its *truths* into *principles* of useful application. They thus mutually support one another and in a manner complete one another, together tending to promote, each in its own way, directly or indirectly, the *common end of public and private prosperity.*

In logical order, science precedes art and art precedes practice, because people ought not to *act* without a *rule of action.* Neither can there be an infallible rule without full *knowledge.* In the historical order however the series is inverted; instinctive action is followed by an empirical art, and then comes the science which finally reconstructs the whole. Verses are made, instruments are played upon, illnesses are cured, houses are built, long before people become acquainted with the musical and poetic arts, or the sciences of medicine and architecture.

It should be noticed that the science of political economy seeks for what are called *natural* laws, not being, like *positive* laws, the result of human invention. They must nevertheless not be confounded with *physical* laws, as they have a *psychological* character, being subject to the influence of the free and intellectual element manifested in the human will. They are also called *general laws,* to distinguish them, according to what has before been said, from the *particular laws* and the *technical processes* of the different arts, which lie in the sphere of industrial economy and technology.

As to the applied part of political economy, it is well to observe that it enlightens the actions of private individuals in the same degree as that of public rulers. It is therefore incorrect to consider political economy, as some do, merely as an art pertaining to government, although it cannot be denied that the most important applications of the science refer to the management of public affairs. On the other hand, that reasoning seems exaggerated which would separate political economy as a science from its most useful applications, on the ground that the art of beneficially governing even the material interests of nations must be guided, sometimes in the highest degree, by considerations very different from those it suggests. For though this observation is without doubt most just, inasmuch as it tends to place in its true light the science and art of *public administration*, it does not afford any argument against the deduction of the principles of economic art from the laws of pure political economy. Indeed those writers, mostly English, as for example, Senior, J. S. Mill, and Cairnes, who argue for the absolute separation of the economic science from the art of government, are inconsistent with their own strict principle—*felix culpa !* to which we owe those admirable illustrations of the fundamental principles of economics to be found in the works of the said writers, and of others.

Having explained our definition of political economy, and specified its *subject*, its *point of view*, its *functions* and its *aim*, we will not here attempt a minute criticism of other definitions. From the great number of these definitions, almost equalling that of economic writers, such a criticism would be necessarily incomplete. Nor would its results compensate for the loss of time it would involve.

We will content ourselves with the observation that the greater number of such definitions err either by deficiency or by excess. Those definitions, for example, err *by deficiency* which state that either *value*, or *exchange*, or *commerce*, is the subject of the science. These are all facts of great importance, no doubt, but none of them sum up the whole class of economic phenomena. For the same reason those conceptions are erroneous, which either refer only to the *abstract*, or only to the *applied* part of economic doctrine.

But more frequently do definitions of political economy err by *excess*. Either they assign to it too wide a subject, as when it is stated that *political economy is the science of wealth* or of material interests, thus confounding it with *economy in general*. Or they confound it with *morals*, with *politics*, or with *law*, subordinating it to other sciences with the false idea of giving it added dignity and importance. Sometimes again they identify it with the entire *social science* or, as many now call it, *sociology*, which has, as we have already seen, a much wider subject-matter, and exceeds the limits of investigations relating only to wealth.

This disagreement, owing chiefly to the mania that some economists have for originality, is certainly deplorable, and is with reason lamented by our own Pellegrino Rossi. Inasmuch as it concerns the limits of the science it serves to alienate the respect of outsiders. Besides, the inconsistency is really smaller than would 'appear at first sight, it having been several times aptly remarked that such differences may often be reduced to questions merely of words. Whence it comes that the same questions are discussed in the same manner and with the same conclusions by writers whose definitions are incompatible. It is also undeniable that equally great discrepancies are to be found in the definitions of other sciences, on the importance and progress of which there can now exist no reasonable doubt.

The same remarks apply to the many phrases which it is proposed to substitute for the term political economy. Almost all these, and some in a higher degree, have the same fault of inexactness which is complained of in that term, while many of them could not obtain an easy acceptance among students. These circumstances make it inadvisable, in our opinion, to introduce innovations in the scientific language more generally in use, which is on the whole well enough adapted to our educational methods.

CHAPTER II.

THE doctrines comprehended in political economy may be distributed and arranged in different ways according to the principle upon which these distinctions are founded ; and they are of more or less importance in proportion to the service they render to an adequate treatment of the subject.

A distinction may first be founded on the nature of the special *function* of political *economy*. This is two-fold : it first investigates the *natural laws* of economic phenomena ; and secondly lays down *guiding principles* for the advantageous management of public and private wealth. Accordingly we have :

(1) *Pure, rational, abstract* political economy, the *science* in the strict sense of the word, which studies the economic order of things, that is the social relations arising from wealth, in and by itself. Its *immediate aim* is purely *speculative*, to discover the intimate nature and the various aspects of the mass of social facts, to investigate their causes, and to trace them to their general laws.

(2) *Applied* political economy, the economic *art*, which studies economic phenomena with the immediate aim

of providing safe rules for administration, or of direct-
ing economic institutions so that they may conduce
to the general welfare. Its aim is therefore immediately *practical*, since it does not investigate the *how* or
why of certain facts, but seeks rules for *doing* certain
things *well*.

Applied political economy is closely connected with
the pure science, as it necessarily presupposes it. Besides the identity of their ultimate aim (*the general well
being*), it is resolved by ultimate analysis into a series
of deductions drawn from truths discovered by rational
political economy. It is not possible to conceive of
ruling principles having any other foundation than that
of an exact and profound knowledge of the phenomena
to which they refer.

And here we must beware of confounding, as is often
the case even with men well acquainted with the subject,
the distinction between *science* and *art* with that, more
commonly discussed, between *theory* and *practice*. For
both science and art belong to the order of ideas and
exist in the sphere of thought, while practice signifies
either *action* or the *skill* acquired by it. The rules
for doing things in the right way, suggested by art,
lead up to and enlighten practice and prevent it from
degenerating into empiricism. But they cannot in any
way be considered identical with it, because they are
wholly ideal and speculative and hence belong no less
than the pure science to the domain of theory.

Another method of classifying the subjects of political
economy (connected with the preceding in many
respects, yet quite distinct from it), is based on a distinction which is made, more especially by German
writers, between :

1. Political economy in the sense naturally belonging to the word, or, as some would call it, *national economy*, which studies the social fact of wealth in its relations to the welfare of the *nation* considered as something different from and independent of the State, or the government to which it is subjected ; and

2. *State economy*, called also *economic legislation* or *economic politics*, which studies the phenomena of wealth in relation to the *economic action* of the State and of other political bodies.

Such action presents two orders of facts, because it may affect either the economic influence of social power on private wealth, or the management of that portion of wealth which specially constitutes the patrimony of the State, the Province, or the Commune. Hence *economic politics* is in its turn subdivided into two parts, namely : (*a*) *economic politics* in the strict sense, which directs the action of public powers with regard to private wealth, and (*b*) the *science of finance*, which sets forth guiding principles for the better administration of the public wealth.

But this science of finance can now be considered as totally distinct from political economy. It is even treated in separate works because of the increased amount and importance of its theories, and also because its principles are not deduced from the laws of pure economics alone. They are also derived from other sources of equal and in some cases of even greater importance, that is, from the principles of law and politics. And in the same way economic legislation draws its inspiration not only from economic maxims but also from those founded on the study of law and politics. It thus becomes a separate science, or rather a part of that other applied science of a more complex kind, the *science of public administration*, now being specially studied in Germany with the extensive and thorough investigation required by the subject.

We have said that the distinction between *political economy in its proper sense* and *economic politics*, is not equivalent to that between *pure* and *applied political economy*. The guiding principles furnished by the economic art refer to private no less than to public affairs. Thus, as has before been noticed, an economic art might exist on the hypothesis of a human society with no political constitution and no need of government, in which case there could of course be no such thing as economic politics.

Another quite different division of economic doctrine considers the various phases and stages, movements and aspects, presented by economic phenomena. It has its root therefore in the intimate structure of the organism of wealth.

On the ground of such considerations J. B. Say, one of the masters of the science, divides its subjects into the three heads of *production*, *distribution*, and *consumption*. He assumes these distinctions even in his definition of the science and in the title of his principal work (Traité, 1803). The *formation* of wealth, its *partition* among men, and its *destination* to the uses of life, present themselves naturally, and in that order, as the three principal aspects under which the movements of social wealth may be studied. This division has therefore been accepted by most economists, as, for instance, Gioja, de Tracy, Rau, and MacCulloch.

Other writers, particularly those of more modern date, add to these three heads that of *circulation*, or as some less accurately call it, the *exchange* of wealth. And the importance of those phenomena of which circulation is the result is indeed very great—phenomena relating to the removal of wealth from one *place* to another (*transport*) and from one *person* to another (*exchange*). These constitute a complete and interesting system, and merit separate examination. They should not be treated as a mere appendix to production (*v.* Say) or to distribution (*v.* Rau, MacCulloch). This arrangement has the support of many writers of authority, as, for instance, James Mill, Florez Estrada, Mangoldt, Messedaglia, and Nazzani.

Other writers, following in the steps of Roscher, add a fifth head, that of *population ;* but this proposal has, and we think with reason, had few supporters. For the important theories which have enriched the recent discussions on this subject have now reached such dimensions as to constitute by themselves an additional science, which some have already distinguished by the name of *Demography*, and others by that (which seems to us better) of *Demology*. Nor are there wanting treatises which embrace all the aspects of the problem of population. But it should not be forgotten that for economic purposes population is only considered in its relation to *subsistence*, that is, from a subordinate point of view, which makes it more fitly treated under the head of *distribution*.

Other innovations tend to simplify or variously modify the threefold division of Say.

Rossi, for example, considers *consumption* to be foreign to political economy, and to belong to *hygiene, morals,* and *domestic economy*, in so far as it refers to the *unproductive consumption of individuals ;* while he wishes

productive consumption, or in other words the employment
of capital, to be treated under the head of production.
The subject of taxation, which he reduces to *unproductive
public consumption,* can be treated under the head of distribution; his final conclusion being thus that *political
economy* should only be divided into the two heads of production and distribution.   This opinion was held in the
last century by Turgot, and among contemporaries is
supported by J. S. Mill in his *Essays* (1844), though
Mill's reasoning differs slightly from that of Rossi.

There are writers, also modern, who, though suppressing the head of consumption, add to the two given by
Rossi that of circulation referred to above.   We may
mention Mill in his *Principles of Political Economy*
(1848); after him A. E. Cherbuliez (1862), H. Fawcett
(1863), and Mrs. Fawcett, in her brief compendium
of her husband's work.

We think it better to retain *consumption* as a distinct
head.   If we take away the foreign matter which, as
Rossi justly objects, is sometimes brought in under
it, and if we take away the *science of finance* which
ought to be studied by itself, there yet remains a considerable body of doctrine which considers consumption
in its true economic function and with regard to its
influence on production and distribution, a subject of
the first importance.   And it should not be forgotten
that consumption, or in other words the practical application of wealth to the uses of life, is the end to which
all production tends.   Thus by giving it its due place
we take away the pretext of those enemies of political
economy who, as we shall see, reproach it with giving
its whole attention to products, regardless of the lot of
those who create and consume them.

We will finally touch upon two other modes of dividing political economy suggested or followed by other writers, but which for several reasons do not commend themselves to us.

The one, widely accepted and applying both to the science and the art, divides them both into two parts : a *general* part where economic questions are treated in relation to industry considered as a whole ; and a *special* part where they are examined in relation to the different industries.

This system has the defect of involving useless repetitions; it presents the danger of bringing into consideration special technical details (agricultural, technological, commercial,) foreign to the science. This is a danger which the most praiseworthy authors have fallen into, *e.g.* Rau, Roscher, Nazzani. It not uncommonly leads to the. consideration of phenomena which are common to all industries in sole relation to one industry, as in the subject of *grande et petite culture*, which is nothing but a particular case of production on a large and small scale. Real specialities of separate industries may either be brought in as examples, or explained in seasonable appendices to, or digressions from, discussions of general economic laws.

Others, and principally Ferrara, wish both the science and the art to be divided into the three branches of *individual, social,* and *international* economy, distinctions evidently suggested by the well-known division of jurisprudence into *private, public internal,* and *international* law.

This system incurs in a still greater degree than the preceding the dangers of repetition, for economic phenomena do not invariably present themselves in these three phases; besides, it tends to incorporate with political economy a great part of private economy. This was clearly perceived by an able pupil of Ferrara, Professor Reymond, who accordingly modifies the system of his master, by suppressing in his treatise the division of *individual economy*. But this is not enough; for there is no analogy between the sciences of political economy and law on which to found the division into social and international economy preserved by Reymond.

And in fact there do not exist from the economic point of view those wide differences between States which we observe in their legal and political conditions —differences which produce important modifications in their subordinate relations. The character of economic phenomena is to a great extent rather *universal* than *national*, while the matters discussed in what is called international economy, such as the questions relating to free exchange, commercial treaties, emigration and colonies, find their natural place under the head of the *circulation of wealth*.

It seems to us necessary in conclusion to draw attention to the true nature of these controversies on the division and order of treatment of the subjects included under political economy. It should be understood that any division whatever must be not only in a measure inexact but also arbitrary, since economic phenomena constitute in reality an undivided unity —an organism in constant motion and not a mere mechanism. On the other hand, science by didactic necessity must proceed with the help of existing analogies, must artificially arrest the motion of phenomena, must break them up into parts, and having separately observed these parts, must endeavour to form them again into an ideal unit which shall conform as nearly as possible to the real unit. Rossi has remarked that production implies productive consumption and even exchange, since most exchanges are effected for the purpose of production. This is a most true observation and one which might with accuracy be extended to other cases.

The value of the various divisions and sub-divisions mentioned in this chapter is a question rather of good arrangement than of intrinsic merit, while the divergences between these various writers are really much smaller than they appear at first sight. Those economists who do not admit the titles of consumption and circulation into their principal division of subjects treat it separately in appendices to other divisions of the science. See for example Mill, Courcelle-Seneuil, Cherbuliez, Rau and many others.

For the rest, we do not wish to deny the importance of such controversies, which, in so far as they result in the better arrangement and classification of the subjects of research and instruction, certainly help to make these subjects more readily apprehended.

CHAPTER III.

ON THE RELATION OF POLITICAL ECONOMY TO OTHER SCIENCES.

IN speaking of the limits of political economy we have already shown how it differs from other sciences which are yet akin to it in that they treat either wholly or in part of the same subject-matter. Those differences cannot do away with the analogies—nor hence with more or less close relations—between these sciences and political economy, relations and analogies which we propose in the present chapter briefly to discuss. At the same time we shall indicate the more recent and important works which deal, either with these relations at large, or with one or other of the said sciences in special connection with political economy.

Having first premised that these relations may be called either *passive* or *active* according as political economy receives or gives information, we will speak more particularly of the relations between political economy and :—

1. *Private Economy.*	4. *Statistics.*
2. *Morals.*	5. *Law.*
3. *History.*	6. *Politics.*

§ 1. *Private Economy,*

While political economy considers both wealth and the industries from which it arises in their relations to society and not in connection either with the conditions of the family or with technical processes, it yet not seldom receives valuable assistance from technology, and from private—more especially from industrial—economy. It is not able either to recognise the natural laws of social wealth nor to deduce from them wise administrative rules without first paying attention to the technical and economic conditions of separate industries.

This assistance is indispensable to political economy when it treats of the division and combination of labour, of machines, of money, of the means of transport and communication, of the formation, the scale, and the organisation of industrial enterprises, &c.

On the other hand political economy, explaining in the mass the general laws of the economic world which cannot with impunity be defied by individuals, throws the most useful light on private economy. The latter, thus finding its complement, corrects by enlarging the purely individual point of view which it *per se* naturally takes, especially in the department of industrial economy. For this reason some recent writers treat diffusely of such economic doctrines as are more closely connected with the principles of industrial economy and in particular with the doctrine of manufacture. The following works deserve special mention :

C. G. Courcelle-Seneuil, *Manuel des Affaires*, third edition, Paris, 1872.

A. Emminghaus, *Allgemeine Gewerkslehre*. Berlin, 1868.

M. Haushofer, *Der Industriebetrieb*, Stuttgart, 1874 (a more copious and complete work than the preceding).

P. Coq, *Cours d'économie industrielle*. Paris, 1876.

Ch. Laboulaye, *Économie des machines et des manufactures*. Paris, 1880. (Reproduction of the well-known work of Babbage.)

§ 2. *Morals.*

Although political economy is a science altogether distinct from morals, yet, especially in its applications, it is closely related to it.

In its applied part political economy is inferior in rank to morals, the supreme precepts of which ought never to be disregarded in the pursuit of mere economic advantage. In the progress of civilisation, wealth is simply a means to the attainment of the higher aim of moral improvement. Therefore in the event of partial conflicts between ethical and economic interests, the latter ought always to give way to the demands of the former. In dealing for example with the employment of women and children in factories, important considerations of a moral kind would justify the energetic action of social powers when economic reasons either do not demand or even distinctly discourage such interference.

We have used the expression *partial* to qualify these conflicts, knowing well that *general* or *permanent* conflicts between morals and economy cannot be imagined. They are rendered impossible by that consoling fact known to philosophers, the ultimate harmony of utility with justice and right. On these points we must beware of two opposite errors, that of necessary and fatal contradiction or antinomy (Proudhon), and the other error of expecting necessary harmony in the minute particulars of economic life (Carey, Bastiat, Ferrara).

But this inferiority of political economy relates only to its applied part, because with respect to the pure science, which seeks for the primary causes of economic and moral phenomena alike, there can be no question of preeminence. Political economy may even give the most useful support to morals, and one who is a Christian moralist and at the same time an orthodox economist has said with good reason that political economy is *the most powerful ally of morality* (Droz).

It does in fact provide a powerful practical argument to influence minds which are not open to conviction from philosophic principles and which have no strong inclination to obey the sentiment of duty. It points out the material advantages to be derived from the exercise of certain virtues, such as industry, foresight, thrift. Further, it makes clear the economic disadvantages of certain vices, such as idleness, improvidence, dissipation, and those still greater ones arising from social institutions repugnant to moral laws (slavery, serfdom, war, &c.).

Political economy rightly studied may thus help to correct the erroneous assertions of some moralists who, judging certain actions morally blamable, bring in false economic considerations to determine the degree of their culpability. One often reads or hears for example that *avarice* is a worse vice than *prodigality*, which may, it is said, be at least partly excused by its beneficial economic effects. As a matter of fact, from the purely economic aspect of the two vices, it is more

correct to say that the lying idle of a certain portion of
wealth is a less evil than its absolute destruction. (On
this point see Clément, *Dictionnaire de l'Économie
Politique—Introduction*, pp. xxiii., xxiv.   Paris, 1853.)

In the last twenty years this very delicate question
of the relations between morals and political economy
has been much discussed, especially in elaborate monographs called forth in the competition for a prize
offered by the French Academy of Moral and Political
Sciences (1857).

We will enumerate the chief of these, with the warn-
ing that in some of them the just balance is not held,
while they recommend as a step in scientific progress
the absorption into political economy of a great part of
ethics, which would in reality be a most undesirable
retrogression.

These are the titles of some of them :—

H. Baudrillart, *Des Rapports de la Morale et de
l'Économie Politique.*   Paris, 1860.

A. Rondelet, *Du Spiritualisme en Économie Politique.*
Paris, 1859.

H. Dameth, *Le Juste et l'Utile.*   Paris, 1859.

M. Minghetti, *Dell'economia pubblica e delle sue attinenze colla morale e col diritto.*   Florence, 1859, 2nd ed.,
1868.   This is a thoughtful work, which adds to its
many intrinsic merits that—too rare in Italy—of an
elegant and correct style.

§ 3. *History.*

Political economy studies the general laws by which
economic facts are governed, while history chronologi-
cally traces the successive development of these facts.

The one is concerned with necessary, the other with contingent matter. And yet it is undeniable that the former science obtains the most important information from the latter, which, as already remarked, is one of its main sources, making clear the laws of economic phenomena in many difficult cases. Even when history does not fulfil this function of completing theory, it yet supplies most useful illustrations of principles otherwise discovered.

On the other hand, political economy gives the history of economic institutions the most powerful support by guiding the choice, co-ordination, and appreciation of facts which would otherwise be entirely inexplicable, or at least could not be comprehended in their full importance.

Contemporary historians appear to be now more fully aware of this, as they give greater attention to economic facts, and strive to qualify themselves for a more sufficient explanation of them by studying the principles of political economy. The works of Grote, Mommsen, Macaulay, and Thiers, are a convincing proof that this is the case.

See Baudrillart's *Prolusion* to the course of lectures given by him in 1864-5 at the Collège de France. (*Journal des Économistes.*)

§ 4. *Statistics.*

The connection of statistics with political economy is analogous to, though closer than, that of history. Statistics are an orderly exposition of social and hence also of .economic facts, summing up their total result when possible in the exact language of figures.

Though not the only means, as some pretend, yet statistics are of the utmost importance in the discovery of economic truths, and in all cases they provide very useful materials for illustrating the theories and applying the doctrines of political economy.

For this reason political economy has profited much by the new direction given lately to statistical science by Quetelet, Guerry, Dufau, Engel, Wagner, Oettingen, Knapp, Lexis, and many others, to whom we Italians may add the illustrious names of Messedaglia, Lampertico, Morpurgo, Bodio, and others who follow in their steps, holding the high place in fame which in another period of the science has been duly awarded to the writings of Gioja and Romagnosi. But at the same time it must not be forgotten that conversely statistics cannot dispense with the support of political economy, which gives the necessary light for the choice, the comparison and the criticism of its data.

And this close bond between the sister sciences is in no way loosened by those imperfections of statistics about which we hear so much on all sides just now, and which are very often exaggerated by the epigrams of the half informed and the prejudices of the vulgar. Such people forget the really eminent services already rendered by statistical investigations and the still greater ones which may be expected from them.

Among the compendiums of *theoretical statistics* which come up to the present state of the science, we may note :

M. Haushofer, *Lehr und Handbuch der Statistik.* Vienna, 1872. (A diligent compilation.)

M. Block, *Traité théorique et pratique de Statistique.*

Paris, 1878, 8vo. (German translation by H. v. Scheel. Leipzig, 1879.)

A. Gabaglio, *Storia e teoria generale della statistica.* Milan, 1880. (Undoubtedly the best work on *statistical method.*)

Among the many treatises of *applied statistics*, it will be enough to name the best known :

G. F. Kolb, *Handbuch der vergleichenden Statistik*, 8th ed. Leipzig, 1879.

And . another, more exact, sober and really *comparative* :

H. F. Brachelli, *Die Staaten Europa's.* Brünn, 1876. 3rd ed.

§ 5. *Law.*

Notwithstanding the differences already mentioned between the legal and economic points of view, consisting in the fact that the science of law confines itself to tracing the sphere of competence which justly belongs to different individuals, yet none the less strong is the link which binds political economy to the different branches of public and private, rational and positive law.

It being impossible in an elementary book to go deeply into such a delicate subject, we will content ourselves with some passing remarks by way of illustration.

I. *International public law.* Political economy points out in a positive manner the material advantages to be derived from an equal adjustment of international relations. It also shows the bad effects of wars and of the old systems of isolation founded on political and commercial hostility, as for instance the *mercantile*, the

prohibitive, the *protective*, and the *colonial* systems.
Thus where wars are inevitable it tends to moderate
their fierceness, proclaiming the principle of respect in
war for private property. This principle is admitted
more in the theory, yet to a certain extent also in the
practice, of modern international law.

And here we may observe that the utilitarian nature
of the arguments put forward by political economy gives
them a peculiar efficacy, so that we may be permitted
to hope with Scialoja that *international justice* may
be one day established as the *outcome of economic
calculation*.

II. *Constitutional law.* The connection existing between the wise political ordering of States and the
economic prosperity of citizens sufficiently explains
the kind of assistance mutually rendered to one another
by political economy and constitutional law. The first
demonstrates how the best economic consequences result
from a set of truly liberal institutions ensuring the
pacific and orderly development of all the elements of
social progress. The second proves the no less important
influence which the wise direction of public economy
exercises over the right adjustment of constitutional
laws. As a proof of these truths it may be seen how
often subversive ideas with regard to economics and
politics are joined in a pernicious alliance which can
only be broken by the rapid diffusion of sound principles
in both the sciences.

III. *Administrative law.* Political economy gives a
sufficient number of principles for the formation of a
good administrative system, without which any constitutional law whatever, however wisely framed, would
be but a dead letter. On the other hand, a well-directed

administration sometimes succeeds in curing the many
evils of a corrupt political constitution.

Indeed it must be noticed that political economy provides secure rules either for the establishment of an
administration or for wisely carrying on one already
existing. This sufficiently proves the necessity for a
study of economics as the basis of a study of administration, though it does not justify the practice of those
writers on administrative law who fill their books with
economic digressions, with the hope of hiding their
want of that positive knowledge which ought to be the
primary qualification of such treatises.

IV. *Civil law.* The connection which binds civil law
to political economy is soon perceived, if we reflect that
the greater part of the doctrines constituting the first
have an essentially economic object, as is the case
with theories which concern *property* and other [1] *real
rights,* such as *hereditary successions, pecuniary engage-
ments and contracts,* &c.

Civil law is of use to political economy in making
known the legal relations originating in various economic transactions, while political economy helps to
give a true and complete notion of many institutions
of which civil law only analyses the external form.

Thus, for example, it is easier to understand fully the
legal distinction between *barter* and *buying and selling,*
when it is perceived that these contracts are economically identical, differing merely in form. And it must
also be observed that economic progress has contributed
to the reform of many clauses in modern civil codes.

---

[1] This term, restricted in English law, has in Continental law
its literal meaning—*all rights over things,* as distinguished from
personal rights. ·

It is enough to mention the now almost general abolition
of restrictive laws on the rate of interest, the many
innovations in the system of hypothecation, the radical
changes in lease-contracts, &c.

Therefore the question of the relations between the
two sciences has been in our time the subject of more
or less subtle and accurate researches. In these many
illustrious Italian writers have taken part, among others
Valeriani and Romagnosi, and somewhat later Rossi,
who in 1838 made a critique of the French civil code.
Still later Minghetti, in the book cited above, treated
ex-professo of the relations between economics and
jurisprudence.

Among foreign writers Rivet deserves praise as the
author of a work entitled :

*Des Rapports du droit et de la législation avec
l'économie politique*, Paris, 1864.

And Dankwardt, who illustrates with much ingenuity
though with obvious exaggeration the influence of economic ideas on certain institutions of Roman law.

H. Dankwardt, *Nationalökonomie und Jurisprudenz.*
Rostock, 1857 et seq.

V. *Commercial law.* In commercial as in civil law,
the jurist studies the legal relations arising from particular institutions (*partnerships* and *companies, instruments of credit, banks, insurances,* &c.), while the economist determines their functions and their social effects.
Thus the progress of political economy has no little influence, especially in our own times, on the development
of jurisprudence and commercial legislation. For example, Einert's book, propounding a legal theory of
the bill of exchange founded on its modern economic
functions, contributed largely to prepare the way for the

German law of 1848 which marked a new epoch in the history of the legislation of *bills of exchange.*

And for this reason some contemporary jurists make frequent use of economic theories to explain the true nature of the institutions of commercial law.

In Germany, for instance, Prof. W. Endemann has done so in his book : *Das deutsche Handelsrecht.* Heidelberg, 1865 (3rd ed. 1876).

With wider and more profound research, Prof. L. Goldschmidt gives us a fine illustration of the advantages to be gained from political economy in his classical work entitled *Handbuch des Handelsrechts.* Erlangen, 1864, et seq. (2nd ed. 1874).

In Italy, Vidari is following in the same line in his *Corso di Diritto Commerciale,* which he has already begun to publish. (Milan, U. Hoepli, Vols. I.-III., 1877-79.)

§ 6. *Politics.*

With politics, the science of good government based upon the principles of social utility, political economy has both passive and active relations. On the one hand it receives from politics more general notions about the rules of government and the nature of civil institutions. On the other it provides indispensable maxims to *economic politics,* a most important branch of the *science of public administration.* For the general principles of politics we may consult among more recent works :

Waitz, *Grundzüge der Politik.* Göttingen, 1862. (Very brief but good.)

Esquirou de Parieu, *Principes de la Science politique.* Paris, 1870. 1 vol. 8vo. (2nd ed. 1875).

J. C. v. Bluntschli, *Politik als Wissenschaft.* Stuttgart, 1876. 1 vol. 8vo.

For *administrative science* in particular :

Theod. D. Woolsey, *Political Science ;* or, *The State Theoretically and Practically Considered.* London, 1878, 2 vols. 8vo.

L. v. Stein, *Die Verwaltungslehre,* 1865 et seq., 7 vols. 8vo. This is a very important work of colossal size, but incomplete and not free from errors. The author most usefully completed and abridged his work in his *Handbuch der Verwaltungslehre.* Stuttgart, 1876. 1 vol. 8vo. (2nd ed).

Among Italian writers we must not forget :

G. Manna, *Partizioni teoretiche del diritto amministrativo.* 2nd ed. Naples, 1860.

C. F. Ferraris, *Saggi d'economia, di statistica e di scienza dell' amministrazione.* Turin, 1880. (Very learned and remarkable essays).

CHAPTER IV.

§ 1.

BY *method* we mean the logical process by which truth is discovered (*i.e.* the *inventive* method) and by which it is communicated to others (*i.e.* the *demonstrative* or *didactic* method).

The study of the inventive method (method in its strict sense) is of the first importance, not only in philosophy but also in the special sciences, where it is often neglected. The didactic method has a purely educational value.

Notwithstanding that the general doctrine of method belongs to the sphere of logic we will touch on it briefly here, in order to render intelligible the many lively controversies which are constantly going on about the method best suited to political economy. And first to explain the distinction between the deductive and inductive methods, which constitute two poles logically opposed.

In the *deductive method* (synthetic, rational, *à priori*), certain general principles being given which are self-evident or known by immediate intuition, the

D

consequences comprehended in them are deduced by a connected chain of reasonings. It thus proceeds from the general to the particular by the help of pure reason, and with no external aid. It is an exact method, leading to certain results, provided that the premisses are true and sufficient, and the deductions correct.

The *inductive method* (analytical, empirical, à *posteriori*) is founded on the observation of certain phenomena; and by means of abstractions stating their analogies and differences, it seeks to discover the laws by which they are governed. It proceeds therefore from the particular to the general with the help of what is called inductive reasoning—reasoning, that is, which is based on experience. It is a less rigorous method than the deductive, and leads to results which in relation to truth are merely more or less probable, it not being possible to arrive by it at absolute certainty.

According to the different uses of these methods we have *deductive sciences*, *inductive sciences*, and sciences which are *partly deductive*, and *partly inductive*.

The purely deductive or exact sciences in the strict sense are specially the mathematical sciences, and in part only the philosophical sciences. Thus they include *arithmetic, algebraic analysis, geometry,* and in fact every branch of abstract mathematics.

The exactness of mathematics is owing firstly to the use of deductive reasoning; and secondarily to the use of a *symbolic language (ciphers, letters, geometrical figures).* This is superior to common language, both from its brevity and elegance and because it indicates all the logical operations which have been performed in the reasoning, thus facilitating the discovery and the correction of such errors as may have marred it. And here we must beware of confounding the accessory (the symbols) with the principal, since it is quite possible to apply ordinary language to mathematics, though we thus lose in brevity and elegance.

Purely inductive sciences are to be found among the physical sciences, which, having until now remained in a purely descriptive stage, are consequently little more than mere generalisations of phenomena. Such, for example, are *geology* and *meteorology*, notwithstanding their recent notable advances. Among social sciences, we have *statistics*, which, although it makes use of what is now sometimes called *mathematical induction*, has not yet passed beyond this first stage.

Sciences partly *inductive and partly deductive* are those which, having found their general principles by means of induction, proceed deductively to discover the consequences of these principles, with the frequent use of calculation. The more advanced physical and natural sciences belong to this group, as for example *chemistry*, *physics*, *mechanics* and *astronomy*. Such sciences, inductive in their beginnings but subsequently reaching the deductive stage, may in a wide sense be called *exact sciences*, in addition to abstract mathematics, which is, as has been seen, purely deductive.

But here we ought to make another distinction, important in itself, and also because it helps people to avoid errors into which they may fall if they follow literally certain nomenclatures, frequent enough in common usage, but somewhat incorrect.

Those sciences which are founded on observation and induction, and which some authors loosely and vaguely call *experimental sciences*, are really divided into two classes according to their very different modes of observation.

These are :

1. *Sciences of observation* (in the strict sense), which study certain phenomena as they naturally present themselves, without subjecting them to any modification. And among these again those sciences in which observations are only made by means of the unaided senses are to be distinguished from those in which it is possible to make use of *instruments of precision*, as *astronomy, meteorology,* &c.

2. *Experimental sciences,* which unite with simple observation the use of *experiments* properly so called, consisting in the artificial production of phenomena with a constant varying of conditions. So, for example, physics and chemistry owe the greater part of their progress to the possibility of experiments, in other words observation carried to a greater degree of perfection.

§ 2.

The method proper to the social sciences, these being as a whole younger and less advanced than the physical or mathematical sciences, is still a much controverted point, and more or less profound disputes still take place, on their logical character, on their nature as deductive or inductive sciences, and on the possibility of applying experimental investigation to them. These disputes rarely lead to any results, being often raised without sufficient philosophic preparation, and especially by dilettanti, who at the least excuse digress from the field of letters into that of the social sciences which they lightly consider as belonging to them.

As we cannot here enter into a discussion of the method to be applied to the social sciences in general, we will name some works which, together with Mill's *System of Logic* and Whewell's *Philosophy of the Inductive Sciences*, treat at large of this subject.

Sir George Cornewall Lewis, *A Treatise on the Methods of Observation and Reasoning in Politics.* London, 1852, 2 vols.

P. A. Dufau, *De la Méthode d'Observation dans son Application aux Sciences morales et politiques.* Paris, 1866.

§ 3.

The controversy on method also rages continually in the special field of political economy. While some hold it to be wholly or in great part a deductive science, others, mostly more recent, call it an inductive science and a science of observation; they consider that until now it has advanced by experiment. Finally others think that it is both deductive and inductive. The difficulty of the question obviously exists only with regard to rational political economy, since no one can reasonably doubt the capital importance of observation and induction to the applied science, and still more to practice, or to effective application in concrete cases.

It appears to us that in the inquiry as to the method best adapted to political economy we must take into account the nature of the science itself, to which the method must necessarily be accommodated, as well as the method successfully followed by the great masters who have helped to construct the science; and finally the analogies, existing up to a certain point, between political economy and some other sciences, mostly physical, the methods of which have now reached a certain point of perfection.

This view is expounded by Cairnes in a profound and too little known monograph, from which we have drawn largely in the present chapter.

J. E. Cairnes, *The Character and Logical Method of Political Economy.* London, 1857. (2nd. ed. 1875.)

Let us turn our attention to the method that has been effectually followed in the discovery of the greater number of those truths, which, even in treatises professing to hold different views as to method, are expounded in nearly the same way. We shall arrive at the inevitable conclusion that the most firmly established theories, and especially those relating to circulation and distribution, the most important and difficult points of the science, are without doubt discovered by the deductive method, starting from a few premisses, sometimes explicitly declared but more often tacitly understood, which may be reduced to the following statements :

1. In the economic order of things the principal motive of human actions is *individual self-interest.* This induces man (a) to avoid pain (fatigue, work); (b) to desire pleasure (wealth) ; (c) hence, to aim at obtaining the greatest amount of wealth with the least amount of labour, or in more general terms, the greatest result with the least effort, which is, as it is now expressed, the law of least resistance.

2. The earth, indispensable to man as a place in which to live and work, and as the source whence he may extract food and raw materials, is naturally limited, (a) in the products which it contains; (b) in

iv.] ON THE METHOD OF POLITICAL ECONOMY. 39

its actual extent; (c) in its relative fertility (different qualities of soils); (d) in its successive fertility (decreasing productiveness at a certain point with every new application of capital and labour).

3. The physical and psychological tendencies of man lead him to multiply his own species with a rapidity which, if it met with no obstacles, would bring about an unlimited increase of population.

From these three premisses, bearing respectively a physical, physiological, and psychological character, the three important theories of *value, rent,* and *population* are derived. Of these, the two first are specially deduced from the first and second premisses, while the last is founded on the second and third. It is therefore impossible to appreciate the scientific consistency of that portion of political economy which rests on deductions from those premisses, without a previous examination of their logical value.

Such an examination convinces us that these propositions result from facts, either of themselves positive and certain, or at least susceptible of strict proof. Indeed it is almost needless to state that the first and third propositions are known by intuition, since they affirm tendencies which we find in ourselves and which are inseparable from our nature, while the second premise may be verified by experience. The fact that instead of an unceasing application of fresh capital and labour to soil of the best quality, cultivation extends to lands of inferior quality, at once proves that there is a natural limitation to the fertility of cultivated land, which is just what is affirmed by the second proposition.

If we then take into consideration only the premisses

from which political economy starts, we shall find that
these premises are certain, either because they are
immediately intuitive or because they may be directly
and strictly proved. We must conclude that in this
sense political economy is more a positive science than
even mathematics, of which the definitions and axioms
are often of a hypothetical character, and still more so
than the most advanced physical sciences, which are
obliged to find their premisses by means of the most
laborious inductions, with no possibility of subjecting
them to direct proof.

It is necessary, however, to add that the said premisses, however true, are incomplete and insufficient
when compared with actual phenomena. For example,
individual self-interest is not the only motive of human
action, even in circumstances of an economic character.
Sympathy, charity, custom, patriotism, more or less
modify or sometimes even paralyse the action of individual interest. The laws of value, of wages, of
emigration, are often affected by the action of these
causes, and of others not taken into account in the
ordinary economic assumptions. In the same way
the progress of agriculture and of those sciences on
which it is founded, tend up to a certain point
to counterbalance or at least to delay the results of
the limitation of land. Sometimes egotism and sometimes foresight co-operate with other circumstances to
temper the force of the principle of population. To
recapitulate :—Economic deductions, starting from just
premisses and proceeding by correct reasoning, lead us
to conclusions which are scientifically true, and which
assume the character of laws. These laws however
have a hypothetical character, because they express

the tendency of certain causes to produce given effects on condition of the absence of certain other causes, which cannot like the former be discovered by *à priori* calculation, and which the science considers as *disturbing elements.*

But the hypothetical nature of its conclusions does not place economic science in an inferior position to the physical sciences. These are also for the most part obliged to limit themselves to stating laws which are merely hypothetical, and inconsistent with actual phenomena, though this inconsistency is no proof of the inaccuracy of scientific investigations. For to illustrate, the actual motion of a projectile presents neither uniform and perpetual motion nor perpendicular accelerated motion nor the perfect parabola, and yet it cannot be cited as a proof of the falsity of the respective laws of motion, gravity, and resistance.

But what does without any doubt demonstrate the inferiority alike of political economy and the other social sciences, compared with the physical sciences, is the fact that in the latter disturbing causes can be eliminated, while in the former this process is not possible. The economist, if he wishes to proceed inductively, is almost always reduced to the simple observation of extremely complicated facts, which are very often the result of agents either hidden or incommensurable. In the sphere of political economy, the practical experiment of the legislator and administrator is the only experiment possible, and that, from the nature of its subjects, must necessarily be restricted within extremely narrow limits and conducted with great caution.

And this inferiority of political economy, in comparison with the more advanced physical sciences greatly exceeds the advantage it possesses in being able to avoid for the most part the lengthiness of the inductive method in the establishment of its fundamental principles. Sir G. C. Lewis has shown this very well in the excellent work cited above. And yet there are many in our days who affirm decidedly that political economy should be reckoned among the experimental sciences.

The hypothetical nature of economic deductions,— founded on premisses which, although true, do not take into account those exceptional causes which modify phenomena in various ways,—necessitates, so to speak, a supplementary use of the inductive method. While observing actual facts, this method tries to discover the disturbing causes, themselves capable of classification and, though variable, obeying laws which up to a certain point are constant.

In other words, the inductive and deductive methods —observation and reasoning—must be combined, with the twofold aim of obtaining a concrete proof of laws found by deduction and of finding some explanation of the probable causes of the variation of phenomena. Such observations, whether for the purpose of proof or of discovery, are either made directly by the economist, or are found collected and more or less elaborated and arranged in *historical* and *statistical* works. Statistics, as some have truly said, has by its recent advances, become a new instrument of political economy.

It must be remarked that these results of the inductive process, if they are well ascertained and refer to a sufficient number of phenomena, serve to modify the original premisses of political economy and hence also its further deductions, thus following in the path constructed by the physical sciences. For the rest, although we thus find our conclusions in stricter accordance with facts, we run the danger of diminishing the scientific exactness of our arguments and the logical value of their results.

To sum up in a few words the conclusion of this investigation which, from its nature, has been somewhat dry and abstruse. Political economy, although a science in great part deductive from its mode of discovering its more general principles, is yet also an inductive science. This is the case not only when it seeks for rules to be practically applied, but also when it undertakes the practical proof of principles deductively found. Induction is also essential to the discovery of new principles, especially of those relating to production, for which, as Mangoldt truly observes, the deductive method is absolutely useless.

So that, as Messedaglia remarks, the question of method in political economy resolves itself into a question of limits. But we will permit ourselves to add that it is none the less complicated and delicate on this account, as is proved by the errors of those who, with little knowledge of the proper use either of deduction or induction, allow themselves to be led away by false and superficial analogies to place political economy among the experimental sciences. Carey, a meritorious economic writer, gives abundant examples of the strange confusions into which those may fall whose ideas as to the method of a science are ambiguous.

§ 4.

Connected with our present subject is the question of the application of the calculus and of mathematical language to economic doctrines. This is not a question of method, as some have erroneously supposed, but simply of the convenience of applying to our science the figures and symbolic forms which are frequently found useful in purely deductive sciences, and in those mixed sciences which have reached the deductive stage. We must limit ourselves to a few observations, such as our absolute incompetence in this branch of knowledge will allow of.

In the first place political economy is not, nor can it ever become, an exact science in the sense of being able to present in all its departments subjects fitted for mathematical calculation. For it is not, as we have already remarked, a purely deductive science, and its premisses are not capable of exact quantitative determination (*weight, number, measure*). They often relate to incommensurable quantities, so that their conclusions cannot always be marked by mathematical exactness. The use of the most delicately adjusted scales has brought quantitative chemical analysis to the highest degree of perfection; the crystallographer can determine the geometrical forms of bodies left to their own intrinsic power of aggregation; but it is certain that political economy can rarely produce such exact results. We know indeed that a diminution in the supply of grain as a rule increases its value in a proportion more rapid than that which would correspond to the actual deficiency of produce; we know, that is, that if the harvest of this year is half that of last year, it is probable that its price will be more than double. But we cannot à *priori* determine the amount of this increase, because it is influenced by other causes than the amount of harvest, and these defy all attempt at measurement. Among such causes are the intensity of the need for food, the variety of products that may serve for the satisfaction of that need, the greater or less disposition to abstain from other expenses and to make use of other foods; and more than all, perhaps, the greater or less fear of starvation, which depends not so much on the actual supply as on the opinion as to that supply held by the mass of consumers, and the effect of this opinion cannot in any way be precisely determined.

Hence those economists err who believe, or affect to believe, that political economy is nothing else than an application of mathematics, and that in time it will be reduced to this.

Notwithstanding, within certain limits and in treating of exactly appreciable quantities, we may apply mathematics to the economic science. At least its symbolic language may be found most useful for the abbreviation and development of certain complicated theories, and for the illustration of certain doctrines by hypothetical cases. For such purposes algebraical symbols are superior to numerical figures, so lengthily and tediously made use of by Ricardo, Ferrara and other able economists. This method has been followed with more or less success by Cournot, Thünen and his critics (Knapp, Brentano, Schuhmacher), and by Whewell, Mangoldt, and Fauveau, not to mention older and in general less correct writers.

We will leave others to judge whether or no this

method has led to the discovery of any important theory by which the scientific inheritance of political economy has been increased. For ourselves we do not think so.

Among more recent writers who are inclined to give a mathematical direction to political economy, may be cited: W. Stanley Jevons, *The Theory of Political Economy*, London, 1871 (2nd edition, revised and enlarged, with a bibliography of mathematico-economic writers, 1879) : L. Walras, *Élements d'Économie politique pure*, Lausanne, 1874. Independently of one another, these writers arrived at almost identical results in the *theory of exchange*.

The following writers do credit to this new branch of mathematics : J. D'Aulnis de Bourouill, *Het inkomen der Maatschappij*, Leiden, 1874 ; G. Boccardo, *Dell' Applicazione dei Metodi quantitativi alle Scienze economiche*, &c. (Preface to vol. 2 of 3rd series of the *Biblioteca dell' Economista*, 1875.)

§ 5.

About thirty years ago, a controversy which had already grown old in the science of law began among the German economists and spread to those of other nations. It arose between the *historic* and *philosophic schools*, relating not to method but to another and no less important question, namely, whether there are in political economy absolute and general truths, or whether there are only partial and relative principles capable of application only under certain conditions of time, place, and civilisation.

Hildebrand (in 1848), Knies more explicitly (in 1853), and at the head of all, Roscher (in 1854) propounded and largely developed the principles of the historical school. In France Wolowski, Roscher's translator, and in Italy Cognetti de Martiis (*Delle Attinenze tra l'Economia sociale e la Storia*, Firenze, 1865), and Schiattarella (*Del Metodo in Economia sociale*, Naples, 1873), declared themselves followers of it.

A few remarks will here suffice as to the tendencies, merits and defects of the so-called historic school, for which we have made much use of Messedaglia's brief but for the most part excellent criticism on the same subject.

In law the historic school recognises no rational principles of absolute and universal validity (a philosophy of law), but only admits the existence of law as the organic product of the national conscience, that is, a positive law. So in political economy the new school denies the existence of absolute principles and of ideal types to which the economic government of states may be conformed. It recognises only a *national economy* peculiar to each nation and period, and thus confined to the particular *physical, ethnical* and *historical* conditions of a nation and its stage of civilisation. The supposed general principles are merely erroneous and incomplete abstractions of the conditions and circumstances prevailing in the country to which their author happens to belong. And so the genuine historical economist ought to content himself with describing the various stages of economic civilisation and finding the principles and applications proper to different periods.

But we may observe on the other hand :

1. That we must not confuse the *truths* of *pure science* with the *principles* of *applied science* or of art.

The former are for the most part absolute and universal.
The latter are always contingent and particular, since
in order to apply them to concrete cases we are obliged
to take into our calculation those varying conditions
of time and place the consideration of which is not
peculiar to the historic school.   For instance, to
propound the theory of free exchange is not to deny
that there are temporary means which must be made
use of in order to apply that system wisely to countries
which have long been subject to protective duties.

   2. That though the circumstances of *time, place,*
and *civilisation* are of their nature changeable, we
ought not to forget that certain natural tendencies of
man and of society were, are, and always will be the
same.   The constant changes taking place in the instruments of war, and in military constructions generally,
cannot be cited as a proof of the impossibility of *military
tactics* and *strategy.*   In the same way the varying
economic conditions already mentioned do not by any
means prove that there are no *natural* laws of *value,
wages, profits, &c.*

   3. That to reduce political economy to a mere
narrative of facts is to destroy its most practical
functions, and erroneously to declare it unfitted to
provide *general rules* for the appreciation and guidance
of economic progress in its various phases.   Nor will
the analogy of the natural sciences, often quoted in
support of the new doctrines, really serve this purpose, since *organic* no less than *inorganic nature* has
its general laws.   And to Roscher's remark that the
food of the infant will not serve the full-grown man,
Messedaglia answers conclusively that the nutritive
functions are the same in both, and that the object of

the physiological science is to determine the laws by which these are governed.

Nevertheless the historic school has rendered itself in many respects most useful to the progress of political economy. Indeed it has given the signal for a salutary although somewhat excessive reaction against the exaggerations of the pure idealists, or, as they are generally called, the doctrinarians, who, even when they were dealing with the applications of the science, were too regardless of actual circumstances. The historic school, and especially Roscher, its distinguished head, has enriched the science with most useful *historical, geographical* and *statistical illustrations,* and with a very ingenious analysis of the known characteristics of the various periods of economic civilisation. Finally it has provided excellent materials and a strong impulse for the construction of a history of *economic institutions* and *theories,* which had been much neglected before, and which would not only enlighten us concerning the *past,* but give us a better knowledge and understanding of the *present,* and even guide us in our building up of the *future.*

Just as Hugo, Savigny, Niebuhr, Mommsen, and their followers have given us valuable works on the *history of Roman law,* so Roscher and some of his pupils have published accurate works on the *history of political economy.* It will be enough to mention the historical works of Roscher, which we shall have occasion to cite further on.

We may then conclude that political economy ought to keep the mean between excessive *idealism* on the one hand and a somewhat antiquated *positivism* on the other. It ought to give the past its due weight and to

E

enlighten the future. It ought to recognise the necessity
for temporary expedients no less than the universality
of certain scientific principles, and hence to perceive
that the narrow point of view of the historic school
must lead to errors.   It will suffice to compare the two
first volumes of Roscher's *system*,—essentially in accordance with the views of more orthodox economists,
—with the books of the ablest followers of the so-called
philosophic school.   We shall thus be convinced that
the many excellent illustrations set before us in his
work have not been able to effect any substantial modification of the general principles taught in Germany
itself by Hermann and Rau.

CHAPTER V.

WHAT has been said in the preceding chapters as to the definition of political economy, its divisions, its proper method and its relation to other sciences, will have already given an idea of its *importance*. In speaking especially of this subject, let us remark that this importance arises from the nature of the *subject-matter* of which it treats, from its general *point of view*, from the *function* which it exercises, and from the *aim* of its inquiries.

Hence it may be inferred that political economy has a twofold importance; *theoretical* with regard to the *pure science* and to the usefulness of the knowledge it gives; *practical* with regard to the *applied science*, and the advantage which may be drawn in public and private life from the guiding principles which it points out.

The pure science of political economy has a large general utility, because it constitutes an indispensable element of wide and solid culture, which cannot be attained without competent knowledge of the laws governing the social ordering of wealth. That complicated and very interesting mass of phenomena,

E 2

constituting one of the most important factors in the growth of civilisation and one of the most notable elements in the life of human societies, ought certainly not to be unobserved or imperfectly understood by those who profess to be cultivated and civilized persons. And such knowledge, at all times very useful, has become in our days almost a necessity, owing to the present constitution of political affairs and the great transformation which all social institutions have undergone. We should remember also the increased importance of the economic element, which has now become the principal basis of political power, in place of elements, independent of the possession of wealth, which prevailed in former times.

Wherefore the study of political economy ought to enter in due proportion into the courses of instruction of every educational institution, and should not be limited merely to those industrial and professional establishments where it is taught with a view to immediate application. Indeed we cannot understand why those youths who are instructed in the laws of physics, chemistry, natural history and geography, should be allowed to remain ignorant of all that relates to social life, and particularly of economics.

The special importance of a thorough knowledge of political economy to students of history, law, and politics is self-evident. The information it gives is indispensable to the complete understanding of many of the facts belonging to these sciences. This may easily be gathered from what we have said before on the relations between political economy and the sciences in question.

With regard to its applications the study of political

economy has a great *practical importance*, both *general*
and *particular*, and in *public* as well as in *private*
life.

And first we will remark that economic laws exercise
a general and irresistible influence on all men considered
as members of civil societies. It is therefore to their
own interest to make at least an elementary study of
them, both that they may procure the advantages to be
derived from a knowledge of them, and still more that
they may avoid the irreparable misfortunes which arise
from their transgression.

Political economy further tends powerfully to enlighten the people on the true causes of many economic
disturbances, which they are apt to consider as arising
from the actions of certain individuals or certain classes
of society. It thus helps to dissipate popular prejudices, which, spreading and taking deep root, would
become a danger to public tranquillity. As for instance
the vulgar opinion concerning the influence of *bakers* and
corn-merchants on *famines*, or the action of *bankers* and
stockbrokers in *monetary crises* and times of *bad credit*.

In private life a knowledge of political economy is
specially needed by *employers, capitalists*, and *labourers*.
Indeed employers and capitalists should possess not
only the technical knowledge necessary for the carrying
on of the special industry with which they have to do,
but also a large amount of general economic information.
This will enable them to follow the right course in the
actual conduct of undertakings, as well as in their
choice and organisation of them. It may even enable
them to avoid failure in the struggle with more experienced and better informed competitors. A thorough
knowledge of the state of the market, the wise arrange-

ment and application of the elements of production, the buying of raw material, the most advantageous sale of the manufactured articles, are all critical points of industrial management, in which the diligent study of economic laws will be found of great use.

In like manner such a study, though merely elementary, would be most useful to common labourers. It would help them to understand the true nature of their interests and the just way to obtain them compatibly with due respect to the rights of others. From political economy they may learn the utility of capital, its true economic function, the necessity of labour, of providence, of saving, the laws of wages, the misfortunes that almost always arise from idleness, the usefulness and conditions of success of savings-banks and the like institutions, of co-operation, &c. The competent instruction of labourers in political economy, imparted in a popular form, besides the said advantages would secure to society the incalculable benefit of freedom from many crises and other dangers. It would form a rampart against those subversive doctrines which are too often published, and which find an easy access into the uncultivated minds and excitable fancies of the working classes.

With regard to this subject it may be remarked that the small diffusion of the fatal errors of socialism in England as compared with France, may be in a great measure traced to the greater propagation of sound economic doctrines in the former country, while in the latter very little has been effected in that useful direction.

Nor certainly is the study of political economy any less important for those who take an active part in the direction of public affairs, especially under the forms of government prevalent among civilized nations in the present day.   Above all are those persons interested in attaining accurate economic knowledge who have any sort of position in the deliberative assemblies and consultative bodies of the state, the province, or the commune; such as the senators, the deputies, the provincial and communal councillors, the councillors of state, and the members of the various councils and permanent or temporary committees and commissions which aid the respective ministers in projecting laws to be discussed by the national representatives.   And since the laws and provisions made by these bodies almost always concern, at least indirectly, the economic interests of the state and of individuals, so it is clear that these cannot be good if their originators are altogether ignorant of the *leges legum* of public economy.   Is it not indeed probable that the wastefulness of certain commercial administrations, which has in our days grown to a point beyond everything blamable, may be at least in part attributed to a false view of the action of economic laws, arising from the want of the necessary scientific preparation?

The organs of executive power also, or, more explicitly, the officials whose business it is to superintend the application of financial, administrative, and judiciary laws, are more or less interested in the study of political economy.   They are called upon to administer or superintend public and private affairs of a more or less complicated kind, or to decide controversies in which there is almost always some economic element.

We may observe in conclusion that in a free country public opinion, manifesting itself legally by means of the press and by the exercise of the rights of association, combination, and petition, has a strong influence on political and administrative action. It follows that there is no cultured and patriotic person who cannot in some way, however indirectly, have an influence in the government of the commune, the province, and the state. Hence it is most important that such persons should not neglect a study which alone can make that influence conduce to the general welfare.

CHAPTER VI.

THERE are many who, not appreciating rightly the arguments given in the last chapter, do not recognise the importance of political economy and are averse to its being studied. These persons, in different ways and with different objects in view, have waged a somewhat furious war against it. Some declare it to be an *impossible* science; others hold it to be at the best *useless;* others finally condemn it for many reasons as *dangerous.* A separate examination of the principal objections of this nature will show that they all lead to absurdities :

Whately, *Introductory Lectures on Political Economy.* London, 1831.

F. Ferrara, *Importanza dell' Economia politica.* Turin, 1849.

J. Kautz, *Die National-Oekonomik als Wissenschaft.* Vienna, 1858, pp. 423—442, and the authors referred to there.

The most radical objection, resolving itself into a denial of the existence of any theory of political economy, is that which asserts that there is no basis

for its solid construction as a science.   It is attempted
to prove this in two ways.   Some, reasoning *à priori,*
say that political economy *cannot exist ;* others, following
the *à posteriori* method, say that it *does not exist.*

The first observe that facts of the industrial class are
of their nature complicated and changeable, because they
depend partly on very different local circumstances (such
as country, climate, &c.), and partly on the free will of
man modified by education, habits, opinions and prejudices.   This makes it impossible to study and to
estimate them correctly.   Phenomena so variable and
interests so complicated cannot have constant laws nor
be referred to invariable principles.

It may be answered that the complication and change-
fulness of social facts in general, and of economic facts in
particular, in no way exclude similarities and analogies
between certain effects nor their recurrence on the repetition of certain causes.   These prove that economic phenomena as a whole form a wise and well-ordered organism.
For the same reasons anatomy and physiology are not
rendered impossible by the fact of physical dissimilarities
between individuals, or of the constantly recurring effects
of disease.   It ought then to be clear that variations
in particular cases do not prevent the existence of
general laws of value, price, wages, interest and profits.
For the rest, even the variations and perturbations of
the economic organism succeed one another with a certain
regularity and present even in their anomalies something normal which obeys constant laws.   Among the
medical sciences we have *morbid anatomy* in addition to
normal anatomy, and *pathology* in addition to *physiology,*
both describing the organs and functions of the human
body in a state of disease.   So in political economy we

have a theory of *perturbations* (*e.g.* famines, monetary and commercial crises, &c.) which is a necessary complement to the theory of the normal development of economic functions.

Those who are satisfied with a merely empirical demonstration of the non-existence of political economy cite in support of their position :

1. The *hypotheses* on which it is founded ;
2. The *abstractions* which it uses ;
3. The *problems* which it leaves unsolved ;
4. The *disputes* which it fails to settle.

As to the said hypotheses, we can at once reply that this is not the case with the whole science. It results from what has already been stated in discussing its method, that many economic principles are deduced from truths which are either self-evident or susceptible of strict proof by means of observation. We may add that hypotheses, when they are not arbitrary, may be the instruments of most valuable scientific discoveries. · Those that are wholly gratuitous and irrelevant will always be found to have originated with some incompetent exponent of the science. For the rest the history of the physical and mathematical sciences teaches us that, though they are truly called positive sciences, many of their theorems rest upon purely hypothetical bases, and many which were once held to be axioms are now called in question.

If we have no *abstractions*, no analyses, no formation of genera and species, but content ourselves with the mere verification of individual cases, we can have no science, but only a barren empiricism. Grammar, logic, algebra, law, also make use of abstractions, which are not only useful but indispensable. And if abstractions, like everything else, can be abused, both in political economy and the other sciences, that is not a valid reason for repudiating the science. *Abusus non tollit usum.*

Unresolved problems may doubtless be met with in political economy and every other branch of knowledge. Some of these are insoluble, *e.g.* the squaring of the circle, the trisection of angles, perpetual motion, &c. Others may possibly be resolved in a more advanced stage of scientific progress. It would be strange to abandon a branch of science because some of its phenomena must remain unexplained, and because the explanation of others has not yet been found.

Further, that reasoning is obviously absurd which would argue the non-existence of political economy from the fact of the interminable controversies of its students. It ought especially to be considered :

1. That such disputes refer for the most part not to the pure science but to its applications. This we shall see to be a natural and inevitable result of the hostility of those private and collective interests which political economy seeks to conciliate and bring into order ;

2. That such disputes are more apparent than real, and touch more on form than on substance. Indeed, if the disputants treated each other with more consideration and good faith, there would be some chance of their cessation ;

3. That these disputes are often about points of minor importance ;

4. That we must not charge political economy with the unreasonableness of some incompetent writers who insist upon calling in question truths which have long since been clearly proved ;

5. That it is scientific disputes and reasonable doubt, very different in their nature from systematic scepticism, which reanimate sciences and lead to the attainment of new and fertile discoveries. And here it may be generally remarked that scientific controversies in their various more or less useful forms are not peculiar to the social and economic sciences. They have arisen, and always will arise, in sciences as to the existence of which there can no longer be any doubt, at least among men of moderate culture. For the rest, though it is true that such controversies attest the imperfection of the science, yet they also prove its perfectibility and prepare the way for its future progress.

There are other classes of enemies to political economy, who do not dispute its existence but its usefulness, and this with great violence and in two different ways. Some say that the truths which it teaches are wholly irrelevant; others that it is possible to acquire the knowledge it gives, independently of any scientific study, by the sole aid of common sense and individual experience.

The former class attempt to prove that it is useless, upon the following grounds :

1. The small importance of its *subject-matter ;*

2. The simplicity of its *premises ;*

3. The negative character of its *conclusions.*

The answer to the first objection is easy. The man of science cannot fail to find a worthy object of investigation in the providential laws which govern the economic world, and which are no less wise and admirable than those which govern the physical world. The importance of such questions becomes more evident when we consider the close connection between moral and material welfare, the first of which cannot be considered by anybody as a subject unworthy of scientific speculation. It will be enough to mention the relation between *poverty, ignorance* and *crime.* Of these three social evils the first, which is also an economic evil, is often a cause of the other two, or at least a circumstance which accompanies and aggravates them.

As to the *simplicity of the premisses* from which political economy starts, with its definitions of utility, wealth, production, &c., we may observe that it is necessary for every science to be founded on simple and well-known conceptions in order that it may proceed by degrees to the unknown and the complex. It is the legitimate boast of political economy that it is able with such humble principles to arrive at results of vast importance to the general well-being. And who, we ask, would argue against the usefulness of geometry, because it begins by defining a point and a line, and proceeds to deduce all its theories from the so-called axioms?

For the rest we should not forget that in the social order apparently the most simple conceptions contain elements for the solution of the gravest and most formidable problems. Ferrara has well said that the idea of value differently understood may lead either to the affirmation or the negation of the right of property. Again, in a still higher sphere the abstract ideas of monarchy, liberty, and nationality, differently interpreted, have been the causes of centuries of war and revolution. In the *Dialogo dell' Invenzione,* Manzoni has proved in an astounding manner how the apparently simple ideas of Rousseau led by degrees to the terrible actions of Robespierre !

It is equally false to adduce the negative character of economic conclusions as a proof of the uselessness of the science. These conclusions are considered by many, and not only by enemies but also by friends of economic studies, to be summed up in the famous but misunderstood and misapplied formula of *laissez faire et laissez passer.*

We may reply by the following remarks :—

Political economy does not only establish principles but also seeks for laws. All its principles are not of a negative character. Some which are really negative, as *laissez faire,* are not admitted in their whole extent by the actual science, but are circumscribed and restricted by considerations which demand careful study. Finally the negative character of a principle or of a precept does not always take away from its importance. On the contrary, to point out the evil effects of certain laws and institutions, the abolition or at least the reform of which is counselled by political economy, is very useful in the abstract and most necessary in the concrete.

The opposition of economists to restrictions on manufactures, to monetary alterations, to official tariffs regulating prices, wages, interest, &c., was certainly most useful, although it almost always aimed at limiting or entirely abolishing the intervention of public authority in certain departments of economic affairs. The passionate resistance of exclusive interests and inveterate prejudices to the carrying out of such measures proves of itself that these wholly negative reforms were anything but ineffective.

The latter class of enemies have little ground for their arguments. They contend that *common sense* and *individual experience* can take the place of economic science, and lead with less trouble to the same or even better results. This *sophism*, connected with the common assertion of the disagreement of theory and practice, is reproduced at every turn in opposition to the study of all branches of moral science and even of the most unpretending technological sciences.

When we compare *theory* with *common sense*, that is, an ordinary capacity for understanding and doing things, and with *individual experience*, that is, the experience acquired in repeatedly doing certain things or seeing them done; when, again, we consider that practice is founded on a certain amount of knowledge empirically acquired by ourselves and by those who help us in our doings, we must conclude that theory resembles practice in being derived from observation and reason. It differs, in that it is the systematic result of the experience of generations, and the fruit, as has been said, of the genius of nations. Practice must of necessity be founded on fewer and less accurate observations and on reasonings less perfect and exact. Therefore to set up practice against theory is as much as to say that the less is equal to the greater, or that the part is larger than the whole. In short, the whole question lies between more or less study, between a mastery of the complete science and that half knowledge which powerfully affects the intellect of so-called practical men, who profess to be totally emancipated from the dominion of theory.

But if on the one hand practical experience cannot take the place of science, it is not the less true that science in its turn is insufficient without the aid of practice. It is only a knowledge of the real applications of the principles of the science that can safely

guide the man of practical action.   It is therefore needful to hold ourselves aloof equally from the so-called
doctrinarians, who refuse the assistance of practice, and
from the *empiricists*, who obstinately close their eyes to
the light of theory.   The pure science explains phenomena
and determines laws ; the applied science gives guiding
principles which practice brings into conformity with
the innumerable varieties of individual cases.   More-
over practice is indispensable because in its absence the
art, in attempting to go beyond its own sphere of *general
principles*, tends to degenerate into *a system of casuistry*
which must be *theoretically superfluous* and *practically
incomplete*.

Economic studies meet with still stronger opposition
from a numerous class of writers who, giving little or
no attention to the question of the soundness of economic science as it exists or to the best way of acquiring
economic knowledge, maintain that the doctrines of political economy are highly *dangerous* both to the individual
and to society, owing to their effect on *religion* and
morality.   This opinion they deduce from :

1. The nature of its subject-matter, which is wholly
material and worldly, *i.e. wealth ;*

2. The sordid character of its point of departure,
i.e. individual self-interest ;

3. The *irreligious opinions* of some cultivators of the
science and their merely *utilitarian morality ;*

4. The intrinsic *immorality* of some of its theories,
as for example those on the *interest of capital*, on
population, on *charity*, &c.

These accusations, we must observe, are often made
with the best intentions and in perfect good faith,
though they are the result either of false reasonin

or of an insufficient knowledge of the true nature of
the science. But we hope to reassure those who, though
desirous of entering upon this study, do not wish to
endanger convictions of a deeper and more important
nature than economic knowledge.

To begin with the material nature of the subject-
matter, we may remark that political economy regards
social phenomena from a purely economic point of
view. Scientific progress cannot be made without the
division and separation of the various sciences. Where
shall we now find the physicist, the chemist, the
naturalist, or the philosopher, who will deny that the
physics and the natural history of to-day are sciences,
because their subject-matter is more circumscribed than
that of the *physics* of Aristotle, the *natural history* of
Pliny, and the *science* of Thales?

We must remember therefore that to limit the field
of investigation of any particular science does not imply
the depreciation, much less the negation, of others, of
which the greater general importance may still be
recognised. Hence, though the economist does not
occupy himself with the attributes of God or with
the supreme principles of morality, his teaching cannot on this account be called irreligious or immoral.
Who has ever thought of condemning as atheists the
mathematician, the technologist, the anatomist, or the
physiologist, because they write volumes in which it
would be hard to find the name of God?

Certainly that economist would be most blameworthy
who should teach that the attainment of wealth is the
one or even the principal end towards which the individual and society ought to direct their activity. And
such a proposition would never be laid down by a

competent exponent of the science. If a strategical writer were to declare war to be the ideal of civil life, or if a writer on physiology were to maintain that man is born only to digest, these equally absurd and immoral statements could not affect the two sciences respectively professed by them.

Again, for many reasons the objection to individual self-interest as a material point of departure is no less invalid.

In the first place *pure political economy* does not invent but merely describes the action of economic laws and their causes. It cannot be denied that the human will is powerfully influenced by self-interest, *i.e.*, the desire for pleasure, the dislike to pain, the tendency to do the least amount of work that will satisfy wants. But it is not the less certain that political economy did not create self-interest nor the abuses to which it may lead. It must not be forgotten that the pursuit of utility, though it may lead to immorality and disorder when it is the supreme motive of human activity, has its proper and legitimate sphere in such economic questions as involve a choice between different modes of action, all morally right. To study the consequences of self-interest, to determine the effect of those actions, moral or otherwise, which in the economic sphere result from that most powerful impulse, does not in the least imply the proclamation of the principle of utility as the only foundation of morality. The economist is no more responsible for the abuses of selfishness because he studies the action of self-interest, than the physiologist is for those of *intemperance* because he studies the laws of nutrition.

Further, it is altogether false to accuse political

economy of encouraging selfishness and an inordinate desire for riches by promoting a bad use of them. Without entering upon the domain of morals, it shows by its arguments that economic evils arise from self-interest when, degenerating into selfishness, it creates *monopolies,* or in other words when the wealth of some producers is gained to the injury of the majority of consumers, *i.e ,* of society at large.

It is well to repeat that political economy, as it has, like other sciences, its special subject-matter and its special aim, has also its special point of departure, which does not conduce either to the negation or depreciation of those premisses upon which other social sciences are founded. It studies certain human actions arising from a principle which is confined within certain limits, and tending also to an object of a limited character—*i.e.*, the attainment of wealth. At the same time it fully recognises the fact that there are other and nobler motives of human action, and more important ends for which man ought to strive in order to attain to the greatest possible perfection of his faculties.

Neither can a valid argument against the science be found in the *irreligious opinions* of some economists, and their wholly utilitarian morality. It is true that several economists, and some of these among the most illustrious, enunciate here and there in their writings propositions which from the moral and religious point of view are blameworthy. But it is also true that such opinions have a purely subjective character and are not bound up with the essential nature of the science. In this respect, the cases of Say, an avowed unbeliever, and Droz, a sincere Catholic, are noteworthy; their economic views and teaching being in accordance. If then we take away the unorthodox passages and those that savour of Benthamite morality from the works of Say, they might gain in morality, but their economic teach ing would remain unaltered.

As to the pretended *intrinsic immorality* of some economic theories, and specially those relating to *interest*, *population*, and *charity*, it will suffice to remark that political economy :

1. Without encouraging *usury*, which is justly condemned by ethics, shows the absurdity and futility of laws forbidding and restricting the receipt of interest on capital ;

2. Points out the dangers that may arise from a *partial excess* of population, and hence counsels *providence*, subject to the supreme dictates of morality ;

3. Points out the *inconsistencies* and *abuses* of certain forms of *charity*, which give help haphazard, without recognising on the one hand the religious and moral obligations of true charity, nor on the other the advantages, some of them of an economic kind, attending a system of relief wisely directed to counteract the *causes*, and not merely to mitigate the *effects*, of *want*.

It is then a false idea that political economy while searching for truths in its own sphere of investigation may find itself opposed to truths of a more elevated kind, which have been arrived at by a different method and with a different purpose. But it is true that it has its own independent sphere, and that it does not propose to itself the direct function of laying down the principles of morality and religion. Therefore it cannot be really affected by such accusations, especially as it has never occurred to anybody to make them with regard to mathematics and other sciences which do not enter upon the ground of theology or ethics.

There is a final group of enemies to political economy who condemn it as *politically dangerous*. This accusation is formulated in two different and contradictory propositions; political economy is declared:

1. By the one group to be an *enemy* of the principle of authority, favouring the absolute *non-intervention* of the state in economic matters;

2. By the other to be an enemy of *social progress* and a supporter of the existing *inequalities* in the economic organism.

To the accusation of the first we reply, to begin with, that truth as such is never dangerous, and that it is necessary to distinguish the conclusions of the science from those hastily put forth in worthless and superficial doctrines. And further the limitation of the economic functions of the State, when affecting matters altogether outside its natural and legitimate sphere of competence, does not in the least weaken, but rather strengthens, the principle of authority, by giving it a true position and assigning to it reasonable limits. And it should be observed that economists, and especially those of to-day, do not propound it absolutely, but with the necessary modifications, and with due regard to conditions of time, place, and civilisation, and to precedents of all kinds.

It is strange indeed that political economy should be considered *hostile to authority* and at the same time *favourable to socialism,* as if the very essence of socialism were not the desire to substitute *authority* for *liberty,* and as if socialists had not declared themselves the fiercest enemies of modern economic science.

Finally, in replying to those who contend that political economy is opposed to beneficial reforms, and is the primary cause of social inequalities, we remark :

1. That, in its *rational part*, as we have already several times asserted, it does not invent nor create, but observes the natural laws of certain phenomena; it does not occupy itself with *that which is* nor with *that which ought to be*, but rather with that which is *constant* and *necessary*, thus bearing an unchangeable relation alike to the *present* and the *future;*

2. That, in its *applied part*, the principles that it propounds are decidedly favourable to *wise reforms*, and only opposed to certain thoughtless and ill-timed changes, which would cause the ruin of civil institutions;

3. That political economy cannot be the cause of social inequalities, which have existed apart from its influence. Indeed this influence has never hitherto been so powerful nor so universal as some seem to think;

4. That with regard to *natural inequalities*, these are the inevitable result of differences in the habits and customs of men; hence they are a useful factor in true social progress. In any case, to condemn political economy because there are the poor,' the idle, the avaricious, and the dissipated, is like accusing anatomy of creating blindness, lameness, and deformity;

5. That if we turn to *artificial inequalities*, the offspring of privilege and corrupt political institutions, we shall find that political economy has never ceased to attack them, and that to it may in part be ascribed those reforms through which such institutions are gradually losing ground where they have not altogether disappeared.

In short, it seems to us that the strong aversion to
the theories of political economy shown both by the
laudatores temporis acti, and by those who with little
modesty call themselves the *men of the future,* may be
considered as an indirect proof, if others were wanting,
of the great usefulness of political economy.[1]

[1] On the subjects treated in this first part, besides the already
mentioned works of Whately, Cairnes, Kautz, &c., the following
may be consulted :—

N. W. Senior, *Four Introductory Lectures on Political Economy,*
London, 1852.

E. Pickford, *Einleitung in die Wissenschaft der Politischen
Oekonomie,* Frankfort-on-the-Main, 1860.

v. Mangoldt, article "Volkswirthschaft," in vol. xi. of the
Deutsches Staatswörterbuch. Stuttgart, 1869, p. 97—126.

v. Hermann, *Staatswirthschaftliche Untersuchungen,* 2nd ed.
Munich, 1870, p. 1-77 of the reprint of 1874.

F. Lampertico, *Economia dei Popoli e degli Stati. Introduzione.*
Milan, 1874.

John K. Ingram, *The Present Position and Prospects of Political
Economy.* London, 1878.

Th. Ed. Cliffe Leslie, *Essays in Political and Moral Philosophy.*
Dublin, 1879.

E. Nazzani, *La Scuola Classica d'Economia Politica.* Milan,
1879.

HISTORICAL PART.

CHAPTER I.

THE CONCEPTION, DIVISION, METHOD, AND SOURCES OF THE HISTORY OF POLITICAL ECONOMY.

P. Rossi, *Introduction à l'Histoire des Doctrines économiques.* In the *Journal des Économistes,* Vol. II. (1842), p. 201—223. (Preface to a historical course given by Rossi during the last years of his teaching at the *Collège de France.*)

Giovanni Bruno, *Sull' Origine dell' Economia sociale, o Teoria della Storia di questa Scienza.* Palermo, 1854, 8vo. (The object of the work is to prove that political economy, as a science, did not exist until after the rise of Christianity.)

H. Baudrillart, *De l'Histoire de l'Écon. polit.*—In the *Journal des Écon.,* Vol. V. (3rd. series), 1867, p. 57—75. (Treating of the method, the characteristics, and the usefulness of a history of political economy.)

The *History of Political Economy* is an explanatory narrative of the origin and development of economic theories considered in connection with social institutions.

It follows from this definition that such a history should not be confined to a mere chronological exposition of the various doctrines held by successive generations. It should also take upon itself the higher task of determining their absolute and relative worth. Taking these different theories singly, it should investigate their origin and growth and observe them as they manifest themselves in disconnected and isolated forms, so that it may be able to build them up into a distinct and consistent system of science.

Further, as to the relations between economic theories and social institutions, we must draw attention to the fact that these are of two kinds.

In the first place writers are almost always influenced, though in different degrees, by the circumstances, ideas, and peculiar institutions, either of the country and period to which they belong, or of some other to which they have specially given their attention. The power of such influences is often not suspected, or even flatly denied, by those who are subject to them. They make unfounded pretensions to philosophic impartiality, which is, in the nature of things, impossible. In fact, if we turn to the essential points of the different theories, and if we eliminate peculiarities of an incidental kind in order to compare these theories with the external circumstances preceding or accompanying their growth, it will be easy to discover in them an underlying aim. Either they *apologise* for certain economic institutions of which the author approves and, so to speak, idealises, or they *attack* certain other institutions of which he does not approve, laying down principles opposed to them. Bacon's saying with regard to certain philosophers may truly be applied to most economists, that they *tamquam e vinculis ratiocinantur.*

In the second place it cannot be denied that these writers in their turn exercise remarkable influence on the opinions of their age and of posterity; influence which leads the way to, and sometimes directly inspires, legislative and administrative reforms of great moment. Among examples of such influential writings, the most memorable is the system of Adam Smith, a powerful factor in the almost complete renovation of economic institutions which began at the end of the last and the beginning of the present century.

In spite of these mutual influences, the history of economic theories ought not to be confounded with the history of economic institutions. They comprise two distinct orders of research, which, though they are both integral parts of the history of political economy in its wider sense, yet have each their proper sphere of competence. Hence the arguments of Blanqui and his followers are incorrect. They deduce the antiquity of political economy from that of economic institutions, thus obviously confounding the science with the objects of its investigations. To assert that where exchanges, money, and taxes exist, economic science must exist also, is equivalent to asserting that astronomy and physiology must have begun with the motions of the stars and the phenomena of breathing and eating.

The history of political economy, considered as a *scientific whole*, comprehends :

1. The *external* history, which narrates the origin and development of economic theories and of the

various economic systems considered as a whole; touching also on their more salient points, without descending to particulars.   It is either:

(a) *General,* when it takes in all periods and nations ; or

(b) *Special,* when it is limited, in time and space, as for example to one epoch, or nation, or system, or to one or two writers ;

2. The *internal* or, as some say, the *dogmatic* history, which studies the formation of particular theories (*e.g. value, money, rent*), and which is often treated as an introduction or complement, in connection with their scientific exposition.   The materials of such a history are scattered abroad in a multitude of monographs. Among authors of general systematic works who have gathered together, within certain self-imposed limits, much interesting information of this nature, Wilhelm Roscher undoubtedly holds the first place.

W. Roscher, *System der Volkswirthschaft.*   Vol. I. Stuttgart, 1854 (14th ed., 1879).   Vol. II., 1860 (8th. ed. 1875).

The purpose and the dimensions of this *Guide* will only allow us to give a *summary of the external history,* accompanied by the indications necessary to lead to a wider and more profound study.

For the convenience of exposition we will divide the external history into three periods :

1. The period embracing *antiquity* and the *middle ages,* which merely presents a *fragmentary treatment* of certain doctrines, almost always regarded from points of view proper to other sciences then existing ;

2. The period which, beginning with the modern era, ends about the middle of the 18th century, and which

might be called the period of *empirical theories* and of the separate treatment of different doctrines ;

3. The contemporary period, reaching from the middle of last century to the present day. It is distinguished by the building up of political economy into an independent body of systematically connected doctrines, which from the nature of their *subject-matter*, their *functions*, and their *method*, hold a distinct position in the group of economic and social sciences.

As to the method to be followed alike in the external and internal history of political economy we have to remark :

1. That the choice of facts must be made judiciously, so that the history should not deal with all economic authors and theories, but only with those, whether correct or not, which are remarkable, either from their intrinsic *value*, their *originality*, or their *influence ;*

2. That the *exposition* of facts of an internal nature, as *books, theories, teaching*, and of *external* circumstances, as *individual* and *social* conditions, ought to be clear, sober, and faithful ;

3. That the *criticism* of the theories ought to be wide and impartial. , It ought to take into account their *originality*, the respective *influences* to which they are subject and which they exercise ; also their *intrinsic merit*, whether in relation to the times in which they were developed, or to the ultimate results of the science in its present stage.

The history of economic theories, though only useful when accompanied by the study of the science as it now exists, is yet a valuable complement of that study. If it be illumined by criticism, it cannot generate systematic scepticism, irrational eclecticism, nor a posthumous apology for antiquated doctrines and institutions. It serves to illustrate the general history of civilisation and to point out the influence that the theories of economists have exercised on social reforms. It also promotes a more thorough examination of separate theories, which cannot be fully appreciated unless they are traced to their sources. Finally, it prepares the way for future legislative reforms founded on past experiences recorded by history.

Those who are desirous of pursuing the historical study of economic doctrines will find it best to begin with those books which treat specially of that subject, and which sum up, at least in part, much that is contained in a large number of works less accessible to the majority of students.

It will be opportune to introduce here a critical notice of the *subsidiary sources* for the *external* history of political economy, as a preparation for a more thorough examination of those primary sources which we shall indicate in the following chapters.

See R. v. Mohl, *Die Schriften über die Geschichte der politischen Oekonomie.* In the work *Geschichte und Literatur der Staatswissenschaften*, Vol. III., Erlangen, 1858, 4to, p. 291, et seq.

The historical dissertations, necessarily brief and often exclusively bibliographical, which are attached to many scientific treatises either as *introductions* or *appendices*, are not sufficient for those who wish to have a thorough knowledge, however concise, of the historical development of political economy. Among works of this sort we may indicate, by way of example, those which form part of the compendiums published in England by MacCulloch; in France by Say, Garnier, and Courcelle-Seneuil ; in Germany by Lotz, Rau, Wirth, and the socialist Marlo (Winkelblech); in Italy by Bianchini, and after him by Trinchera; in Spain by Florez Estrada and Carballo y Vanguemert; in America by Perry, etc.

Passing to works exclusively occupied with the *general external history* of political economy, the following merit special notice :

Ad. Blanqui, *Histoire de l'Économie politique en Europe, depuis les Anciens jusqu'à nos Jours, suivie d'une Bibliographie raisonnée des principaux Ouvrages d'Économie politique.* Paris, 1837-38. Two vols., 8vo. 4th ed. (edited by A. Ott), Paris, 1860.

Alb. de Villeneuve-Bargemont, *Histoire de l'Économie politique; ou, Études historiques, philosophiques et religieuses sur l'Économie politique des Peuples anciens et modernes.* Paris, 1841. 2 vols., 8vo.

Travers Twiss, *View of the Progress of Political Economy in Europe since the Sixteenth Century, etc.* London, 1847, 8vo.

Julius Kautz, *Die geschichtliche Entwickelung der National-Oekonomik und ihrer Literatur.* Vienna, 1860, 8vo.

E. Dühring, *Kritische Geschichte der Nationalökonomie und des Socialismus.* Berlin, 1871, 8vo. 3rd ed., 1879.

In the histories of Blanqui and Villeneuve we have many faults to find. There is a want of any clear conception as to their general aim, and a confusion between the history of theories and that of facts. They make frequent digressions into general history, and their information, especially with regard to economists earlier than the *Physiocrats*, is scanty. Their

investigations are superficial, their criticisms uncertain,
and their materials wanting in order. The history of
Villeneuve was never very popular, and is now wholly
forgotten, whether from the infelicity of its style or
because the author's main object is too evidently to
oppose to what he calls the *English* political economy,
a *Christian political economy*, by the introduction of
inappropriate religious discussions.

Blanqui's history, on the other hand, enjoyed no small
fame, whether from the excellence of its style or because there had not been for a long time before any
better works treating the subject with the same fulness.
Or it may have been because later works, being written
in tongues unintelligible to a good many economists,
did not succeed in displacing it.

The work of Twiss is more a historical prospectus
than a history. It is too concise, and deals only with the
last four centuries, while Blanqui and Villeneuve turned
their attention in a measure to antiquity and the middle
ages; neither does it show a competent study of the
original works. But it is worthy of praise, if for no
other reason, for its clearer perception of the difference
between the history of theories and that of institutions.

Immeasurably superior to all those preceding is the
work of Professor Kautz. Making diligent use of
special histories of political economy already existing,
and having frequent recourse to the original sources, he
has presented us with a learned and ample narrative of
the historical vicissitudes of the principal scientific
systems of political economy, both ancient and modern.
The success of the book is marred, however, by a want
of temperance in the notices of secondary works, and of
acuteness, in its judgments and criticism; also by the

arbitrariness of its classifications, by the want of scientific
precision, and by the fact that the author, struggling
with the serious difficulties of a foreign language, falls
into empty declamatory periphrases. Besides, by no
fault of the author, the many *special works* published in
the last twenty years cause the greater part of the
book to be out of date.

The more recent history of Dühring is distinguished
by merits and defects of a very different kind. Its ex-
cellences consist in its philosophic acumen, the clearness,
precision, and elegance of its language, and the fulness
of its information with regard to certain economists,
especially Carey, and the socialists of the present day.
Unfortunately, these qualities are obscured by faults of
a very serious nature. In the first place the author has
an exaggerated admiration for the specious doctrines of
List and Carey. Then he is so ignorant of the principal
materials for his subject as to neglect, almost entirely,
not only the works written towards the end of last
century, but also the monographs published by contemporary economists. Finally he judges the more illustrious
modern writers, and especially his own countrymen, with
a tone of presumptuous depreciation, turning, to speak
plainly, a great part of his history into a vulgar libel.

Still less importance must be attributed to three compendiums of the history of political economy, of which
one was published in 1851 by Molster, in Dutch ; a
second, rather better, by De Rooy, also in Dutch and in
the same year; and a third in Swedish by Balchen, in
1869. They all follow more or less in the steps of
Blanqui, with the addition of some meagre bibliographical notices of Dutch and Scandinavian books.

A source of fuller and more exact information on the

progressive development of economic theories is to be found in the numerous monographs which, more particularly in the last thirty years, have been published, on the *special history* of political economy at various times and in various countries. From these we may construct a general history more in accordance with the latest results of investigation.

As we cannot name all of these, some of which will be mentioned in the following chapters, we will content ourselves with references to the principal works concerning the history of political economy among the more civilized nations.

Giuseppe Pecchio, *Storia dell' Economia pubblica in Italia*, or *Epilogo critico degli Economisti italiani, preceduto da una Introduzione*. Lugano, 1829. (Reprinted several times.)

This work, the earliest of the special economic histories, has become, with the help of a French translation, the only source from which foreigners get their information about Italian economists. It is really little more than a brief summary of the works and biographical notices contained in the collection of Italian economists of the sixteenth, seventeenth, and more particularly of the eighteenth century, made by Baron P. Custodi, under the patronage of the Italian Government. (*Scrittori classici italiani, d'Economia politica*. Milan, 1802-1816, 50 vols. 8vo.) To this Pecchio has added a general introduction, many political and literary digressions, and some comparisons with English and French economists of the 19th century.

There is a still briefer work on the economists collected by Custodi, containing no biographical information, but written with greater critical acumen, and with a knowledge of our own writers quite surprising in a foreigner. Notwithstanding some defects and errors of judgment, this book would certainly cause the somewhat flimsy work of Pecchio to be forgotten, if it were not written in Dutch. The title is :

N. G. Pierson, *Bijdrage tot de Geschiedenis der econo-mische Studien in Italie gedurende de 17° en 18° eeuw.* Amsterdam, 1866.

A German translation or rather *plagiarism* has ren-dered the work more widely accessible. This is :

Schwarzkopf, *Beiträge zur Geschichte der national-ökon. Studien in Italien, etc.* Strassburg, 1872.

W. Roscher, *Zur Geschichte der englischen Volkswirth-schaftslehre.* Leipzig, 1851-52. (A learned and ele-gant exposition of the changes undergone by political economy in England during the sixteenth and seven-teenth centuries.)

M. Colmeiro, *Historia de la Economia politica en España.* Madrid, 1863. 2 vols, royal 8vo. (Little known, but very rich in information on the history of economic theories and institutions in Spain up to the end of last century.)

Et. Laspeyres, *Geschichte der volkswirthschaftlichen Anschauungen der Niederländer, etc.* Leipzig, 1863, 4to. A most learned work on the Dutch economists of the 17th and 18th centuries, which inspired another work, superior in point of critical acumen, and on a larger scale, but left unfinished by the death of its author. It is called :

O. van Rees, *Geschiedenis der Staathuishoudkunde in Nederland, etc.* Utrecht, 1865-68. · 2 vols. 8vo.

But the most remarkable work which we possess on the history of political economy in one of the most cultivated nations of Europe, is without doubt Roscher's : *Geschichte der National-Oekonomik in Deutschland.* Munich, 1874. 2 vols. 8vo.

On the other hand we have to deplore the want of a good history of political economy in France, a subject which, in its earlier part, presents much greater interest than the history of German economists, to which Roscher dedicated fifteen years of laborious research.

Some inquiries have been made into the development of economic theories among certain nations of a later civilisation. It will be enough to mention two monographs on Hungarian economists :

J. Biedermann, *Das Studium der politischen Oekonomie in Ungarn, etc.* Kaschau, 1859. (Briefly written, but clear and well arranged.)

Jul. Kautz, *Entwickelungs-Geschichte der volkswirth— schaftlichen Ideen in Ungarn, etc.* Buda-Pesth, 1876. 8vo. (A German translation, abbreviated from the original Hungarian, was published in 1868.)

CHAPTER II.

POLITICAL ECONOMY IN ANCIENT TIMES AND IN THE MIDDLE AGES.

SOURCES :—

J. Kautz, *Die geschichtliche Entwickelung* etc. Vienna, 1860, p. 51-222.

Political economy, considered as an independent science, with well-marked boundaries to its field of research, and with its proper method of investigation, is an entirely modern science; it is indeed little more than a hundred years old. But it must not be thought that the various theories which have gradually enriched this science were wholly unknown to those eminent thinkers of the ancient world and the middle ages, to whom we owe so much. Besides their works on philosophy, history, politics, and jurisprudence, we have their codes of laws as an undying witness to their wisdom in civil matters. Even now these codes form a very important part of the written law of the most advanced nations of Europe and America.

Hence, we are well repaid in turning our attention to the early manifestations of scientific thought in the direction of economics. We must never forget, however, that these are merely *fragments,* treating of *isolated theories.* And even within these narrow limits, social wealth is not studied by itself, but from the point of view of those other *philosophies,* social and religious, which mainly constituted the intellectual culture of the period.

§ 1. *Political economy in antiquity.*

Sources :—

Du Mesnil-Marigny, *Histoire de l'Économie politique des anciens Peuples de l'Inde, de l'Égypte, de la Judée et de la Grèce.* Paris, 1872. 2 vols. 8vo. 3rd ed. 1877.

(To be consulted with great caution, because it starts with the pre-conceived idea of a retrospective apology for the protective system.)

Francesco Trinchera, *Storia critica dell' Economia pubblica,* etc. Vol. I. (all published). *Epoca antica.* Naples, 1873. 8vo. (Very poor, compiled with no reference to modern philology.)

We cannot conceive of an economic science, which shall be systematic, independent, complete and practical, without the idea of the existence of natural laws governing the phenomena of social wealth. But the ancients were prevented by various circumstances from attaining to this idea. Such were their social conditions, their philosophic and religious opinions, their conviction that all the actions, economic and otherwise, of citizens, should be looked at in reference to the state. For the state, notwithstanding the various forms that its constitution assumed among them, was always considered omnipotent.

Furthermore, the social organism was corrupted by the custom of slavery, perverting and debasing wealth at its very source. Then there was the predominant spirit of war and conquest, robbing the most civilised and powerful people of the fruits of peaceful industry. There was also the political constitution itself. In Greece and Rome all the thoughts of the citizens were turned to politics, and even their ideas of the liberty which they desired were false. They conceived of it merely as a larger participation in the functions of the state. Their ideal of the state was that it should be omnipotent. Hence they considered that its duty was to suppress every form of individual independence, and all minor social combinations. Again, the philosophic and religious theories of paganism held the arts of production in the greatest depreciation. They considered all kinds of industry, with the sole exception of agriculture, perilous to the health of the body, the culture of the intellect, and the exercise of domestic and social virtues.

A.—The East.

F. Eb. Kübel, *Die soziale und volkswirthschaftliche Gesetzgebung des Alten Testamentes,* etc. Wiesbaden, 1870, royal 8vo.

Giacomo Lumbroso. *Recherches sur l'Économie politique de l'Égypte sous les Lagides.* Turin, 1870, royal 8vo.

We gain some idea of the economic theories of the early nations of the East from their sacred books. From the point of view of modern science, these books present very little that is remarkable. Their economic teachings may generally be reduced to certain moral precepts on the virtues of industry, temperance and thrift, on the worthlessness of riches, which ought

only to be desired that they may be employed in
sacred uses, or to help the poor and suffering. Manufactures and commerce were almost always despised and
neglected; agriculture, on the other hand, was held in
much esteem and, as in Egypt and India, it made considerable progress. The division of labour was not
carried out with the elasticity that comes from liberty.
It was, so to speak, crystallised in the system of *caste*,
which hardened the national fibres, and prevented any
progress in social institutions; these institutions consequently preserved the character of uniformity and
immobility. The statesmen and learned men of China
appreciated more correctly the function of commerce,
and had a sufficiently exact idea of the nature of money.
They understood it to be the representative of fixed
and generally recognised value, and the instrument of
circulation. But their ideas on the laws of production
were not equally clear. Although they appreciated
the importance of labour, they did not recognise the
economic functions of capital. And they not uncommonly fostered idleness and improvidence, in the
confidence that the gods provided believers with the
necessaries of life.

B.—Greece.

K. H. Rau, *Ansichten der Volkswirthschaft.* Leipzig,
1821, 8vo. p. 3-21.

W. Roscher, *Ueber das Verhältniss der Nationalökonomie zum klassischen Alterthume.* In the work:
Ansichten der Volkswirthschaft. Leipzig, 1861, p. 3-46.

J. C. Glaser, *Die Entwickelung der Wirthschafts-
verhältnisse bei den Griechen.* Berlin, 1865, 8vo.

L. Cossa, *Di alcuni Studj Storici Sulle Teorie econo-miche dei Greci.* Milan, 1876. In the *Rendiconti del R. Istituto Lombardo di Scienze.* Vol. IX, No. VII. (Critical notice of the monographs on the said subject.)

Many states in ancient Greece, being endowed with various natural advantages, among others a good maritime position, attained to a high degree of mercan-tile and political power. Up to a certain point this necessarily drew the attention of several of their emi-nent thinkers to the causes of this prosperity. Never-theless, for the reasons above indicated, and because politics stood before everything else both in theory and practice, the researches of the Greeks on economic phenomena were always subordinate and accessory either to the theory of the state (πολιτική), or to that of house-hold government (οἰκονομική). In both these branches they were more occupied with men than with things, and more with freemen than with slaves, to which latter class almost all actual industrial operations were abandoned.

Nevertheless, certain Greek writers, and notably Aristotle, were not without a clear conception of a special doctrine of wealth and its acquisition, (χρηματιστική) sub-ordinated to the two sciences above-mentioned. Of this theory as they conceived it, we have only a few scattered fragments. And these are almost lost in works of history, and more frequently in those of practical philosophy, of which, in the Greek idea, Ethics, Economics and Politics formed the principal elements.

Among historians, Herodotus is not without some interest for us. But Thucydides stands first, from the greater subtlety with which he estimates the economic element and its great influence on political and social

facts. Roscher was the first to point out his economic
merits, perhaps with an excessive enthusiasm, both in
the above-named work, and in a later academic discourse,
entitled : *Disputatio I de Doctrinae oeconomico politicae
apud Graecos primordiis.* Lipsiae, 1866, 4to.

There must also have existed before Aristotle and
Plato numerous works treating of the problems of
domestic economy in general, and also of certain productive arts, especially hunting, mining and agriculture.
And there may have been controversies on certain special
points of *chrematistics*, particularly on the differences
between the idea of wealth and that of money. The
economic and political question of slavery provoked
disputes which are vividly depicted in the writings
of Aristotle. Among works belonging to these categories
which are now lost we may mention that of Apollodoros
of Lemnos, *on Mining;* of Chares of Paros, *on Agriculture;* of Hieron and Callicratidas, *on Domestic
Economy.*

In particular see :—

L. Stein, *Die staatswissenschaftliche Theorie der
Griechen vor Aristoteles und Platon.*—In the *Zeitschr. f.
d. ges. Staatswissenschaft.* 9. Jahrg. (1853). Tübingen,
p. 115—182.

A comparatively larger mass of information on the
scientific views of the Greeks with regard to the theory
of social wealth, may be gathered from their philosophical works. Many of these have come down to us
entire, or at least in their essential parts. This cannot
be said of the works of the most ancient philosophers,
nor of those of the school of Pythagoras, to which not
only statesmen and legislators, like Philolaos of Thebes,
but also theoretical politicians, belonged. As far as we

can learn, however, none of these philosophers occupied themselves with investigating the nature of wealth and the causes of its development. The *sophists*, who arose out of the Ionic school, had a more practical influence. Many public men became imbued with their teaching, among whom Hippodamos of Miletus and Phaleas of Chalcedon are worthy of mention, whose theories, at least in part, are examined in the second book of Aristotle's *Politics*.

In his speculations on the constitution of the state, Hippodamos, who was also an architect of merit, proposed that the state should be composed of ten thousand citizens, to be occupied partly in agriculture, partly in manufactures, and partly in the arts of war. Its territory was to be divided into three portions, devoted respectively to the service of the gods, the maintenance of warriors, and the exercise of agriculture.

Phaleas on the other hand propounded a community of goods, as the best means of obtaining peace and public tranquillity. He thought that as such a system could easily be introduced into an entirely new state, it could likewise be applied to one already constituted, by a law ordaining that the rich should give dowries to their daughters, but should not receive them with their wives, while the poor, being of course unable to give dowries, would gain by this arrangement. Socrates proposed as the scope of philosophy practical life as it is with its various relations. Hence the merit doubtless belongs to him of having given a more useful direction to the investigations of philosophy in general, and therefore to those also which related to the phenomena of wealth. But the learned men of his school occupied themselves with economic products in their connection with ethics and politics. They did not consider them in themselves but merely as an instrument for gaining the higher ends of human life, so that most of their reflections belong rather to *economic ethics* than to *political economy.*

Among those writings preserved to us, which throw light on the opinions of Socrates as to economic products, we may first give our attention to a dialogue entitled *Eryxias.* It is found among those of Plato, but it is easy to see that it is not really written by him. Some philologists ascribe it to Eschines, and others, apparently with more reason, to a later Socratic writer of minor importance. The author argues that men ought not to look on wealth as the object by which they may attain happiness. Its possession does not necessarily bring happiness, since a rich man more than any other needs wisdom to make a good use of what he has.

C. H. Hagen, *Observationum oeconomico-politicarum in Æschinis Dialogum, qui Eryxias inscribitur.* Pars prima. Regiomonti, 1822, 8vo.

Far more useful, as giving a complete and exact idea of the economic opinions of the Greek philosophers and learned men generally, are the writings of Plato, of Xenophon and still more of Aristotle.

Rob. v. Mohl, *Die Staatsromane.* In his *Geschichte und Literatur der Staatswissenschaften,* etc. Vol. I. Erlangen, 1855, 4to. p. 171—76.

Ad. Frout de Fontpertuis, *Filiation des Idées économiques et sociales de l'Antiquité,* etc. In the *Journal des Économistes,* 30th year, 3rd series (September 1871), p. 356—382. (Both explaining the economic doctrines of Plato ; the second that of Xenophon also.)

Bruno Hildebrand, *Xenophontis et Aristotelis de Oeconomia publica Doctrinae illustrantur.* Part 1. Marburg,

1845, 8vo. (The second part concerning Aristotle has not been published.)

J. C. Glaser, *De Aristotelis Doctrina de Divitiis.* Regiomonti, 1856, 4to (Insufficient).

W. Onken, *Die Staatslehre des Aristoteles.* Leipzig, 1870—75, 2 vols. 8vo. (Wide critical exposition of the political doctrine of Aristotle.)

Plato (429—348 B.C.) in his *Republic* depicts an ideal state, based on the system of community of goods and of wives, and governed by wise men and philosophers. He divides the population into three principal classes, rulers, warriors, and labourers, while the produce of the soil is distributed between citizens, slaves and strangers. In the *Laws* he sets forth his economic views, conforming them rather more to the actual conditions of the time. He gives proofs of great profundity in dealing with certain points of theory, and especially in his political exposition of the ancient state in all its greatness. He defines wealth as the possession of more than other people. He distinguishes good gifts which are *human* (as health, beauty, strength, wealth) from those which are *divine* (wisdom, virtue, temperance), and those which serve for pleasure and luxury from those which are profitable. He appreciates the importance of labour and of the division of labour, without foreseeing its more remote consequences. He understands the functions of money as the instrument and token of exchange, and the consequent advantage of it to commerce. He is further of opinion that to preserve good order in the state it is advisable to exercise a prudent guardianship over commerce, manufactures, and agriculture. The last he values more especially, giving many precepts with regard to the profitable pursuit of it. He recognises the

tendency of men to acquire private property, and therefore inclines to a system of the greatest possible
equality. To this end he proposes that the extension of
territory as well as the increase of population should be
restrained within very narrow limits ; also that external
commerce should be regulated in such a way as not to
prejudice the purity of customs and the integrity of the
national character.

Rather less profound, but certainly more positive
than Plato, was Xenophon (446—356 B.C.), the author of
many historical writings and of some small works on
Domestic Economy, such as the *Chase,* the *Revenues of
Attica,* etc., in which he enters into some particulars of
the economic life of nations and states. *Wealth,* according
to his definition, consists in the excess of *goods* over
wants. By *goods* he means all *useful things.* He
recognises as the elements of production *nature,* which
provides materials, and *labour,* which modifies them,
and is approved by him so long as it is skilfully directed
to legitimate purposes. Like Plato, he perceives the
advantage to be gained from the division of employ-
ments, and his ideas about the manufacturing arts and
commerce are more correct. He cannot get rid, however, of the notion of the superiority of agriculture, which
he considers the healthiest occupation both for the body
and the mind, and the most useful in increasing wealth.
He describes the conditions of soil and climate, the
methods of cultivation and organisation of labour, which
seem to him best adapted for its success. Up to a certain
point, he anticipates the modern theory of the limits of
agricultural production, seeing that the successive application of labour to land gives progressively decreasing
results. He does not rise above the common prejudice

in favour of slavery, but he recommends that slaves should be well treated. Finally, he has some comparatively advanced ideas on money and prices ; but in treating of the relative values of the precious metals, he falls into an error with regard to silver, attributing to it a constant value, independent of increased production.

As has already been said, Aristotle holds the first place in economic knowledge among the Greek thinkers. A patient, acute, and experienced observer, he not only greatly advanced speculative inquiries concerning wealth, but summed up in himself all the economic knowledge of antiquity. He laid down boundaries which limited the researches of the most illustrious mediæval thinkers. His economic theories are set forth in the *Ethics* and *Politics*, the *Economics* having been compiled in the succeeding centuries. He divides the patrimony into wealth destined for consumption and wealth destined for profit. Again, he distinguishes wealth consumed by the proprietor from that devoted to exchange. This leads him to the important distinction between value in use and value in exchange,—between primitive economy and the economy of a money-using people, observing that the latter is proper to a more advanced civilisation, in which there exists a more minute division of labour. He appreciates correctly the functions of money, as a measure of value and an instrument of exchange, adopted by universal consent as a means of effecting the needful exchanges at any given time. He does not fall into the error of confounding money with wealth, remarking that it is possible to die of hunger, as Midas did, while owning vast quantities of the precious metals. On the other hand, he has a false conception of capital and of interest, which he condemns as an unjust usurpation,

holding it impossible that money can produce money.
He divides the population into farmers, artisans,
traders, and those who perform personal services, such
as warriors, priests, judges and magistrates ; but he ex-
cludes from a share in the government of the State those
who, being solely engaged in the arts directed to increase
wealth, are doing base work, unworthy of the truly free
man.   He defends slavery by affirming that the position
of slaves is naturally servile, though he admits that if
the harp could play, and the shuttle could weave, of
itself, there would be no need for servile aid.   He
thinks that population ought to be exactly propor-
tioned to territory, since a thinly scattered population
would endanger the independence of the State, while one
too abundant would endanger internal tranquillity, order,
and safety.

C.—Rome.

F. B. G. Hermann, *Dissertatio exhibens Sententias
Romanorum ad œconomiam universam sive nationalem
pertinentes.*   Erlangen, 1823, 8vo.

The classical writers of Rome, particularly the philosophers, did not devote themselves to economic
questions with the same diligence and acuteness as those
of Greece, whose opinions on this subject the Latins
reproduced with little variation.   Hence there is not
much of interest to be found in a collection of economic
passages from the Latin authors.   Such a collection,
incomplete, by the way, is given by Hermann in a brief
and juvenile work of his, very unworthy of the fame
which he afterwards gained by arduous investigation
into the more profound conceptions of the science.

Among Roman writers whose importance in economic matters is relatively great, we may cite Cicero, Seneca, and Pliny the elder. The first, when young, translated the *Economics* of Xenophon, and repeatedly expressed his well-known opinions in favour of agriculture and in opposition to manufactures and trade. Further, in his *philosophical*, *political*, and *rhetorical* works there are some wise observations on economic questions, which have been collected by a learned Dutchman, Calkoen.

Calkoen, *Over eenige staathuishoudkundige Gevoelens en Stellingen in de Geschriften van Cicero, etc.* In the *Bijdragen tot Regtsgel. en Wetgeving* of van Hall, 1831–32, Vol. VI., p. 413, et seq.

Seneca's ideas on the use of wealth are inspired by the stoic philosophy of which he was an expositor. He is the enemy of avarice no less than of dissipation and luxury; he is averse to conquest, slavery, and war, and favourable to frugality, temperance, and work.

In his *Natural History*, Pliny recognises the greater productiveness of cultivation on the large scale, but deplores the evils arising in districts cultivated by servile labour. He condemns luxury, and opposes the exportation of money in exchange for foreign goods. Specially noteworthy is his exposition of value, its causes and movements.

Somewhat more important, with regard to certain points of theory, if on no other account, are the *Roman agriculturists* (*scriptores rei rusticae*), especially Cato, Varro, and Columella. Living in a time of economic and moral decay, incipient or advanced, they strove to bring back their countrymen to happier and healthier agrarian conditions. Their technical precepts are chiefly inspired by the desire of making agriculture

H

more rational, of spreading a knowledge of the agrarian customs of other peoples, and especially of the Carthaginians, of reviving the love for country life, of stirring up proprietors to undertake personally the cultivation of their farms, and discouraging the system of leaving vast estates to servile cultivation.

We get an impression of more clearness and originality from the economic theories of the Roman Jurists, chiefly preserved in the *Corpus Juris*. It is true that we cannot properly form from these, by the arbitrary welding together of fragments, a compendium of economy on the modern pattern. Tydemann, a Dutch writer, attempted to do this with great weight of learning, but with little judgment, making no distinction between theories and opinions often removed from one another by centuries. Nevertheless, we do find in the writings of the Jurists most interesting passages, which deserve special elucidation. This was happily attempted by Scheel in a brief essay which makes us wish for a larger work. And it should be mentioned that some of the more important passages long since attracted the attention of many learned men. As, for instance, the well-known fragment of Paul on the origin of money, which exercised the analytical talent of our Pompeo Neri. (*Leg.* 1 *Dig. de contr. empt.* XVIII., 1.)

J. G. Tydemann, *Disquisitio de Œconomiæ politicæ notionibus in Corpore Juris Civilis Justinianeo*. Lugduni Batavorum, 1838.

H. v. Scheel, *Die wirthschaftlichen Grundbegriffe im Corpore Juris Civilis Justinianeo*. In the *Jahrbücher für Nat.-Oekon. und Statistik* of B. Hildebrand, Jena, 1866, Vol. I.

Pompeo Neri, *Osservazioni sul Prezzo legale delle Monete*

(1751). In the *Economisti classici italiani.* Ancient part, Vol. VI. p. 324, et seq.

§ 2. *The Middle Ages.*

L. Cibrario, *Della Economia politica del Medio-evo,* libri tre, 5th ed. Turin, 1861. Two vols. 8vo. (This work does not deal with theories.)

H. Contzen, *Geschichte der volkswirthschaftlichen Literatur im Mittelalter.* 2nd enlarged edition. Berlin, 1872, 8vo. (A compilation somewhat superficially and hastily written.)

L. Cossa, *Di alcuni Studj recenti sulle Teorie economiche nel Medio-evo.* In the *Rendiconti del R. Istituto Lombardo di Scienze e Lettere.* 2nd series. Vol. IX. (1876), art. 4 and 5. (Critical account of modern works on the subject.)

The middle ages was a period of fierce struggle between the old pagan ideas and the modern world, which had been radically transformed by the influence of Christianity. By proclaiming the unity of the human race and the equality of men, Christianity condemned slavery and serfdom, and led the way to their abolition. By moderating the harshness of paternal rule, raising the moral and social position of women, and reforming the system of successions, it reconstituted the family. By creating and diffusing charitable institutions, by preaching to the rich the duty of charity, and to the poor that of gratitude and resignation, it improved the condition of the less prosperous classes. Thus it laid the foundation for a more satisfactory organisation of the production and distribution of wealth.

But this fruitful and renovating process met in existing ideas, prejudices, customs, and laws, with

hindrances which delayed the full effect of the incipient
reforms. In the period before the Crusades, disturbed as it was by constant struggles between Pope
and Emperor for political supremacy in Christian
Europe, and by wars, more restricted but none the less
fierce and unceasing, between the feudal lords, the
development of manufacturing and commercial industry
was impeded. There could be no guarantee for order
and liberty in the midst of continual war, robbery, and
violence. Industry suffered not a little from the deficiency and insecurity of the means of exchange, transport, and communication. Even agriculture languished
under the weight of intolerable burdens and the miserable
condition of the cultivators, who were bound to the soil
and oppressed by the exactions of the feudal system.

It was only in the latter half of the middle ages that
the emancipation of the towns and the growth of the
burgher class, together with the fresh sphere for trade
opened by the Crusades, gave new life to manufactures.
Organised under a system of strong self-governing cor-.
porations, which alone could resist the oppressions of
feudal lords, manufacturing industry soon became—
firstly, in the Italian republics, and latterly, in Flanders .
and the German Hanse towns—a powerful element in
economic prosperity and civil progress.

It was about the beginning of the eleventh century
that there arose in Italy those economic institutions,
which, even at this distance of time, rouse our admiration. These institutions were upheld by those statutes
and customs of commercial, banking, and maritime law,
which, having been first introduced into the laws and
ordinances of the seventeenth and eighteenth centuries,
are largely embodied in existing commercial codes.

But the revival of economic studies in the middle ages only dates from the eighteenth century. It was due in a great measure to the study of the *Ethics* and *Politics* of Aristotle, whose theories on wealth were paraphrased by a considerable number of commentators. Before that period we only find moral and religious dissertations on the proper use of material goods, the dangers of luxury, the undue desire for wealth, etc. This is easily explained when we take the following circumstances into consideration, namely : the prevalent influence of religious ideas at that time ; the strong reaction against the materialism of pagan antiquity ; the predominance of "natural economy " ; the small importance of international trade ; the decay of the profane sciences, and the metaphysical tendencies of the more solid thinkers of the middle ages. Later on, when industrial conditions had grown better, when public safety was increased, when the love of knowledge had been developed, when jurisprudence had been reformed and its scientific study revived, and when *scholasticism* had reached its highest point, the wisest students of philosophy turned their attention more frequently to the investigation of economic phenomena, discussing their relations to the doctrine of ethics and the management of public affairs.

It is not surprising that among the economists of the middle ages the highest place is held by the *theologians.* In sermons, dogmatic and moral compendiums and summaries, and sometimes in special works on the *sacrament* of *penitence,* they were led, while treating of the payment of debts, to examine the nature of commerce and the known characteristics of certain contracts and mercantile operations, in order to distinguish acts

that were lawful from those that were unlawful and
sinful.

The *philosophers* and *jurists*, most of them being
also ecclesiastics, are especially noteworthy. Following in the line of the two works of Aristotle, above
mentioned, they discussed the nature and functions of
money. They asserted the unlawfulness of interest on
money-loans, arguing from its so-called barrenness, from
the prescriptions of the *Corpus Juris Canonici*, and
from the interpretation of certain passages of Scripture.
Later also a subtle distinction was formed in support of
the same doctrine between *infungible* and *fungible* things.[1]
It was said that as the *use* of the former cannot be
transferred without the *ownership* being changed at the
same time, it is not lawful for the lender to demand interest in addition to the restitution of the principal, such
a demand being a claim for *double compensation*.

W. Endemann, *Die national-ökonomischen Grundsätze
der canonistischen Lehre.* Jena, 1863, 8vo.

Ch. Jourdain, *Mémoire sur les Commencements de
l'Économie politique dans les Écoles du moyen-âge* (1869).
In the *Mémoires de l'Acad. des Inscr. et Belles-Lettres*,
Vol. XXVIII. Paris, 1874, p. 1–51.

W. Endemann, *Studien in der romanisch-canonistischen
Wirthschafts-und Rechtslehre*, 1st vol. Berlin, 1874, 8vo.

---

[1] A *res infungibilis* is the subject of a contract or "obligation,"
which can only be discharged by the return of the thing itself. A
res fungibilis is the subject of a contract or "obligation" which
can be discharged by the delivery of a similar thing, and must in
consequence be always ascertainable by measurement, etc. The
commonest instances of *res fungibiles* were things which perished
in use, and indeed *res fungibiles* are generally confounded with
things *quæ usu consumuntur*. Austin, Jurisprudence, p. 807, ed. iv.
Mackeldy, § 369–374. Digest. XII. i. 6.

The political writers of the thirteenth and fourteenth, and more particularly of the fifteenth centuries, are not without interest. Their numerous writings, all very similar in substance, treat of the government of princes and of republics. They do not enter much in detail into the application of legislation to industries. Here and there, however, they give precepts for good economic and financial government.

V. Cusumano, *Dell' Economia Politica nel Medio evo. Studi Storici.* Bologna, 1876.

Many men of letters, too, of this period pay some attention to the economic element, and observe its influence on the right adjustment both of the house and the State. Some of these were authors either of *Encyclopedias*, like Brunetto Latini, or of works on *domestic economy*, like Leone Battista Alberti. Some were historians, as, for example, Giovanni and Matteo Villani.

E. Gebhart, *Les Historiens florentins de la Renaissance et les Commencements de l'Économie politique et sociale*, 1875. In the *Séances et Travaux de l'Académie des Sciences morales et politiques*, 34th year, p. 552–590.

It being impossible to give an accurate account of the economic literature of the middle ages, we must content ourselves with simply enumerating the more noted writers.

A. *Thirteenth Century.*

Albertus Magnus (1193–1280), and Duns Scotus (1245–1308), two eminent *schoolmen*, must be mentioned. The first was the master, the second the subtle antagonist of St. Thomas Aquinas (1226-1274), the greatest philosopher and theologian of his time, and also the most remarkable economic writer of the thirteenth century. The *Summa*, the pamphlet *De Usuris*, and the Commentaries on Aristotle, deserve special consideration, and to a certain point also, the book *De Regimine Principum*. The authencitity of this last work, however, is very doubtful, it being probably in great part written by his pupil, the Friar Tolomeo da Lucca (1236-1317). St. Thomas may be considered as the link between the economic doctrines of ancient Greece and the Christian-Guelf political theories set forth in a good many works in the thirteenth and following centuries. In the writings of St. Thomas we find indeed paraphrases of the Aristotelian doctrines on *money* and *interest*. On these doctrines he and his imitators founded their condemnation of the depreciation of the standard and of the usury which was concealed in many mercantile contracts to evade the severe rules of canon and civil law.

Among the minor schoolmen, Henry of Ghent was the author of a work, since lost, *De Mercimoniis et Negotiationibus*, in which he showed a somewhat juster understanding of *commerce*, its *lawfulness* and *utility*, than most of his contemporaries.

B. Fourteenth Century.

The *political writers* of this time followed in the steps of St. Thomas, as for example, Egidio Colonna in his book *De Regimine Principum*. Certain writers on *Roman law*, among them Bartolo di Sassoferrato (1313-1359), propounded comparatively correct ideas on money and some other subjects. At the same time the *canonical* writers and *theologians* somewhat modified their views on the theory of interest. Other learned men

examined with much subtlety and surprising exactness
the economic functions of money, courageously and with
sound judgment condemning its depreciation.   To this
class belong :—

1. Jean Buridan, who was governor of the University of Paris in 1327.   In his questions on the *Ethics of
Aristotle*, he gave, as Jourdain observes, a short treatise
on the economic functions of money.

2. Nicolas Orêsme, Bishop of Lisieux (died 1382),
who, before 1373, wrote a fuller and more remarkable
discourse on the same subject than any which had preceded it, *De Origine, Natura, Jure et Mutationibus
Monetarum.*   It was reprinted in 1864 by Wolowski,
and commented on by Roscher, who speaks of Orêsme
as "a great French economist" of the 14th century.

We will pass over other schoolmen of less importance,
only mentioning the two professors of the theological
faculty of Vienna, Henry of Langenstein (*Henricus de
Assia,* died 1397), and Henry of Hoyta (died 1392).   The
first was the author of a treatise, *De Contractibus et de
Origine Censuum,* and the second of a book *De Contractibus, scilicet redditibus.*   More worthy of notice are :—

1. The famous chancellor Jean de Gerson, who, like
Buridan, turned his attention to the theory of *value.*
He argued, in accordance with the opinions of his time,
in favour of an *official valuation* of the price of all goods.

2. Giovanni Sercambi, the historian and political
writer of Lucca (1347-1424).   In his *Avvertimento politici,*
published before 1400, he figures as one of the earliest
upholders of the so-called *protective system.*

C. *Fifteenth Century*.

The spread of literary culture, the progress of industry, the new credit-institutions, and the legislative reforms, necessarily had a great influence on economic literature. Though still controlled by theologians, it grew wider in its scope, and in its technical and political applications.

Among the writers, more numerous than before, who were remarkable for their diligence in the study of economic phenomena, we will only mention three theologians and two political writers. They are commented on by Roscher, Funk, Contzen, and Cusumano, in certain monographs already described by us (See note already given respecting *Alcuni Studj recenti sulle Teorie economiche del Medio-evo*, p. 99).

St. Bernardin of Siena, (1380-1444), and St. Antonine, Archbishop of Florence (1389-1455), were both theologians of great fame, belonging to the first half of the 15th century. Their theories on economic subjects were rather more correct than those of preceding writers. St. Antonine in his *Summa Theologica*, and St. Bernardin in his sermons, *De Rerum Translatione ; De Mercatura in genera ; De Temporis Venditione ; De Examine (Pretii) Rerum Venalium ; De Voragine Usurarum*, explain certain points of the doctrines of production, circulation, and distribution. Their observations on the nature of *capital*, the causes of *value*, and the nature of *interest*, deserve special attention.

Another theologian, who was also a philosopher, Gabriel Biel (died 1495), a professor at Tübingen towards the end of the 15th century, wrote a *Collectarium Sententiarum* in four books (*Tübingen*, 1501, i. .vol. folio). He was chiefly remarkable for his theory of money, which was afterwards reprinted separately under the title, *De Monetarum Potestate simul et Utilitate Libellus* (Magonza, 1501). It was quoted by several writers of the following century.

Of the many political writers who now and then turned their attention to the economic management of the state, we must notice Filippo Beroaldo (1453-1505), Bartolomeo Platina (1421-1481), Giovanni Gioviano Pontano (1426-1503), and more especially :—

1. Francesco Patrizzii of Siena, bishop of Gaeta (died 1494), the author of two works, *De Regno et Regis Institutione* (Paris, 1567), and *De Institutione Reipublicæ* (Paris, 1565).

2. Diomede Caraffa (died 1487), a Neapolitan writer, published at the request of Eleanor of Aragon, Duchess of Ferrara, a treatise : *De Regentis et boni Principis Officiis.* It contains some important remarks on agriculture and corn, money and commerce, and more especially on financial arrangements. With regard to the last he advises, under certain conditions, the farming of taxes, an idea which was singular enough at that time.

CHAPTER III.

In the *second period* of the history of political economy, which includes the 16th and 17th and the first half of the 18th centuries, economic questions were discussed with greater breadth. The point of view proper to the science became more and more separated from that of other sciences, to which it had been subordinated in the previous period. But there is not as yet any complete or really systematic treatment of the science as a whole. The various theories are not yet brought into connection with their fundamental principles. They only form, as it were, a conglomerate of disconnected monographs, superficially conformed to those rules of economic government which make up the so-called *mercantile system*. In the legislation and commercial customs of the 16th century and the last half of the 17th, the influence of this system was very great.

§ 1. *Political Economy in the* 16*th Century.*

A complete revolution took place during this period, in circumstances and institutions, opinions and theories alike. It may be mostly explained by those great events which divide the middle ages from modern times. These were : The fall of the Roman Empire in the East ; the great geographical discoveries ; the invention of powder and of printing ; the revival of classical studies ; the so-called religious reformation, etc. Besides these facts of political and social importance, there were others of a purely economic character. There was the abundant supply of the precious metals flowing from the newly discovered mines of America, and the increasing prevalence of monetary over "natural" economy, a special characteristic of the middle ages. There was the rise and spread of institutions founded on credit. There was the confiscation of the wealth of religious bodies in Protestant states, causing an increase of misery which called for a reform of beneficent institutions. Again there was the introduction of standing armies, and the growing needs of public finance in the absolute monarchies which formed themselves on the ruins of the old feudal systems, and which steadily grew in unity and strength. And there were the new trade connections between the Old and the New Worlds, demanding new institutions to maintain them.

This revolution of changing circumstances and opinions had a strong influence upon scientific speculation. In the century of which we are speaking it burst the bonds of metaphysics, and took a more practical and positive direction. Thus it was led to investigate the phenomena of wealth, especially those belonging to *circulation*. A glance at the many works by writers on *general politics*, belonging to the 15th century, and more particularly to the last thirty years of it, clearly shows the greater attention given at that time to economic problems.

This remark does not apply indeed to the greatest

politician of the period, Niccolò Macchiavelli (1469-
1527). But in him it certainly was not the aptitude but
the inclination to consider the economic side of political
facts and problems that was wanting. We have his own
declaration of his inexperience in the treatment of
questions relating to *wool* and *silk*. We have further
proof in the careful and diligent investigations of Knies,
a modern economist of considerable merit. He searched
the works of the Florentine secretary for observations
on economic matters, with little or no result.

In the historical, and more especially in the political,
works of Francesco Guicciardini (1480—1540), which
have been discovered recently, we find a greater number
of economic passages. In these works he describes the
vicissitudes of Italy, and of Florence in particular, and
gives political advice to statesmen. At the same time
he appreciates with much penetration the political importance of the fierce financial struggles in which the
rival parties of Florence strove to damage one another.

But it was the French politician, Jean Bodin
(1530-1596), who in the fifteenth century held the first
place with regard to political economy, administration,
and finance. In his work, *De la République* (1576),
and most fully in the last of its six books, he discourses
at large of the economic organisation of the state.
This, he thinks, should be suited to the natural conditions of soil and climate. It should be regulated by
a moderately restrictive legislation with regard to the
customs duties, and by a financial system based on the
taxation of products. These theories must of course be
judged in relation to the time to which they belong.
They have been learnedly explained by :—

H. Baudrillart, *J. Bodin et son Temps. Tableau des*

Théories politiques et des Idées économiques au seizième Siècle. Paris, 1853, 1 vol. 8vo. The remarks in this work on the economic theories of the fifteenth century are somewhat insufficient. But it contains much information on the life and general writings of Bodin, and a minute analysis of the treatise *De la République.*

In the last years of the 15th century an Italian politician devoted himself to the problems of economic government. This was the Piedmontese Giovanni Botero, abbot of San Michele alla Chiusa, and secretary of St. Carlo Borromeo. Among his writings we may name the *Ragione di Stato* (1592) and a small work on the *Cause della Grandezza delle Città* (1598), in which he expounded theories on wealth, the relative importance of industries, commercial politics, population, colonies and taxation. These are all worth the attention of the economic historian, though they do not justify the exaggerated praise given to them by Botero's biographer, Galeani Napione.

Finally, we must mention two other political writers of this period. In his work, *De Monetae Mutatione* (1609) Mariana, a Jesuit, dealt with the questions of money and prices, showing himself to be in favour of the restriction of international commerce. And Gregory of Toulouse in his book *De Republica* (1597) summed up the economic notions of his time. He was however wanting in originality, and a critic of the following century said of him, "*multa ingerit, pauca digerit.*"

With this group of political writers who expounded theories relating to the government of states as they actually existed in their times, we must contrast another class of writers. These were partly men of letters, partly philosophers, partly popular agitators in times of war and other political disturbances. Their object was to describe an ideal state, organised on a system of community of goods, after the model of Plato's *Republic*.

First in order of time, and celebrated also for having given the name of *Utopia* to the political scheme and economic organisation described by him, is the famous chancellor of England, Sir Thomas More. (*De novo Reipublicae statu deque nova insula Utopia, &c.* 1516.) Then there was the strange Florentine writer Antonio Francesco Doni (1513—1574) with his *Mondi celesti, terrestri ed infernali* (1552—1553), 2 vols. 4to, and the philosophers Telesio (*De Rerum Natura*) and Giordano Bruno (*Spaccio della Bestia trionfante*). In Germany Sebastian Frank, the communist of the *reformation*, wished to extend this movement to a thorough trans·formation of social order.

Rather more interesting are the theological and economic controversies relating to *usury, instruments of credit*, and the *monti-di-pietà*, or pawnbrokers' shops. Such controversies followed and partly arose out of the discussions and commentaries occasioned in the middle ages by the canonical and civil prohibition of *interest* on money-loans. The strictness of ᵗhis prohibition became modified by the necessities of trade, the growth of commercial enterprise, the constantly increasing importance of productive in comparison with merely consumptive credit. Thus *loans, companies*, and *institutions of credit* arose under various forms, and gradually succeeded in emancipating themselves from the old prohibitive laws. Among these institutions we may mention *bills of exchange, insurances*, the so called *montes sacri* and *profani*, and *mortgages*.

The canonical theory with regard to such economic matters was based on the conception of a loan as an essentially gratuitous contract. An examination of the new institutions led the upholders of this theory to the admission that the creditor may demand a compensation for his service under certain conditions. As when for instance he can plead an ensuing *loss*, a *cessation of gain*, the *risk of partnerships*, the *cost of transport of money* from one place to another. But these compensations must not, they said, be confounded with *interest*, which is unlawful.

Among Protestant theologians Luther was as strongly opposed to usury as the Catholic writers, while Melanchthon, Zwingli, and especially Calvin were more indulgent.

We next have a numerous group of writers treating especially of *bills of exchange* and *monti di pietà*. On the first subject the Dominican Tommaso da Vio, called also Cardinal Gaetano, opens the series with his Latin dissertation *De Cambiis* (1499). In this work he take great pains to distinguish true and lawful exchange from the *Cambio secco*,[1] or dry exchange, which is unlawful because it disguises a loan at interest. Later on the subject attracted the notice of legal writers. The many works which deal with it, notwithstanding differences in

---

[1] "Dry exchange was an evasion of the Usury Laws, by means of Bill of Exchange, which the borrower drew on a fictitious person at Amsterdam, or any foreign town, at the then current rate of exchange, which he delivered to the lender. At maturity, the Bill was returned protested from Amsterdam, and the borrower charged with re-exchange and incidental expenses; and in this way twenty or thirty per cent. was made, the bill never having been out of the country."—Kelly, *Summary of the History and Law of Usury*, p. 18. London: 1835.

I

detail, are all inspired by the same ideas. We may specially mention that of the Siennese Tommaso Buoninsegni (died 1610), a merchant at first and then a monk (*Dei Cambii.* Florence, 1573), and another by the Padre Fabiano Clavario of Genoa. The *Breve notizia dei Cambii* (1581) by Bernardo Davanzati (1529-1606), gives a simple description of the mechanism of exchange. This work is better known to economists, because it is included in Custodi's collection, and to men of letters because of the elegance of its style.

A far more lively controversy was excited by the *monti di pi tà*, which had spread in Italy during the second half of the fifteenth century. In the following century a demand arose for their introduction into the Low Countries. These institutions lent money on security, at first gratuitously, and afterwards for interest. They were fiercely opposed by the Dominicans, on the ground of the unlawfulness of interest. On the other hand, they were defended by the Franciscans from a charitable point of view, as being a refuge for the poor from the heavy usuries of private money-lenders, chiefly Jews. Among theologians, the already-mentioned Cardinal Gaetano and Barianno, an Augustinian monk (*Tractatus de Monte Impietatis,* Cremona, 1496), were enemies of the Monti. De Rosellis and Padre Bernardino da Busto (*Defensorium Montis Pietatis,* 1497), defended them.

But the favourite subject of the economists of the 16th century was that of money. Their attention was called to it by the discovery of the American mines, and by the still existing abuse of the adulteration of money by sovereigns. Some observations of the economic kind are made by learned men, while discoursing, like Budaeus, Agricola, and Alciati, on ancient money, or, like Borghini, on modern money. The writers on *natural history*, too, in dealing with the *precious metals* come across economic questions. They sometimes even discuss them, as, for example, the German writer Julius Agricola, in his book *De Re metallica* (1535). The subject is more thoroughly treated by jurists, who discuss with much subtlety the legal consequences of altering the monetary standard. Hence they are led to definitions of the nature and functions of money. These, however, they do not always clearly understand. They confound the essential qualities of money with the stamp of the sovereign, which is merely an attestation of its value. Among these legal writers the following are noteworthy : Alberto Bruno d'Asti, Antonio Sola, and Gaspare Tes- auro, all Piedmontese ; the Savoyard Favre, and the Germans, Johann Aquila and Reinero Budelio, whose works have been often reprinted in special collections.

Without denying the importance of these writings, the economist will doubtless find certain other treatises more interesting, in which the same subject is treated from a more purely economic point of view.

The earliest of such writings proceeded from a worthy successor to Buridan and Orêsme in the 14th century, the celebrated astronomer Copernicus. About 1526 he wrote, at the command of Sigismund I. of Poland, a treatise with the title *De Monetae Cudendae Ratione*. It was printed for the first time in 1816, and again in 1864 by Wolowski. In it he expounds correctly the con- ception of money. He opposes monetary depreciation, pointing out the economic and legal disturbances which arise from it. And he makes many useful proposals for the reform of the monetary system in the Prussian provinces, at that time subject to Poland.

A. Montanari, *Nicolò Copernico.* Padua, 1873. (2nd ed. 1877).

Almost contemporary with Copernicus was an anonymous German writer, author of *Gemeine Stimmen von der Müntze*, 1530; *Apologie*, etc. 1531. He defended the sound monetary policy of the Albertine line of the princes of Saxony against the accusations made by the partisans of the Ernestine line. His ideas on wealth, commerce, and money, are very correct and have been praised highly by Roscher.

W. Roscher, *Ueber die Blüthe deutscher National-ökonomie im Zeitalter der Reformation.* In the *Berichte der Sächs. Gesell. der Wiss., Phil.-hist. Classe.* 1862, p. 145, et seq.

Half a century later, the already mentioned Davanzati in his *Lezione delle Monete* (1588), and Gaspare Scaruffi of Reggio (died 1584) in his *Alitinonfo*, written in 1579 (Reggio, 1582), deplore the disorders in the currency. Davanzati is superficial, but his style is brief and elegant. The other, though more profound and competent, is tedious and lengthy. They both propose the adoption of a uniform monetary system, with a double standard based on a proportion of value of 12 to 1 between gold and silver, approximately corresponding to the actual proportion at the time.

The subject of the rise of prices, being related to that of money and even entering in a large measure into monetary questions, was touched upon, though not very successfully, by some of the writers above mentioned. The disturbing effects of such a variation of prices on economic relations made themselves especially felt in the second half of the 16th century. This gave rise to some interesting special treatises, the object of which was to investigate the causes of the movement, and to suggest opportune remedies.

The erroneous assertions of a certain Seigneur de Malestroit were the occasion of two brief discourses in reply by Jean Bodin, the French politician mentioned above (p. 110). (a). *Réponse aux Paradoxes de M. de Malestroit touchant l'Enchérissement de toutes les Choses et des Monnaies*, 1568. (b). *Discours sur le Rehaussement et la Diminution des Monnaies*, 1578.) These pamphlets were afterwards incorporated in his *République*. He points out as the principal causes of the rise of prices : the abundance of money caused by the increased production of silver in America ; the growing importance of external commerce ; the large business done by the bank of Lyons ; monetary alterations, etc. He considers that all these circumstances would be turned to better advantage by a fiscal system promoting the growth of national manufactures in opposition to the excessive consumption of foreign goods.

An anonymous English writer W. S. (probably William Stafford), who was evidently acquainted with the writings of Bodin, treated of the same subject in a dialogue. *A compendious or briefe examination of certayne ordinary complaints*, etc. London, 1581. His manner of treatment, a more popular one in his own country, differed from that of Bodin. That is, he expounded with greater fullness the effects of the rise of prices, without laying much stress on the influence of the increased production of silver. But he also proposed as a remedy a restrictive policy with regard to international commerce. The pamphlet has been often but inaccurately quoted by historians of political economy. Professor E. Nasse gave an accurate and learned notice of it in his memoir :

Ueber eine volkswirthschaftliche Schrift aus der Zeit der Preisrevolution, etc. In the *Zeitschr. f. die ges. Staatswiss.* 19th year (1863), p. 369–391.

Another group of English writers is worthy of particular consideration. Writing towards the end of the sixteenth century they dwelt on the subject of the colonies and their relations with England. They thought that these relations should be so adjusted as to promote national industry as much as possible. They left unnoticed the subject of the importation of the precious metals, which was the ruling principle of the colonial system of Spain and Portugal. Among these writers Sir Walter Raleigh stands the first (*Essay on Trade*, 1595). We may mention besides, Gilbert, Hakluyt, Peckham and Carlisle. Like the economists of the following .century, they demanded restrictive measures with regard to foreign trade, and in favour of English manufactures. But they show themselves comparatively superior to the later writers whose restrictive proposals are based upon a false conception of the nature of money.

We find at this time some economic writers in Spain, a country which is generally looked upon as incapable of producing any original scientific speculation. Towards the middle of the sixteenth century the theologico-economic question of the right of the civil power to forbid begging gave rise to many polemical writings. To this question were allied the delicate economic and administrative problems relating to the organisation of public beneficence. Among the many writings mentioned by Colmeiro in his *Storia della Economia politica in Ispagna* (p. 83), it will be enough to mention the following : *Deliberacion en la Causa de los Pobres* (Salamanca,

1545), by the famous theologian, Domenico Soto, containing a fierce denunciation of every restriction on mendicity and vagabondage : *De lo Orden que en algunos Pueblos de España se ha puesto en la Limosina*, etc., (Salamanca, 1545) by Padre Giovanni di Medina, who advocates the prohibition of begging, and the erection of workhouses : finally, the works of Michele de Giginta (*Tratada de Remedio de Pobres*, Coimbra, 1575) who timidly proposes as a compromise, the non-compulsory erection of workhouses.

§ 2. *The Mercantile System.*

Ad. Held, *Carey's Socialwissenschaft und das Merkantilsystem.* Würzburg, 1866, 8vo.

J. C. Glaser, *Die soziale und politische Bedeutung des sogen. Merkantil-Systems.* In the *Jahrb. für Gesellschafts- und Staatswissenschaften*, Vol. XI. (1869), pp. 300, et seq.

H. J. Bidermann, *Ueber den Merkantilismus*, Innsbruck, 1870. (This work corrects many prevailing errors about the mercantile system, but goes too far in defending it.)

Certain general theories relating to the economic administration of states, and particularly to the organisa tion of a commercial policy, formed that body of doctrine to which the economists succeeding Adam Smith gave the name of the *mercantile system* or the *balance of trade*. These theories were gradually set forth by writers of the sixteenth century, more especially of the last ten years of it (*e.g.*, Bodin and Stafford), and more competently by others belonging to the first ten years of the next century. In the various expositions of them there were many discrepancies in the details, and many incoherences and contradictions. In part they reflected popular opinion; in part they generalised the ruling ideas of most of the positive legislation of the time; in part they sought to influence legislation in the direction of a more complete application of their theories. The mercantile system was also called the *restrictive system*, and by some writers *Colbertism*, after the statesman who, though not its author, made the largest, ablest, and most important experiment in the application of its principles to the government of a great nation.

The conclusion at which the supporters of this system arrived, and which they stated more or less explicitly, was that *the economic well-being of a State is in proportion to the quantity of money which circulates in it.* They started from the idea, obviously true both in domestic and industrial economy, that whoever has at his disposal a large quantity of money possesses the means of procuring every other kind of wealth. Further, their attention was turned to the growing importance of the mechanism of circulation. This growing importance was the result of various circumstances. There was an increase in the production of the precious metals, especially of silver. Trade was increasing more and more. Rich and powerful colonies were arising beyond the sea. There was an almost complete transformation of the old " natural " economy. Again, they observed that commercial and political power was concentrated in the hands of those nations which, standing first in the manufacturing and commercial arts, set in motion a comparatively large quantity of money, either drawn from their own mines, as in the case of Spain and Portugal, or attracted by their trade, as in Italy, Flanders, Holland, and later in England.

From the principle stated above, it followed as a logical consequence, that the *fundamental canon* of political economy should be to *preserve* and to *increase* as far as possible the quantity of money actually in circulation.

The historical investigations of certain writers of merit have shown that these were the ideas in which the *mercantilists* agreed. With some rare exceptions they did not profess the strange error attributed to them, that *wealth consists of money and of money alone*. Many centuries before, this absurdity had received an allegoric confutation in the fable of *King Midas* and a scientific confutation in Aristotle's *Politics*. There is another incorrect statement which has been made by later critics. They say that these writers are distinguished from the theorists of antiquity and from the *physiocrats* of the eighteenth century, by the small esteem they entertained for agricultural industry, which they thought should be neglected in comparison with manufactures and commerce. On the contrary, we find in the writings of the sixteenth and seventeenth centuries many passages showing the opposite opinion. Thus Bodin deplores the injuries which agriculturists sustained from usury, and advocated for their benefit the reform of the system of mortgage. And Botero constantly insists that *a sovereign should encourage and promote agriculture.* Obrecht again, a writer of the seventeenth century, calls agriculture *aliarum rerum parentem et nutricem,* while his contemporary Klock affirms that *suo labore omnes alit vir rusticus.* And, what ·is more important, we find that authors writing in the interests of eminently agrarian States do not confine themselves to proposing measures for the restriction of foreign manufacturing competition. They propose also that the exportation of agricultural produce should be encouraged, and its importation forbidden, for the benefit of land-owners and cultivators of the soil.

These writers then agreed in maintaining that where silver and gold abound there can be no lack of any of the necessaries of life. They were also agreed in demanding that governments should do all in their power to procure an abundance of money. But they did not all agree as to the measures best suited for the attainment of this end. There was no doubt among them that those countries which could help themselves to gold and silver from their own mines were economically better situated than other countries, provided that they knew how to keep the money so easily acquired. But the greater number of them did not approve of those foolish and violent measures against the exportation of money resorted to by certain States. Such measures were indeed absurd and impracticable, as it was impossible to convict offenders. And many mercantilists of the highest authority in England, Italy, France, and elsewhere, began by reprobating these unwise laws. They wished to substitute for penal laws a system of economic provisions better calculated to obtain an abundance of money, and to promote the welfare of industry.

This combination was to be based on an exact relation between imports and exports, so regulated that the latter should exceed the former in value. The difference, they thought, would be balanced by an excess of imported over exported money. To this end they proposed two kinds of provisions, the one tending to increase exports, the other to diminish imports.

They wished to have *prohibited*, or at least discouraged by high duties, the *importation* of products manufactured in countries which were adapted to the development of manufacturing industry. These products, being of more value than others, would procure a greater quantity of money. On the other hand, the more subtle mercantilists wished that the introduction of foreign *raw materials* which could be manufactured in the country should be permitted and even encouraged. They hoped that the subsequent exportation of the manufactured articles would more than compensate for this outflow of money. In the same way they advocated the free importation of *necessaries*, so as to get cheaper labour and consequently smaller expenses of production in comparison with foreign competition.

In order further to encourage the exportation of manufactured products, the mercantilists made the following proposals. They demanded for such products exemption from duties, and sometimes even the grant of *bounties* from the state treasury. They proposed the arrangement of commercial treaties, in which the country should obtain favourable conditions without undertaking excessive responsibilities. Again, they proposed the establishment of a *colonial system*. The manufacturers of the mother country were to have a monopoly of the colonial market. The colonial producers of raw materials were to have either the absolute monopoly of the mother country's market, or at least a favourable arrangement with it.

Experience has shown the sad effects of a commercial policy based on the supposition of a necessary hostility between nations. Modern science too has proved the erroneousness of the mercantile system, whether considered as the ideal of economic government, or as applied to a nation advanced in industry and civilisation, Nevertheless at certain times and under certain conditions this system has given notable advantages to industrial organisation and progress, playing the same part as absolute monarchy has done in the sphere of politics. Colbert's system (1661—1683) and Cromwell's *Navigation Act* contributed not a little to the economic greatness of France and England.

The mercantile system then certainly exaggerated the importance of money, and in our days it cannot be brought to life again by apologies which must necessarily be out of date. But neither can it be confuted merely by the vulgar adage that money is not wealth, although it asserted, as some economic compendiums do, that money is just as much wealth as any other commodity. It was right in considering money as wealth *sui generis*. But it did not recognise its *instrumental* character, overlooking the following facts among others; that its value is not in proportion only to its *quantity*, but also to its *rapidity of circulation* : that its function in *exchanges* may be deputed in part to other *instruments of credit*, less costly and more convenient ; that it may sometimes be scarce and sometimes excessive; that *liberty* is the best means of bringing it in where it is wanted, and letting it flow out where it is in excess; that for a country to have a perpetually favourable balance, that is, always to sell more goods than it buys, is a chimera and an impossibility ; that it is an unwise thing to found commercial treaties on the principle of *reciprocity*, by which we deny ourselves benefit because others deny it to themselves; that international debts are settled in money only as regards comparatively small and unimportant differences.

In short, the mercantile system proposed to itself an end which was in part impossible, and attempted to obtain it by means which often led to very different results. For instance, bounties on exportation occasion loss to the contributors, and duties on importation raise prices for the consumers. Such disadvantages, in an advanced condition of economic civilisation, far surpass the benefits which under other circumstances might be obtained from such measures.

In the history of Colbert's administration we may best study the practical results of this system. See especially :—

Pierre Clément, *Histoire de Colbert et de son Administration*, 2nd ed. Paris, 1875, 2 vols. 12mo.

G. Cohn, *Colbert vornehmlich in staatswirth. Hinsicht.* In the *Zeitschr. f. die ges. Staatsw.* Vols. 25 and 26 (1869-70), p. 369-434, 390-454. (A short and accurate monograph, giving later critical accounts of the sources of information.)

§ 3.   *Political Economy in the Seventeenth Century.*

The economists of the 17th century may be divided into three classes. In the first class are included the more or less unqualified upholders of the mercantile system. The second class, anticipating ideas which were more fully developed in the following century, oppose the balance of trade system, and declare themselves partisans of free trade. The writers of the third class occupy themselves with special questions, or render valuable service by the elucidation of certain theories not directly connected with what is called *mercantilism*.

Among the supporters of the mercantile system the following important writers lived in the first ten years of the 17th century, namely, in Italy, Antonio Serra ; in France, Antoine de Montchrétien; and in England Thomas Mun.

Antonio Serra was a Calabrian and a native of Cosenza. He was suspected, on insufficient grounds, of a share in the conspiracy of Tommaso Campanello against the Spanish government, and found himself in the Papal prison. Here he wrote his *Breve Trattato delle Cause che possono fare abbondare li Regni d' Oro e d'Argento dove non sono Miniere.*   Naples, 1613, 8vo.

For nearly a hundred and fifty years Serra was unnoticed.   Then Galiani, Salfi, and a crowd of Italian and foreign authors, declared him to be the first economist in order of time, while Ferrara denies any economic merit to him.   His book certainly deserves a high place among the writings belonging to the first half of the 17th century. He was not the first to expound the theory of the mercantile system, and certainly not the first to oppose it, as some have strangely asserted.   But he gave a sufficiently remarkable exposition of it, and confuted certain errors made by the more extravagant mercantilists. His belief in it was so strong that he declared that disbelievers should be treated as madmen.   His strictures were chiefly directed against a mercantilist named Marc' Antonio di Santis of Nocera.   This writer had maintained the obsolete theories of the alteration of money, the prohibition of its exportation, and the artificial regulation of the course of the exchanges, and had suggested corresponding measures to improve the economic condition of the kingdom of Naples. Serra could not get rid of the ruling idea of the balance of trade system. But with more perception than the ordinary mercantilists he set himself to show that money can only abound in those states where happy external conditions, the industry of the inhabitants, and the stability of government, favour the development of manufactures and commerce. He quoted as examples Venice and Genoa, which in economic conditions were at that time strongly contrasted to the Neapolitan provinces. (See the conscientious and learned monograph by T. Fornari ; *Studii sopra Antonio Serra e Marc' Antonio di Santis*, Pavia, 1879.)

A Norman writer, contemporary with Serra, but less well known, professed opinions which were much to the same effect but expounded more at length. This was Antoino de Montchrétien, Sieur de Vatteville. He dedicated to the young king Louis XIII., and to the Regent Marie de Medicis, a voluminous work entitled *Traité de l'Économie politique*, Paris, 1615, 4to. The subjects specially discussed in it are the theories relating to commerce, both on land and sea, and to colonies. His treatment of these theories aroused the enthusiasm of Duval, his commentator, who, ignoring or depreciating earlier and contemporary writers, declared Montchrétien to be the most eminent among the fore-runners of political economy.

Jules Duval, *Mémoire sur Antoine de Montchrétien, Sieur de Vatteville, Auteur du premier Traité d'Économie politique*, Paris, 1868, 8vo.

Thomas Mun, a London merchant, had more fame and influence. *England's treasure by foreign trade*, pub-lished after his death in 1664, and his *Discourse on*

English Commerce, came to be looked upon as text books in England. They were subsequently translated into Italian by Genovesi. In the *Wealth of Nations* they received a general confutation.

In Mun's writings the mercantile system, freed from the gross exaggerations of vulgar opinion, is shown to its greatest advantage. It becomes national, from the special references made to the interests of England and more particularly to those of the East India Company. This has been pointed out by MacCulloch and Roscher, by both of whom its theories have been specially criticised.

The followers of the mercantile system were very numerous during the second half of the seventeenth century, and mostly so in Spain and Germany. We find in their publications very little originality, and far grosser errors than in the above-mentioned text-books.

Among the Germans Gaspar Klock was a lengthy compiler of undigested information. (*De Contributionibus*, 1634, *De Ærario*, 1651). The following deserve special mention : Becher ? (*Politischer Discurs*, 1668); Von Hörnigk, who followed in the lines laid down by Becher, applying the mercantilist canons to the conditions of Austria (*Oesterreich über Alles*, 1684); and Baron Wilhelm von Schröder (*Fürstliche Schatz-und Rentkammer*, 1686), the most remarkable of them.

There were certain writers, too, in France, Italy, Spain, Holland, and more especially in England, who opposed the prejudices of the mercantile system, both in its theoretical forms and in its administrative consequences. They were at first but few in number, and never had any influence. They formed more correct conceptions of the nature of wealth and of the right

administration of industry, and they professed, more
or less widely, the theories of *free trade*.

L. Cossa, *La Teoria del libro Scambio nel secolo XVII.*
(1873). In the *Rendiconti del Reale Istituto Lombardo di
Scienze e Lettere.* Series II., Vol. VI., No. XII.

In France Émérique de Lacroix (*Le nouveau Cynée*,
1623), and in Spain Alberto Struzzi, a writer of Italian
origin, proclaimed in the abstract the necessity of free
trade. At the same time certain French authors, who
have remained anonymous, showed the injuries which
had been done to industry by the too rigid application
of the system of Colbert. A reaction against this system
set in soon afterwards, which attained larger proportions
in the following century.

But these writers, and several others who came after
them, are obscured by an illustrious group of English
authors who flourished in the second half of the seventeenth century. The latter represented more advanced
ideas and made more profound analyses of economic
phenomena than any writers before their time. Besides Hobbes and Locke, there were the three distinguished writers, Sir Joshua Child, Sir William Petty,
and Sir Dudley North. These men had a strong influence on the physiocrats and on Adam Smith
himself, which historians for a long time did not
recognise.

Sir Joshua Child, a merchant, was the author of *Observations concerning Trade and Interest of Money* (1668), and
of *A New Discourse of Trade* (1690). He was not wholly
emancipated from the theory of the balance of trade,
and with certain limitations he was favourable to the
Navigation Act, the colonial system, and to the creation
of privileged trading companies. But his ideas on

matters concerning food-commodities are comparatively
wide, and he specially insists on the advantage of a low
rate of interest to economic prosperity.   This had
already been pointed out by Culpeper (*A Tract against the
High Rate of Usury*, 1623 ;   *Useful Remarks on High
Interest*, 1641).   Child supports his argument by the
example of Holland, and proposes the false remedy
of a legal reduction of interest.

The economic, financial, and statistical works of Sir
William Petty show a still more marked advance.
Quantulumcumque, or a Tract concerning Money, 1682 ; *A
Treatise of Taxes and Contributions*, 1679 ; *Essays in
Political Arithmetick*, 1682 ; *Political Anatomy of Ireland*,
1691.   Especially remarkable in these works is the
attempt to fix the value of an ordinary day's labour as
an absolute and constant measure of value, and the
conception of labour as the only element of production, so
that every kind of wealth may be economically resolved
into labour.   These opinions are obviously erroneous,
because capital combines with labour in determining
the value of products.   Nevertheless they form part of
a noteworthy progress in the scientific analysis of production, and are the key-note of a doctrine that was
for a long time characteristic of English economists.

Though inferior to Petty in economic learning and in
width of view generally, his contemporary and political
friend Sir Dudley North (*Discourses upon Trade*, 1691)
was far more explicit in his treatment of the freedom of
exchange, being its most energetic defender in the seventeenth century, from a cosmopolitan and not from a
merely national point of view.   He considers money to
be a commodity of the same nature as other commodities, its quantity varying with commercial conditions.

When money is abundant the prices of commodities rise, and more money is exported. When it is scarce, prices fall, and more money is imported. Thus with nations as with individuals, money is only important as a means for obtaining things which are wanted for direct consumption. The important matter is to increase the amount of raw produce and manufactured articles. Hence the mistake of imposing duties on the exportation of money, and the evil of any kind of measure tending to favour particular branches of industry, the individual gain being counterbalanced by a loss to the nation at large.

The anonymous author of *Britannia Languens* vigorously opposed the Navigation Act. He was not in favour of free trade, but was perhaps superior to North in profundity of learning.

These writers then combated the ideas more generally received, without finding any favour from their contemporaries. But the principles which they laid down were more fully discussed and illustrated in the following century. In the meantime certain other authors examined, with a good deal of success, some special economic theories.

Turning to political treatises we find them more numerous and longer, but inferior to the writings of the sixteenth century both in general merit and in economic value. They discuss at greater length administrative matters relating to the social ordering of wealth, taking sometimes a practical point of view, sometimes the ideal one of Platonic communism. There were two representatives of the latter view in the seventeenth century. One was the English republican, Harrington, author of *Oceana* (1640), dealing chiefly with the excessive concentration of land in the hands of a few people. The other was the celebrated Dominican of Calabria, Tommaso Campanella, who gave out his famous work, *Civitas Solis*, in 1643.

A more fruitful line of thought, with regard both to theories and their applications, was followed by certain Dutch jurists and publicists. The following are specially noteworthy :—Ugo de Groot (Hugo Grotius), the eminent originator of theories bearing on the law of nature and the law of nations; Graswinkel, who in a political work published in 1651, propounded the theory of the free exportation of corn, opposing the system of the State purchase of corn and defending agricultural interests; the two brothers, Jean and Pierre de la Court, and more especially the latter, who was the author of writings which were for a long time thought to be De Witt's. His ideas on commercial policy given in these works are very broad, and he opposes with much weight of learning the abuses of *corporations in arts and trades*.

In Holland also many writers, following the French author Claude Saumaise, maintained the lawfulness of interest, meeting with a good deal of opposition. An interesting controversy about *monti di pietà* (public pawnbroking institutions), arose out of this, and occasioned several writings of some theoretical interest. An account of them is given by Laspeyres (mentioned above), and a fuller one by Veegens.

I. D. Veegens, *De Banken van Leening in Nord-Nederland*. Rotterdam, 1869, 8vo. p. 124—266.

Finally there was in the Netherlands a small number of publicists of considerable merit. They group themselves round the illustrious name of Wilhelm Usselinx, and they deal with the colonial question under its various aspects.

There were also special economic subjects which were discussed in other countries. Passing over points of minor importance, we must note the many works on the subject of money published in France, England, and Germany. Among these; the first place doubtless belongs to the works of the eminent philosopher, John Locke. Although to a considerable extent a believer in the theory of the balance of trade, he expounded with much acuteness in two of his works the theory of money and financial administration. These works were carefully studied, and formed the point of departure of writings which came out in the following century in Italy and elsewhere. There were however in Italy, in the seventeenth century, writers of some merit on monetary questions, independent of Locke. Of these, Geminiano Montanari, professor in the University of Padua (1633—1687), is superior to Turbolo, an obscure mint-director. Montanari wrote two works about 1680, which were only printed seventy years later in the *Raccolta* of Argelati. Their merits are numerous, notwithstanding their obvious leaning to Bodin's opinions.

An earlier work by Romeo Bocchi of Bologna is not mentioned by any historian of the science. Its title is as follows :—

Romeo Bocchi, *Della giusta universale Misura e suo Tipo*. Vol. I. *Anima della Moneta*. Venice (Pinelli), 1621, 4to.—Vol. II. *Corpo della Moneta*. Venice (Giotti), 1621, 4to.

§ 4. *Political Economy in the First Half of the Eighteenth Century.*

In the first half of the eighteenth century the most diligent historian cannot trace any marked progress in economic science taken as a whole. The crude ideas and exaggerated applications of the restrictive system gained in importance. To the blind faith in the influence of money on national wealth there was added, during a certain period, an equally exaggerated confidence in the miracles to be worked by its substitutes, and especially the bank-note. Hence the ruin and disappointment caused by the so-called system of the famous Scotch adventurer, John Law, and the excessive reaction which followed it. During the regency of Philip of Orleans he controlled the French finances for nearly four years, making extreme abuses of credit.

Besides monographs by Thiers, Daire, Cochut, and Horn, the following works may specially be consulted :

J. Heymann, *Law und sein System.* Munich, 1853. 8vo. (This work specially examines Law's theories.)

A. Lavasseur, *Recherches historiques sur le Système de Law.* Paris, 1854, 8vo.

J. J. Clamageran, *Histoire de l'Impôt en France.* Vol. III. Paris, 1876, 8vo. p. 157—204.

As the progress of a science is often, though not always, nor everywhere, nor to the same extent, attended by progress in its public teaching, we may notice that during the first ten years of the eighteenth century economic theories began to be a subject of academic lectures. This took place almost at the same time in England and Germany. But the origin and tendencies of the new teaching were very different in the two countries.

In England, or rather in Scotland, from 1729 to 1747, Francis Hutcheson was giving lectures on moral philosophy from the Glasgow chair. Dealing also with philosophical and political law he was led to illustrate certain points of economic doctrine, and especially the theories of *value* and *price*. There are traces of these theories in his Latin Compendium entitled : *Philosophiæ Moralis Institutio Compendiaria, etc.* (Rotterdam, 1745, 8vo.) A certain historical importance attaches to them. Adam Smith, the pupil, and subsequently the successor, of Hutcheson, must have heard these lectures, and it may be, as some have observed, that they awoke in him the love of this branch of learning. It has been pronounced a memorable fact that political economy first made its appearance at the Scotch universities in the guise of an appendix to a course of moral philosophy. But it must be added that the intrinsic merit of Hutcheson's economic lectures is very small. The book above mentioned is nothing but an extract from the work of the German, Samuel Puffendorf : *De Jure Naturæ et Gentium* (1672), in which the theory of price is developed with much acuteness.

In Germany, the origin of economic teaching was what would now be termed bureaucratic. For the instruction of officials in the political, the administrative, and especially in the financial department of the State, there gradually arose a complex group of studies, to which was given the special name of Chamber-Sciences, because the upper administrative departments were called chambers. These so-called Chamber-sciences included (*a*) private economy in its various branches, agricultural economy, the economy of forestry, the economy of mining, technology, etc. ; (b) the elements of administrative science, or, as it was then called, of *police*; and (c) those few theories of general economics and finance out of which the economic science afterwards arose. King Frederick William I. of Prussia founded two chairs of Chamber-Sciences about 1727, one at Halle, the other at Frankfort-on-the-Oder, and appointed two famous jurists to them, Gasser (died 1745) and Dithmar (died 1737), who treated specially of the subjects belonging to finance. But the best writers during this period are to be found, not in Germany, but in England, France, and up to a certain point in Italy.

In England the idealist philosopher, Berkeley, in his periodical publication *The Querist* (1735) marked the point of departure for a fresh awakening of economic studies which had been neglected during the first few years of the century. But the theory of free trade had been propounded, more competently than by Dudley North, by an anonymous writer in *Considerations on the East India Trade* (1702). A little later Joseph Harris, an official in the London mint, published anonymously *An Essay on Money and Coins* (London 1757—58, 8vo.). This celebrated work, one of the best writings on the subject of money in point of learning, clearness, and precision, was reprinted a few years ago, and was recently commended by Professor Jevons. The foundation of the Bank of England by a Scotchman, William Patterson, gave rise to numerous instructive writings, of a controversial character, at the end of the seventeenth century and the beginning of the eighteenth. In these works we can trace the germs of many modern theories and controversies on the operations of credit. Notices of these books, accompanied by criticisms, some of which are partial and inaccurate, may be found in *The Literature of Political Economy* (London, 1845, 8vo.), by J. R. MacCulloch, partly reproduced under the article *Banque* in Coquelin et Guillaumin's *Dictionnaire de l'Économie politique.* Paris, 1852—53, Vol. I., p. 140.

The French economists living at the beginning of the eighteenth century deserve to be placed before those of other nations, if we judge them from their width of view rather than from their exposition of particular theories. Special eminence belongs to the great Marshal de Vauban and to his friend Pierre le Pesant, Seigneur de Boisguillebert. In his *Dixme royale* (1707), Vauban painted in bold and vivid colours the misery into which France had fallen during the last years of the reign of Louis XIV., and proposed as a remedy a thorough reform of the system of revenue. Boisguillebert was the author of various writings—*Détail de la France,* 1697; *Factum de la France,* 1707; *Traité des Grains,* etc. He understood better than Vauban how to combine his financial projects, and he gives an analysis, which is good in many respects, of the nature and characteristics of wealth. Though by no means free from errors,—one of which is the small importance attributed to money, the effect of a reaction against the mercantile system,—this analysis may be considered as preparing the way for a larger method of economic investigation. In the sphere of applications, Boisguillebert is perhaps the most eminent of the direct opponents of *Colbertism.* His recent biographers are mistaken in saying that his position in this respect was that of free trade. It was really that of *agrarian protection.* He did not ask for absolute freedom of exportation and importation, in order that consumers might benefit by low prices and the abundance of all kinds of commodities. He merely demanded free exportation for corn in the interests of the agricultural classes, hoping that the price of food would rise, and with it the value of land. At the same time he wished its importation to be forbidden, or at least that high duties should be laid on imports from abroad.

J. C. Horn, *L'Économie politique avant les Physiocrates*. Paris, 1867. One vol. 8vo.

F. Cadet, *Pierre de Boisguillebert, Précurseur des Économistes*. Paris, 1870. One vol. 8vo.

G. Cohn, *Boisguillebert*. In the *Zeitschrift für die ges. Staatswiss.* Vol. XXV. (1869), p. 360, et seq. (This work contains less detail, but gives on some points more accurate expositions and more impartial judgments than the preceding.)

The works of the noted publicists, Melon (*Essai politique sur le Commerce*, 1734), and Dutot (*Réflexions politiques sur les Finances et le Commerce*, 1735, 1738), show many signs of the influence of the mercantile system. Their general views are less elevated than those of the above-mentioned writers, and mostly limited to the subjects of money and credit, their ideas on these matters being to a certain extent favourable to Law's system. Melon defended monetary alterations within certain limits, while Dutot opposed them. This controversy was echoed in Italy, where their works found translators, commentators, apologists, and adversaries.

Économistes financiers du XVIII° *Siècle.* (In the *Collection des principaux Économistes*, of Guillaumin.)

Montesquieu's greatest political work (*De l'Ésprit des Lois*. Geneva, 1748, 2 vols. 4to.), is rich in concise and ingenious remarks on the connection between the system of government and economic conditions, more especially that of finance. But he does not rise much above the ideas and prejudices of his time.

During the first ten years of the eighteenth century the condition of Italy was far from flourishing, and social matters were little studied. Towards the middle of the century, however, certain reforms set on foot by the Italian princes seem to point to a remarkable progress of ideas.

Among those politicians who deal, at least incidentally, with economic questions, Paolo Mattia Doria, a Genoese writer, is noteworthy. He lived at Naples, and was the friend of Vico. His book, *Della Vita civile*, was written in 1710.

Of greater importance, at least comparatively, is the Perugian Abbot, Leone Pascoli, who in 1733 published anonymously his *Testamento politico di un Academico fiorentino*, which he had written in 1728. In this book he suggests many plans for the revival of trade in the Papal provinces, all based on the ideas of the mercantile system.

A greater and well-deserved fame belongs to the *Discorso sulla Maremma sienese*, written in 1737, but not published till 1775, by Archdeacon Salustio Antonio Bandini di Siena. He describes in dark colours the miserable condition into which the Maremma had fallen, partly through its unfavourable climate, and partly through the decay of agriculture there. This latter circumstance was in great measure owing to the bad government of the Medici, and particularly to the wretched economic and fiscal system in force. He proposes a complete reform of commercial and financial legislation, based on the free exportation of agricultural produce and the simplification of taxes. For the latter purpose the taxes are to be levied from the landowners and paid in kind. They are to be farmed by the Communes, who are to levy them among themselves according to their capabilities. Gorani, Custodi, and Pecchio try to prove that he was a forerunner of the physiocrats. But, as Ferrara has shown, this merit cannot be claimed for him. He certainly holds, however, a very honourable position among contemporary economists, and he well deserves the feeling akin to worship with which he is regarded in Tuscany, where his book led the way to the reforms of the Grand Duke Leopold.

The *Saggio sul Commercio* (1750) of the Roman banker Gerolamo Belloni, was a good deal read in its time, but it is inspired by crude mercantilist ideas. The noted and versatile writer, Scipione Maffei, of Verona, published in 1744 a book, *Sull' Impiego del Denaro*, which made some stir. It is not very original, its materials being to a great extent drawn from a work by a Dutch writer, Broedersen. Later, Concina, Ballerini, and other theologians, attacked Maffei, bringing up the old theories against interest. The controversy went on until Pope Benedict XIV. interposed with the Bull, *Vix pervenit*.

Carlo Antonio Broggia was a Neapolitan merchant; or rather, if Settembrini is to be trusted, a Venetian, who had settled at Naples. He published at Naples, in 1743, a treatise on money, taxes, and political action in sanitary matters. It is badly written and not free from

errors, and in its treatment of the money question contains nothing remarkable. But it may be considered
as the first methodical work on taxation published in
Italy, a fact which, to our mind, has not been sufficiently
taken into account by the historians of Economics. He
was opposed to fiscal exclusiveness, to loans, to free ports,
and to the direct taxation of industry. His financial
system is based on two sources of income. First, the
taxation of the returns to capital, both fixed and cir-
culating (*upon fixed incomes at the rate of a tenth part*).
Secondly, duties on internal (excise) and external
consumption. Only in cases of extraordinary need
would he allow voluntary contributions, and only
within strict limits a capitation tax.

CHAPTER IV.

Towards the middle of the last century the really modern era of economic science began, brought in largely by the progress of philosophy and of the social sciences. The favour with which the various sovereigns of Europe began to look upon it, contributed also to its advance. They started administrative reforms, and granted facilities for wider instruction in the civil sciences. Those who were learned in these matters became their advisers and fellow-workers in plans of reform. Most of the countries of Europe felt the influence of this growth of economic knowledge.

The chairs of Chamber Sciences were multiplied in Germany and Austria, where two men summed up the economic learning of the time. One was Justi, who, in 1752, taught at the Theresianum of Vienna and shortly afterwards passed on to Leipzig. The other was Sonnenfels, who, in 1763, occupied a chair at the University of Vienna. They both published economic treatises, in which the theories of a modified mercantilism are expounded with much learning, and which—especially that of Sonnenfels—contain schemes of reform greatly in advance of the times.

CHAP. IV.]   THE PHYSIOCRATIC SCHOOL.   143

A little later, chairs of political economy were founded
in Italy. Genovesi taught at Naples with great success, 1754-1769; the celebrated Beccaria at Milan,
1768-1770; Paradisi, better known in literature, at
Modena, 1772-1780; and Sergio at Palermo, 1779-
1806.

L. Cossa, *Sulle prime Cattedre di Economia politica in
Italia.* In the *Rendiconti del R. Istituto Lombardo di
Scienze e Lettere.* Series II., Vol. VI. (1873), No.
VIII.

But the stronger and more direct movement towards
progress of which the physiocratic political economy
was the sign, did not originate in these chairs, from
which the lecturers gave forth the doctrines of the
balance of trade. This may be seen from the works of
Justi (1755), and from Genovesi's *Lezioni d'Economia
civile* (1765). We may add to these, since they are
written in the same spirit, though not by professors,
the *Éléments de Commerce* (1754),. and other works
by Forbonnais, the conscientious historian of French
finance, with Sir James Stewart's long treatise, *Inquiry
into the Principles of Political Economy.* London, 1767,
2 vols. 4to. In all these books the remarkable progress
of certain special doctrines is noteworthy. But the
special doctrines are not brought into connection with
any clearly determined general principles, so that we
merely have a collection of monographs, and not really
systematic works.

The foundations of a genuine system of political
economy, or rather of social science considered more
especially from the economic side, were laid by an illustrious school of French writers living in the reigns of
Louis XV. and Louis XVI. Quesnay, a physician

(1694-1774), was the founder of the school. Turgot, the philosopher, the publicist, the economist, the statesman (died 1781), was its greatest representative. A complete and impartial history of the physiocrats has been given by a French writer.

Notice abrégée des différents Écrits modernes qui ont concourru en France à former la Science de l'Économie politique. In the *Éphémerides du Citoyen, etc.* Paris, 1769. (A rich collection of materials.)

A selection of the best works of the physiocrats was made by Eug. Daire for the *Collection des principaux Économistes* (Paris, 1846, royal 8vo.), and by Francesco Ferrara for the *Biblioteca dell' Economista* (1st series, Vol. I. Turin, 1850, royal 8vo). Daire's criticisms, though good in other respects, are exaggerated in their praise. Ferrara errs on the other side, but his observations have many merits notwithstanding.

G. Kellner, *Zur Geschichte des Physiocratismus. Quesnay, Gournay, Turgot.* Göttingen, 1847, 8vo. (The extracts given in this book are good, but the conclusions are thoughtless and superficial.)

Jos. Garnier, art. *Physiocrates,* in Vol. II. of the *Dictionnaire de l'Économie politique,* by Coquelin and Guillaumin. Paris, 1852-53. Two vols. royal 8vo. (This article contains much valuable information on various writers and their works.)

Et. Laspeyres, *Quesnay, Turgot und die Physiocraten.* In the *Deutsches Staatswörterbuch* by Bluntschli and Brater, Vol. VIII. (1864), p. 445-455. (Giving a brief, clear, and accurate exposition of the physiocratic doctrines.)

L. de Lavergne, *Les Économistes français du 18ᵉ Siècle.* Paris, 1870. One vol. 8vo. (This work contains careful biographies of certain physiocratic authors.)

The following are the best of the works illustrating the doctrines of Turgot :—

A. Batbie, *Turgot Philosophe, Économiste et Administrateur.* Paris, 1861, 8vo.

A. Mastier, *Turgot, sa Vie et sa Doctrine.* Paris, 1861, 8vo.

Tissot, *Turgot, sa Vie, son Administration et ses Ouvrages.* Paris, 1862, 8vo.

H. von Scheel, *Turgot als Nationalœkonom.* In the *Zeitschr. für die ges. Staats.* of Tübingen. 24th year (1868), p. 243-270. (Giving a short and interesting critical summary of Turgot's economic theories, though the author's object is also to depreciate the merits of Adam Smith.)

François Quesnay, the founder of the physiocratic school, was the son of an advocate who lived mostly in the country. He was at first a surgeon, and afterwards devoted himself to medicine, in which he acquired a certain fame. Louis XV. made him his doctor, and was much attached to him. It was only in 1756, when he had reached the age of 61, that Quesnay wrote for Diderot and d'Alembert's great Encyclopædia the two articles *Farmers* and *Corn.* These contain the germs of the new doctrine. They consist of an apology for agriculture and a defence of the interests of the peasants, who suffered from feudal exactions, from the concentration of property in the hands of corporations, from the system of high rents, from the want of capital, from the privileges possessed by large trading companies, and from the prohibitions and high duties on the exportation of agricultural produce. For the cure of these

L

evils the author demands full liberty for cultivation and trade.

But the characteristic features of Quesnay's system show themselves more completely in his *Tableau économique*, in the *Maximes générales du Gouvernement économique d' un Royaume* and in the *Problème économique*. These were followed by the *Dialogues sur le Commerce et sur les Travaux des Artisans*, explaining more clearly the principle of industrial liberty. Finally in the *Droit naturel* (1768), he attempts to connect his economic theories with the current philosophical ideas relating to law and politics.

Quesnay's followers are called sometimes *economists* from the nature of their studies, and sometimes *physiocrats* (χράτησις τῆς φύσεως) from their reverence for *natural laws*. The main principles of his system are as follows :—

The world is governed by invariable laws, physical and moral, derived from the order of nature, and constituting what is called *natural law*. Man ought to study this law and not to disturb its action, endeavouring to bring positive law into conformity with it. He will thus avoid the painful results which bear witness to the existence of natural law when it is disregarded. The two chief institutions of positive law are *liberty* and *property*. The production of wealth is subject to the same natural laws ; material goods are the product of natural forces operating on the soil, which alone can produce new material. Territorial industry, as it was first in order of time, must also be first in order of merit and importance, because its produce is greater than the labour and expense of obtaining it. Therefore it alone is productive—that is, it yields a *net produce*

equal to the difference between the gross produce and
the expenses of cultivation.   This net produce is at the
disposal of the farmer, those portions being deducted
which are respectively claimed by the landlord (*rent*),
and by the state (*taxes*).   Manufacture, which trans-
forms the raw material obtained by territorial industry, is useful and necessary, but it does not produce any new commodities.   It merely increases the
value of commodities already existing, by an amount
equal to the value of the labour expended on them.
Competition prevents a greater increase of value than
this.   The manufacturer can only obtain a higher price
by saving from the necessary expenses of his maintenance, by government favour, or by unusually advantageous circumstances.   Any special advantages possessed by him, however, cause a corresponding loss to
farmers and a diminution of the landlord's rent.   Hence
manufactures, and, for the same reason, trade, are barren
and unproductive industries.   The wealth of a country
is not increased by money, the mere instrument of
exchange, but by an abundant produce from its own soil.
On these considerations Quesnay founds his division of
the population into three classes :

1. The *productive* class, or the cultivators of the soil.

2. The *controlling* class, or the landowners, who do
not work themselves.

3. The *barren* class, consisting of those who are not
included in the other two classes.

Applying his principles, Quesnay demanded complete
liberty for cultivation, and for the sale, both at home and
abroad, of the products of the soil ; the abolition of all
restrictions on persons or on commodities by which cultivators were bound ; the multiplication of roads ; the

spread of instruction ; the grant of encouragements and rewards. Manufactures and trade were to be freed from all hindrances to their full development, such as corporations, monopolies and regulations. Free competition would then lower the price of manufactured products for the benefit of the farmers, who could thus increase their gains. The system of *indirect taxation* was unjust and harmful, since all burdens on production must necessarily fall on net produce; a *single direct tax* on land rent should be substituted for it, as being the most rational and the least costly of all taxes.

The new teaching set forth in Quesnay's aphoristic and somewhat Sibylline style, very soon became popular among the cultured classes of France. It was vulgarized in hundreds of high-flown writings by enthusiastic disciples, who coloured it with the current philosophy, and showed it to be compatible with the greatest respect for the absolute power of sovereigns. Strong opposition was aroused by the exaggerations of Quesnay's admirers, who affected the prophetic strain, not being content to take the more modest tone of men of science. Notwithstanding this, the traces of physiocratic doctrine on subsequent events and ideas are ineffaceable, although in the following period it was modified by various corrections and additions.

Among the pupils and admirers of Quesnay was the Marquis of Mirabeau, *l'ami des hommes*, who wrote lengthy declamatory works, examining all the particulars of physiocracy. Mercier de la Rivière and the Abbé Baudeau developed the doctrine, more especially on its political side. Le Trosne and Dupont de Nemours (the collector of Quesnay's writings, and Say's contemporary), enlarged the conception of liberty, which at first was only applied to agricultural industry. The same order of ideas was followed by Condorcet, Condillac, Raynal, G. Garnier (Adam Smith's translator), and up to a certain point by Jean Jacques Rousseau, who published in the Encyclopædia an article, the tendency of which was physiocratic.

There were several followers of the system in Germany, but they were inferior in merit to the French physiocrats. Among the chief of them were Schlettwein, Mauvillon, Iselin, a Swiss, and the Markgraf Karl Friedrich von Baden. The Markgraf was probably the author of a somewhat rare compendium, *Abrégé des Principes de l'Économie politique*, 1775 ; and he attempted to apply the system of unique taxation to two villages in his State. But this experiment was badly carried out and still worse received, and it soon came to an end. Emminghaus justly shows that it cannot be considered as testimony against the ideas that inspired it.

A. Emminghaus, *Karl Friedrich's von Baden physiokratische Verbindungen, Bestrebungen und Versuche.* In the *Jahrb. f. Nat. Oekon.* Vol. XIX. (1872), p. 1, *et seq.*

In Italy the physiocratic influence was only complete and decided on a small number of writers. Among these the Tuscan, Ferdinando Paoletti (1717—1801), the parish priest of San Donnino, at Villamagna, paid special attention to the subject of the free exportation of corn (*I veri mezzi di rendere felici le società.* Florence, 1772.) Gaetano Filangieri (1752—1788) borrowed from the physiocrats all the ideas contained in that part of his *Scienza della legislazione* which treats of *political* and *economic laws* (1780). Count Giuseppe Gorani of Milan maintained in several writings the idea of *unique taxation.*

Still less influence had the physiocratic school in England, where the illustrious philosopher and historian, David Hume, published his economic essays in 1752. In these he treats of commerce, of money, of commercial jealousies, of the balance of trade, of interest, of taxation, and of the public debt. His theories, expounded with much originality and ability, were duly appreciated by Adam Smith, of whom he was one of the greatest English precursors.

Jean Vincent Gournay, a learned merchant (1712—1759), held a notable position among the physiocrats, on account, not of his writings, but of his culture, his connections, and his influence. Educated by the works of Petty, Child, and De La Court, and by his own travels, he became, in 1749, Intendant of Commerce, and independently of Quesnay, whose friend he afterwards became, he arrived at almost identical results. Persuaded that the misfortunes of France came from the want of economic liberty, he fell into the opposite extreme. His well-known aphorism of *Laissez faire, laissez passer*, became the creed of his school, and is still that of many economists. He denied Quesnay's assertion of the barrenness of manufacture and commerce, but maintained the principle of a unique tax on land-rent.

The honour of having attempted the application of economic principles to government belongs to Turgot. This experiment he first made on a small scale, as Intendant of Limoges ; and then, though only for a short time, as the minister of Louis XVI. If he had remained in power he would have peacefully brought about many of those reforms which were afterwards accomplished with violence by the Revolution.

Before 1755 Turgot had busied himself with economic

investigations, and had expounded with much clearness and subtlety certain questions of applied economics. When hardly twenty he wrote some letters about *paper money* to the Abbé Cicé. In these he confutes with vigour and precision the opinions of Terrasson who, following Law's ideas, believed that the State might safely substitute paper for metallic money. In a fragment on *Value and Money*, he states with much profoundness the distinction between value to individuals and value to society.

Having embraced the physiocratic theories, Turgot made a masterly exposition of them in his *Réflexions sur la Formation et la Distribution des Richesses*, written in 1766. It may be considered as the best economic treatise that had yet been published, both for the worth, —at least the comparative worth—of its theories, and the brevity, clearness, and elegance of its style. Though the system expounded in this work is based on the physiocratic doctrines, Turgot's originality is observable in certain respects, and especially in his philosophical ideas, and the systematic arrangement of his materials.

With regard to philosophy, the distinction between Turgot and the other physiocrats and the fundamental principle of all his deductions is that of the rights of individuals. He observes that in many special questions, as in those of *mining property* and *interest on capital*, these rights do not coincide perfectly with the public interest, although they are not really opposed. He endeavours to solve the problem of the reconciliation of these two elements of social progress by determining the limits of their respective spheres of competence. In those cases where the individual initiative does not suffice, he advocates the intervention of the collective

power, both in material questions and in those concerning intellectual and moral culture. And in his own
administration Turgot showed that he knew how to promote the prudent action of the State, as for instance in
his measures relating to food and to poor-relief.

As to the systematic arrangement of materials, it was
Turgot who clearly separated economics from politics,
law, and ethics, with which it was confounded by the
other physiocrats. He thus succeeded in doing what
Genovesi had tried to do in his teaching some years
before. The traces of this attempt may be seen in the
latter's *Lezioni di Économia civile*, published in 1765, a
year before Turgot's *Réflexions*. Only Genovesi, though
clear-sighted and possessing wide knowledge in many
particulars, was too much fettered by the errors of
the mercantile system to be capable of arriving at a true
system of political economy. He calls the science *civil
economy*, understanding by the term *political economy* the
art of governing the State.

Beginning with territorial industry, Turgot shows how
the unequal distribution of land is the chief cause of
economic progress. The soil being cultivated by others,
the proprietors are enabled to turn to different occupa-
tions and social functions. They are also able to pay
the taxes, and thus to bear the burdens of the State. He
then examines various kinds of relations between pro-,
perty and labour, describing their development through
the five stages of *slavery, serfage, vassalage,* the Roman
colony system, and *leasehold*. The necessity for exchange gives rise to the idea of value, and then to that
of money as a measure of value and an instrument of exchange. But money is only a small part of the capital
which is necessary to every undertaking. He then

proceeds to analyse the various modes of employing capital in agricultural, industrial, and commercial undertakings, and the functions of the different classes occupied in them. In the course of this investigation he finds occasion to make many subtle and accurate observations on the functions of money as the instrument of purchase and of production, as capital and as a commodity. He also demonstrates the reasonableness of interest, which depends, not on the quantity, but on the disposability of capital.

But we must not, in admiration of the great merit of Turgot's treatise on economics in general, forget his many interesting writings, official and private, on special subjects. Among these, three—those on *mining property*, on the *interest of money*, and on *freedom in the corn trade*—have become classical, from the high order of the principles which animate them and the subtlety of their scientific deductions.

Most of the works by opponents of the physiocratic school are comparatively unimportant. We certainly find in them many good critical remarks on the erroneous ideas of the exclusive productiveness of land, the barrenness of manufactures and commerce, and the justice and expediency of a unique tax on land. But they rarely show any progress in scientific development. They nearly all consist either in a reproduction of mercantilism or an attempt to reconcile the system of the balance of trade with that of net produce.

To this species of economic eclecticism the Italian economists of the time for the most part devoted their efforts. They accepted many of the physiocratic doctrines and were obviously much influenced by the physiocratic school. But they did not fully appreciate the logical connection of the system. They did not see that when certain premisses were granted they led of necessity to the consequences which Quesnay, Turgot, and the other French physiocrats had expounded in all their bearings.

The French theories had very little influence on Genovesi, who still maintained with thorough conviction the doctrines of the restrictive system, in respect both to internal and international trade. Here and there in his lectures he dwells on the benefits that trade may gain from liberty, and vaguely expresses other opinions of a more liberal nature. But these remarks have no connection with his general theories. The best known of his lectures is that concerning the corn trade, in favour of which he demanded full freedom, with the approval of the Government, which was then wishing to widen the principles of its action. By its orders a book of Herbert's was translated into Italian, in which the subject was treated from the same point of view as that taken a little later by Quesnay. But notwithstanding his admirable intentions, his wide learning, and indefatigable industry, Genovesi is very inferior to the physiocrats. Ferrara has made some very good observations on him, of which the substance is as follows : Genovesi gathered together all the information he could find, and arranged it under sections and heads, making a work which concentrated the results of twenty centuries and seemed too complex to be contained in one book ; on the other hand, Quesnay and Smith endeavoured to find for these scattered fragments a common origin, a relation of ideas, where the Neapolitan professor had only strung paragraphs together with no connection. Thus the most learned among the Italian economists of that century summed up the older learning on the subject, but did not help in its further progress. His sympathies were with Child, Petty, Hume, and with two Spanish mercantilists, Ustaritz and Ulloa. Hence it is a strange mistake to compare him to Adam Smith, and a still stranger one to depreciate Adam Smith in comparison with him as Bianchini has done. But neither can we agree with Ferrara in his low estimate of Genovesi's lectures. We ought in fairness to compare them with certain books published shortly before by Forbonnais (1754), and Justi (1755), and others published rather later by Sonnenfels (1765), and Stewart (1767), which were intended, like Genovesi's writings, to gather together the economic knowledge of the time. In comparison with these Genovesi's merit stands out clearly. His lectures were translated into German (1776), and into Spanish (1785), a proof that he was widely esteemed. It was certainly to a great extent his enthusiastic and efficient teaching which stirred up that interest in social subjects so general in Naples during the last ten years of the eighteenth century, and which furnished the materials for the writings of Filangieri, Palmieri, Briganti, Pagano, Galanti, Delfico, Torcia, and many others, zealous promoters of the cause of scientific progress and social improvement. Nor should we forget that Genovesi's pre-eminence was recognised even outside Naples and Sicily. Among others, Beccaria and Verri, though for the most part superior to him, quote him with a good deal of praise in their writings. And for mere erudition Genovesi did not only stand first in Italy, but was one of the most learned economists in the eighteenth century.

Giacomo Racioppi, *Antonio Genovesi*. Naples, 1871,

one vol. 12mo.   (A meritorious work, biographical and critical.)

The illustrious criminal jurist of Milan, the Marchese Cesare Beccaria (1738—1794), was a man of more profound ability, and with considerable aptitude for mathematics.   He wrote a bright little book on money (1762). He was one of the contributors to the *Caffè*, a literary, social, and political periodical (1764—1765), and professor of "Chamber Sciences" in 1769—1770.   From 1771 onwards, he was Councillor, first in the Supreme Council of Economists, then in the Magistrato Camerale. In this latter position he found occasion for writing many works relating to economic administration (for example on *provisions*, on *money*, and on *weights* and *measures*) of which only some were published.   The others will be brought out shortly by the Royal Institute of Science and Literature in Lombardy.   His *Lezioni di Économia politica*, given in 1769, were not published till 1804, when Baron Custodi included them in his *Raccolta di Économisti italiani* (in vols. xi. and xii. of the modern part). Beccaria was a great admirer of the publicists and economists of France, with whom he had some personal intercourse in a short visit paid to Paris in 1766.   But he only partially accepted the physiocratic doctrines, and wavered between these and the mercantilist theories. His deductions are closely drawn, and he has more idea than Genovesi of what a methodical work should be. But he has no more power than Genovesi of grasping the fundamental principles of the science.   His *Elementi*, though incomplete, contain some good and ingenious remarks on the solidarity of human interests, on the function and importance of labour, and on the nature of capital.   We find there too a vigorous attack

on corporations in arts and trades, on monopolies and
privileges, and good ideas in general about internal
industrial liberty. With regard to international trade,
however, Beccaria is a decided protectionist, though not
admitting the prohibitions which Genovesi held to be
indispensable.

Count Pietro Verri, also a Milanese (1728—1797) was
the contemporary and friend of Beccaria, his colleague
in public offices, and his fellow-worker in the economic
reforms brought about in Lombardy under Maria
Theresa and Joseph II. He was inferior to Beccaria in
philosophic culture, and a less accurate though more
facile writer. He left a good many works on economic
subjects; one calling attention to and explaining the
flourishing condition of Lombardy before the Spanish
rule (1768) ; others proposing certain useful reforms in
the monetary system (1762), and more emphatically in
the system of purchasing corn by the State (1769). His
*Riflessioni sulle Leggi vincolanti, principalmente nel Com-
mercio dei Grani*, written in 1769, and printed in 1796,
is among the best monographs on the subject. He here
advocates unfettered liberty, both for the importation
and exportation of corn. The *Meditazioni sulla Économia
politica*, published anonymously (Leghorn, 1771), is of
a more general character. It is a compendium of the
science, easier and more clear than Beccaria's *Elementi*,
and generally rather remarkable at that period. For the
rest, it is based on an economic eclecticism which starts
from the idea of net produce, and admits industrial
liberty, though it advocates protective duties, and rejects
the unique tax system. The *Meditazioni* of Verri is certainly the best Italian compendium of economics published during the last century ; but, coming some years

after Turgot's *Réflexions*, it has very much less merit
both in substance and form. The little book had much
success, notwithstanding. It was reprinted several
times, and criticized, but with some severity, by Count
Carli. It was twice translated into German, three times
into French, and once into Dutch. These circumstances
have enhanced the importance of the book and raised
the author's reputation. His name as well as that of
Beccaria is associated with those reforms in economic,
administrative, and financial laws, brought about, as we
have before said, by Maria Theresa and Joseph II.

Giammario Ortes (1713—1790), a Venetian priest, is
the most illustrious among the Venetian economists of
last century. He was an original and profound genius,
but his style was unpolished and not free from para-
dox. His standpoint was a solitary one, but he was
influenced, though he did not think so himself, by the
general position and progress of economic studies at the
time. He was the author of numerous writings which
appeared anonymously, and which have been collected
and annotated with much care by Custodi, Cicogna, and
Lampertico. Among these, two are especially remarkable, namely, an Apology for Free Trade in the
Economia nazionale (1774); and the *Riflessioni sulla
Popolazione delle Nazioni* (1790). In the latter work he
gives theories on the question of population opposed to
those almost universally in vogue at the time, and in
great part analogous to those which were rather better
expounded by Malthus a few years later. But the
general system of this author is based on the false supposition that the wealth of a country always consists of
a determinate quantity, bearing a certain proportion
to the number of which the nation is composed.

Fedele Lampertico, *Giammario Ortes e la Scienza economica al suo Tempo.* Venice, 1865, 12mo.

Among other Venetian economists of the time, we may mention Mengotti di Fanzaso, Zanon of Udine, and the Istrian Gian Rinaldo Carli. Carli was president of the Magistrato Camerale at Milan, and was active in the economic reforms of that State. His works are most excellent, especially those on the subject of money. There are also other writers, who are hardly known, as Nani, Donati, Capello, Costantini, Coronelli, Mocenigo, Manin, Scola of Vicenzo, and the Istrian Marchesini. Their works, not without merit, show that even during the last days of the Republic, there existed some enthusiasm for those studies which contribute to the well-being of States.

The works of Briganti and Palmieri,—Neapolitans— and of Count Donaudi delle Mallere of Piedmont, cannot be compared with the earlier writings of Genovesi, Beccaria, Verri, and Ortes. But we find instead some excellent monographs. The question of money, especially, was very well expounded by Ferdinando Galiani, Pompeo Neri, Pagnini (Locke's translator), G. B. Vasco, a Piedmontese, and others. On the subject of *food commodities,* the best writers were Neri, Verri, and the Tuscan, Fabroni. There were also special treatises on taxation in general, and land-taxes in particular. Among these is an administrative work which has been much praised, published by Pompeo Neri, President of the Giunta which carried out under Maria Theresa the famous Milanese census. The fundamental ideas of this work were briefly summed up by Carli (1771).

No less praise should be accorded to Lodovico Ricci

(1742—1799), the author of an excellent work *Sulla Riforma degli istituti Pii* (1787,) containing wise and prudent maxims on the organisation of public poor-relief. Even now it may be profitably consulted. The same question had been discussed at Modena, half a century . before, but only incidentally and from the ecclesiastical point of view, by the illustrious Antonio Muratori (*Della Carità cristiana*, 1723, 4to). Perhaps Ricci might also be recognised as a distinguished financial writer, if his work *Dei Tributi* (3 vols. folio, 1783) were published. It is at present quite unknown to economic historians.

Thus we see that during the last half of the eighteenth century, Italy was rich in industrious and worthy economists, full of zeal for the public good, and working together for the principles of civil reform. Doubtless France and England stood first in economic science, but Italy could claim an honourable position among cultured and enlightened nations.

CHAPTER V.

ADAM SMITH was not the founder of the economic science, nor even the framer of a doctrine resting on fixed foundations, and complete in all its applications. But he was undoubtedly the greatest economist the world has ever seen. He gathered together and co-ordinated all existing materials relating to individual theories. He corrected the exaggerations of the physiocratic school, while retaining whatever was good in its system. He enriched the science with several theories hardly approached before his time, and gave a better form to many others. Again, the method which he pursued was especially well adapted to economic investigations. Finally he deduced from the principles of the science the most important applications which could be made from them to the economic and financial government of States; uniting with a genuinely liberal and independent spirit that moderation and maturity of mind which distinguishes men of genius from those who are blinded by party spirit, and by the tyranny of prejudices and exclusive ideas. It has been excellently observed by Roscher that Adam Smith stands in the centre of economic history; and that whatever was

M

written before and has been written since may be considered respectively as the preparation for, and the complement of, his doctrine. It is surprising that there has been as yet no complete monograph on this eminent author,—biographical, bibliographical and critical— which might impartially determine his scientific value, in relation to the later progress of the science.

The essays of Blanqui (1843), Cousin (1850), and Monjean, are by no means adequate to these demands— nor those, more recent and more accurate in parts, by Lavergne (1859), by Laspeyres (1865), by Du Puynode (1865), by Oncken (1874), by Chevalier (1875), by Inama, by Luzzati, by Bagehot (1876), and by Helfnich (1877).

The longest and most accurate biography is one by Dugald Stewart, *Account of the Life and Writings of Adam Smith*, in the *Transactions of the Royal Society of Edinburgh*, Vol. iii. Part I. (1793), p. 55–537. It has been reprinted several times, and is contained, with some additions, in the second volume of the works of Stewart, edited by Sir William Hamilton (London, 1858).

McCulloch enriched the biography of Adam Smith with some fresh particulars, which are given in the Introduction to his edition of the *Wealth of Nations* (London, 1828, 4 vols. 8vo), and again in his *Treatises and Essays* (2nd ed., London, 1858, 8vo).

J. F. B. Baert, *Adam Smith en zyn onderzoek naar den rykdom der Volken.* Leyden, 1858. (This is a very accurate work, and full of information, but wanting in acuteness of criticism.)

G. Ricca-Salerno, *L'economia politica di Adamo Smith.* In the *Archivio Giuridico*, Vol. xvii., Bologna, 1876, p. 301—320. (The best Italian essay on the subject.)

Aug. Oncken, *Adam Smith und Immanuel Kant. Der Einklang und das Weschselverhältniss ihrer Lehren über Sitte, Staat und Wirthschaft,* Part I. ₁This work shows the connection between Adam Smith's economic ideas and his moral and political theories. It is, however, frequently inaccurate.

W. von Skarzynski, *Adam Smith als Moralphilosoph und Schöpfer der Nationalökonomie.* Berlin, 1878, 8vo. (This writer is too ready to depreciate Adam Smith in comparison with the physiocrats.)

Adam Smith was born at the village of Kirkcaldy, in 1723. He studied at the University of Glasgow (1737-40), and then at that of Oxford. In 1748 he went to Edinburgh, where he gave lectures on rhetoric and lite-rature, and gained the friendship of David Hume. The philosophical and moral sciences had more attraction for him than literature, and at Glasgow, where he had first pursued those sciences, he obtained in 1751 the chair of Logic, and in 1752 that of Moral Philosophy. From 1752 to 1763 he was teaching moral philosophy. He divided the subject into four parts, natural theology, ethics properly so-called, political law and political economy. At that time Hume's *Economic Essays* had appeared, and they must have helped to fix Adam Smith's attention on the problems of the social ordering of wealth. There were also many writings of the French physiocrats which he probably consulted. While he was teaching at Glasgow, he published (1759) his work on the *Theory of the Moral Sentiments.* This ethical treatise was founded on the principle of *sympathy.* It agreed generally with the theories professed by the Scotch school, of which Hutcheson and Reid were the leaders, and Adam Smith himself one of the most

intelligent and active followers. The manner and the
amount of his economic teaching, and the relations between his opinions at that time and those of the French
school are points which remain obscure. Some of his biographers have asserted, but without producing adequate
proof, that the principles laid down by the illustrious
Scotchman in 1776 are in perfect accordance with those
taught from the Glasgow chair more than twenty years
before. It is much to be wished that some critic should
consult the manuscripts of his lectures, which are said
to be preserved, so as to discover what truth there is in
this assertion. Having left the University in 1764,
Adam Smith became tutor to the young Duke of Buc-
cleugh, and accompanied him in journeys on the conti-
nent, more especially in France. They stayed for nearly
twelve months in Paris, where Adam Smith was much
in the society of Quesnay, Turgot, and other philosophers,
publicists, and economists, making many cordial friends
among them, and acquiring a more thorough knowledge
of the economic doctrines of the French school. Return-
ing from abroad in October, 1760, he retired to his
native village, Kirkcaldy, and after ten years of preparation published his great work.

Adam Smith, *An Inquiry into the Nature and Causes
of the Wealth of Nations*, 1776, two vols. 4to.

Smith's work was translated into the principal
languages of Europe. The first Italian translation was
published at Naples, in five vols. 8vo, 1780; but the
best is that in Ferrara's *Biblioteca dell' Economista*.
Praise has been given, among the French translations,
to that by the Count Garnier, and among the German
translations to a recent one by C. W. Asher (Stuttgart,
1861, two vols. 8vo). Among the annotated English

editions we may name those of Buchanan and McCulloch. Jeremiah Joyce made an abstract of the *Wealth of Nations* under the following title : *A Complete Analysis of Adam Smith's Inquiry*, etc. London, 1797, 12mo (3rd ed. 1821).

The fame of Smith's work grew rapidly, and gained for him the post of Commissioner of Customs for Scotland, which he held until his death, in 1790.

The *Wealth of Nations* should not be considered as a scientific treatise written merely for educational purposes. Its aim was, rather, a wide treatment of the principal economic questions, given in such a manner that they might be readily apprehended by every cultivated person. The work is divided into five books. The first two are specially concerned with general theories of pure political economy. The third is mainly historical. The fourth contains a wide criticism of the mercantile and physiocratic systems. The fifth is devoted to questions of application, especially in the department of finance.

Following the example of Turgot, Adam Smith does not confound political economy with law or politics. In his investigations, however, he embraces both the pure and the applied science, and treats at large of many administrative questions which are now generally severed from political economy, as their decision rests on principles which are not purely economic.

According to Adam Smith, human labour is the chief source of wealth, wealth being defined as all material objects which make up the necessities, the conveniences, and the pleasures of life. Hence to produce wealth is to add utility and value to material objects. All kinds of labour are not productive, nor even some which are *necessary* or *useful.* The labour of clergymen, of magistrates, and of domestic servants, for example, from the economic point of view are unproductive. Productive labour is employed in *agriculture, manufacture,* and *commerce.* These are all equally useful and productive, and mutually dependent on each other's progress, as they all alike consist in the preparation and transformation of material products. Adam Smith's system was called *industrial,* because it started from the conception of labour and industry. The *mercantile* system started from the idea of *money.* The *physiocratic* system started from the conception of land. The two last erred in the direction of exclusiveness, not recognising the productiveness of all material industries.

Like Turgot, Adam Smith carefully studied the problem of *value,* and arrived at the capital distinction between *value in use* and *value in exchange.* The first bears relation to the capabilities of things in satisfying human wants. The second arises from the fitness of products for mutual interchange. Things which, like air, water, light, etc., are universally accessible, have no value in exchange. Value in exchange is founded on and measured by the human labour needed to acquire things and to render them serviceable.

In treating of the causes of efficiency in human labour, Smith especially insists on the results of the *division of labour,* which he analyses minutely. Combined with *exchange,* which renders it possible and causes it to be brought to greater perfection, this division is one of the most powerful factors in economic and social progress. Its effects, the causes of its efficiency, its limits, and its principle, are all examined. With this subject, as is well-known, the work opens, the manufacture of pins being particularly referred to by way of illustration. Not less profound, and perhaps more complete, is his analysis of the nature, the forms, and the kinds of capital, and of the laws of its formation and its functions. Here his subtlety, his originality, and his circumspection, are especially striking.

Like the physiocrats, Adam Smith advocated the greatest possible liberty in the mechanism of production and of trade. Descending to applications he absolutely condemned slavery, serfage, feudal and other such restrictions, monopolies, corporations, regulations, the legal determination of prices and wages, bounties, prohibitions, high protective duties, and the like. In his opinion, the great corollary of economics was liberty, which he deduced from far wider premises than the physiocrats. Their starting-points were the advantage of the rural classes and the necessity of increasing the net produce of the soil. His were individual self-interest and the harmony of the general interests.

In his treatment of circulation he gives analyses which are enriched by illustrations and historical digressions on the precious metals, on money, prices, credit and banking. Under distribution he explains the laws of rent, of profits, and especially of wages, pointing out with much penetration the causes of the apparent disproportion between labour and its reward in various localities and professions.

With regard to the natural and economic functions of the State, Smith does not merely recognise its negative province of defence and repression. He assigns to it a wide scope in relation to public works, education, etc. Starting from the fact that the needs of civil societies oblige the State to appropriate a portion of individual profits so as to employ it for the public benefit, he goes on to discuss the following matters. First, the nature of public expenditure. Secondly, the various forms of taxation, and their economic effects. Thirdly, the different systems of public loans, in the discussion of which he especially insists on the dangers and abuses of State credit.

By the work of Adam Smith political economy lost the exclusive character which the physiocrats had given to it, and was freed from the disguise of the sibylline language which they affected. It gained a definite position among the social sciences, and acquired a definite object. It assumed a special function, and adopted a convenient method. It laid a stone on the great edifice of social progress. But it must not be thought that the new science was perfectly constituted by Adam Smith. The *Wealth of Nations* did not comprehend the whole body of economic theories. If it were so, Smith would have done for economics what no single man has ever been able to do for any science, physical or moral.

The defects of the book are many, and by no means small, notwithstanding the wealth of demonstration and illustration which it displays. It fails as a didactic work, and indeed it was not considered in this light by the author. It has few definitions ; they seem almost to be designedly avoided. The language is popular rather than scientific, and there is no systematic arrangement. The interesting digressions into history, statistics, and politics, are too frequent and are foreign to the subject. In short, harmony and proportion are wanting— the necessary conditions of scientific exposition. And further, with regard to essential doctrines, Smith goes

too far in his reaction against the bureaucratic tendencies of the time, though not always, nor to the
same extent as some who claim to be his followers.
But he limits the action of the social power to the
defence of persons and property, a merely negative
function ; to the diffusion of instruction, a subsidiary
function ; and to the execution of certain public works,
for which the individual initiative would not suffice.
Again, Adam Smith, like the physiocrats, was wrong in
his purely material conception of wealth ; he allowed
very little importance to incorporeal products.   Lastly,
he neglected some of the most important economic
theories, those of value, population, rent, and international exchange.

The censures which modern German writers have
passed on him are, however, not justified. They at-
tribute to him the exaggerations of some of his disciples,
who make the idea of unlimited economic liberty the
basis of a theory very different from his. They maintain that economic science ought to be reconstituted
on entirely new foundations, laying down legal and
moral principles as the groundwork for wider and more
complete theories. These ideas are set forth in a work
by Prof. Rösler, which has the merit of acuteness, but
is pretentious, and in great part inaccurate.

H. Rösler, *Ueber die Grundlehren der von Adam Smith
begründeten Volkwirthschaftstheorie*, 2nd ed. Erlangen,
1871.

The work of Adam Smith contained the germs
of new theories which served to correct prevailing
errors and to fill up gaps. As an Italian writer has
said, it comprehends, if not all, certainly the greater
part of the science, manifested in its fundamental

principles by reasoning of a universal and permanent nature.

During the fifty years which followed the publication of Smith's book, the theories for which he pleaded did not find a ready or a wide acceptance in practice, which was still pledged to the old traditions of the restrictive systems. But they descended gradually to a select body of men who, first in England, then in France, Germany, Italy, Russia, the Low Countries and elsewhere, set themselves to explain, to comment upon, to arrange, to complete, and in some particulars to rectify them.

The first place belongs to England, both in originality and in the work of correcting and completing Smith's system. In the period in question that country may boast of the illustrious names of Malthus and Ricardo.

Thomas Robert Malthus (1766–1834) was the author of several economic works. He is immortalised by his explanations of the theory of population (*Essay on the Principles of Population as it Affects the Future Improvement of Society*), by his attacks on Godwin's communism, and on the vicious system of legal charity. With regard to the first subject, he pointed out that many evils which were falsely attributed to political causes were really the inevitable result of the disproportion between population and the means of subsistence. His doctrine, imperfect in statistical expression, but at the bottom economically sound, has survived the abuse and the equivocations with which people sought to confute it. His *Principles of Political Economy* and his *Definitions* are inferior in merit; and his restrictive ideas about the corn trade are erroneous.

. David Ricardo was a rich and skilful banker (1772–

1823). In his *Principles of Political Economy*, he briefly expounds the doctrine of production, and chiefly occupies himself with the theories of distribution and circulation. In these subjects he shows much originality, though he is wanting in clearness, and reasons too much in the abstract. But he made important investigations on the laws of value and of profits, on the elasticity of taxation, on money, on banking, and on private and public credit generally. But Ricardo's fame rests on the theory of rent, which had already been expounded by Anderson (1777), by West (1815), and by Malthus, but with less profundity and fulness. This doctrine was for a long time misunderstood by economists, and is even now opposed by many ; according to Mill it is their *pons asinorum*. It has become with much difficulty an acquisition of the science; but economists are endeavouring now to formulate it with greater precision and breadth.

There were others who contributed to the progress of economics in England. The illustrious Jeremy Bentham opposed, after Turgot, restrictive laws on the interest of money, and convinced Adam Smith himself, when not yet decided in favour of absolute liberty. Among writers of less importance, James Mill was the author of a work in which the theories of Adam Smith, Malthus, and Ricardo, are explained with precision and brevity.

James Mill, *Elements of Political Economy*, London, 1821, 3rd ed., 1826.

To a French writer, J.-B. Say (1767–1832), we must ascribe the merit of having developed in a clear, orderly, and attractive manner, the truth contained in Adam Smith's work. The principles of the new science of

economics were made familiar to the learned men of
Europe in Say's *Traité d'Économie politique*, Paris, 1803,
two vols., 8vo. (6th ed., prepared by H. Say, 1841, royal
8vo), and in later writings of less merit. He expounded
these principles with great clearness, and with rigorous
logic argued from them to their results. His definitions
and examples were framed with great care, and he
illustrated with some originality the theories of immaterial products, markets, and consumption. On the
other hand, Say advocated the limitation of the functions of the State to an even greater extent than Smith.
Not having much legal knowledge, he underestimated
the importance of these functions. Again, he was wil-
fully blind to the progress which the theories of value
and distribution had made through the work of
Ricardo.

Say taught economics publicly at the *Conservatoire des
Arts et Métiers* and at the *Collège de France*. Among
his contemporaries were Tracy, Droz, Charles Comte,
and Ganilh. The first wrote a compendium of political
economy as a complement to a philosophical treatise
inspired by the theories of the sensational philosophy.
Droz was a Christian philosopher and an excellent
economist. Charles Comte, Say's son-in-law, was the
author of a good monograph on *property*, and of a
Treatise on Legislation which was not finished. Ganilh's
numerous writings deserve praise in some special points,
but they are imbued with the narrow views of protection.

In Germany many excellent men of science and
professors modified the so-called *Chamber Sciences* with
the results of Adam Smith's doctrine. This was done
at first without much originality, as in the works of
Sartorius, Lüder, Kraus and Schlözer. Later on there

were some praiseworthy attempts to determine more
precisely the fundamental conceptions of the science,
the most successful being those by :

G. Hufeland (died 1817), *Neue Grundlegung der
Staatswirthschaftskunst*, Giessen, 1807–1813, two vols.
8vo ; and

J. F. E. Lotz (died 1838), *Revision der Grundbegriffe
der Nationalwirthschaftslehre*, Coburg, 1811–14, four
vols. 8vo.

Among the compendiums of this period the following
may be consulted :

L. H. von Jakob (died 1827), *Grundsätze der
Nationalökonomie*, Halle, 1805 (3rd ed. 1825). Clear
but not profound.

J. F. E. Lotz, *Handbuch der Staatswirthschaftslehre*,
Erlangen, 1821-22, three vols. 8vo (2nd ed. 1837-38).
An extensive treatise taking in the science of finance.

The *Cours d'Économie politique*, written in French by
the German Heinrich Storch (died, 1835), for the use of
his pupils the Grand Dukes Nicholas and Michael of
Russia, made the doctrines of Adam Smith known in
that vast empire. In pure economics the author shows
little originality. But with regard to applications he has
been praised for the careful attention with which he
treats the subjects of *slavery, banking, paper money,* &c.

In Holland Smith's teaching was expounded by Count
Hogendorp and by Gogel, illustrious patriots and
publicists. It was given forth in Switzerland in
Sismondi's first work (1803), and a little later by Count
Szecheny in Hungary. Lastly in distant America,
Franklin and others in the United States, and Da
Silva-Lisboa in Brazil, sought to adapt it to the
circumstances of another civilization.

CHAPTER VI.

ECONOMIC science, having been built up by Adam Smith upon solid foundations, has been gaining ground ever since, as an element in general culture, and especially as the most important of the social sciences. During the last fifty years the progress of economics has been very rapid. The science has triumphed over the numerous adversaries who fought against its diffusion for quite opposite reasons ; some fearing its influence in hastening civil reform, others knowing it to be hostile to disorderly, ill-timed, and dangerous attempts to upset the existing economic order.

In this revival of economic studies the leading nations were England, France, and Germany. They were followed by Italy, Switzerland, Belgium and the Low Countries, all eager for progress. In the last ten years Spain, Portugal, Russia, the Scandinavian States and Hungary, have taken part in the movement. It has been spread by the public and private teaching of the science afforded in many of the higher class educational institutions. In some countries its teaching has been extended even to some of the secondary schools, and more thoroughly to those devoted to industrial and professional instruction.

The progress of legislative reform, resulting from the progress of political economy, has led to the further advance of the science. The effects of more enlightened economic legislation have been specially important. Such effects are, for instance, the extension of the means of transport and communication; the organisation and multiplication of credit institutions; the growing liberty of manufacturing industry and of home and foreign trade; the emancipation of territorial property from feudal restrictions; the reorganisation of public poor-relief; the reform and simplification of the system of taxation and public finance in general.

In like manner the circle of students of political economy has been widened by the consolidation of the representative classes, and by the liberty of printing, association, and union, which have resulted from it. Having a more or less direct interest in the management of public affairs, these classes have a special motive for cultivating the branches of knowledge which investigate those phenomena most closely connected with the general welfare.

§ 1.—*England.*

After the time of Adam Smith and his earlier disciples, political economy became almost a popular science in England. The influence of its principles may be observed in improved institutions, and in the foundation of colleges and other educational institutes for working men, which, however, were not quite so numerous as has been sometimes stated. These did much good in arresting the inroad of socialist theories, which have therefore never taken such firm root in England as in its neighbour, France. Economic knowledge was perhaps even more effectually diffused in *reviews, magazines*, and other periodical publications designed for the spread of general culture and for the treatment of questions of the day. There were periodicals for different political opinions as well as for different classes. The *Quarterly Review*, the organ of the Tories ; the *Edinburgh Review*, that of the Whigs; *Fraser's Magazine*, the *Westminster Review*, the *Fortnightly Review*, &c., radical organs, were the most popular. Among special publications, which were fewer in comparison, were the *Journal of the Statistical Society* (appearing every three months) and the *Economist*, a weekly newspaper, occupying itself chiefly with monetary, banking, and commercial questions. There were also several journals representing the interests of the working classes and of the institutions which had been created for their benefit.

The Manchester League, — promoted by Cobden, Bright, and others, maintaining a persistent agitation, and supported by Sir Robert Peel and his successors, Earl Russell, Mr. Gladstone, &c. — succeeded in bringing about great reforms in economic and financial politics. The Corn Laws, the Navigation Act, and protective duties, were abolished ; the income-tax was re-introduced ; many taxes were either abolished or lowered. Other reforms greatly improved the condition of the working classes, as for instance the numerous factory acts, the liberty granted to combinations of workmen, the legal recognition of trades unions, the laws relating to friendly societies, co-operative societies, building societies, &c. On the one hand, hurtful forms of government intervention were done away with. On the other hand, the action of the State was more energetic in certain directions, in spite of doctrinal objections made by those who exaggerated the theory of absolute freedom. It supervised public instruction, banks of issue, and railways. It created post-office savings-banks and government life insurance. It undertook the telegraph service, and improved many other public services more or less closely connected with the economic prosperity of the nation.

The writings of Thomas Tooke (1773–1858) were partly contemporary with, and partly later than, those of Malthus and Ricardo. He was the author of the celebrated *History of Prices*, continued by William Newmarch ; a work which is a rich storehouse of facts and theories about the doctrine of circulation, and more especially that of credit (1838–57, six vols. 8vo.). Colonel Robert Torrens (1784–1864) was the author of an *Essay on the Production of Wealth* (1821), and of several monographs. He maintained, with Lord Overstone, Norman, and McCulloch, those restrictive theories (*currency principle*), with regard to banks of issue, which are opposed to those (*free banking principle*) which were professed by Tooke, Wilson, Fullarton, and Mill. The *currency principle* was the theoretical basis of the famous Act of 1844, which increased the privilege of the Bank of England. Economic knowledge was diffused in Ireland by Richard Whately, Archbishop of Dublin (died 1863), the author of some preliminary lectures on economics (*Introductory Lectures*, 1831). J. R. McCulloch, a learned, clear, and laborious, though not a profound writer, published manuals of economics and finance, a dictionary of commerce, and a bibliography

N

of political economy. He 'promoted investigations on
the early English economists, which were encouraged
by the *Political Economy Club*, created in London by
nineteen economists in 1821. A more original and
acute thinker was Nassau William Senior (1790–1864),
twice professor at Oxford, in 1826 and 1847. He wrote
a most excellent article, *Political Economy* (1836), in
the *Encyclopedia Metropolitana*, and several very interesting monographs on the measure of wages, absen-
teeism, and especially on the international distribution
of the precious metals. We owe to him also a complete
analysis of *cost of production*. He was less happy in
his *wages fund theory*, which is now almost completely
disproved.

But the first place among English economists belongs
undoubtedly to John Stuart Mill (1806–1873). He is
known as an eminent philosopher principally by his
System of Logic ; he is equally distinguished as a publicist
by his books on *Liberty* and *Representative Government*,
and as an economist of the first rank by his *Essays on
some Unsettled Questions of Political Economy*, 1844 (2nd
ed. 1874), written in 1829–30. In these he explained
his theories on method in economics, the influence of
consumption on production, the conception of productive
and unproductive consumption, profits, and interest.
He gives more particular attention to the laws of international trade, subtly investigating the distribution of
commercial profits among the different nations. Later
on, he published his classical work, *Principles of Political
Economy, with some of their Applications to Social Philosophy*, London, 1848, two vols. 8vo. (6th ed. 1865, two
vols. ; People's edition, 1873, one vol.). Even now this is
the best English treatise on economics. It accords in the

main with the doctrines of Smith, Malthus, and Ricardo, but these are amplified, corrected, and enriched by Mill's separate investigations. He consulted less-known works by Rae, Chalmers, Wakefield, &c. Such economic questions as bore most directly on his own time and country occupied his attention more especially ; and particularly those which concerned wages and the condition of working-men generally. Though an eclectic, he was at bottom temperate, notwithstanding some ardent phrases and some concessions, more apparent than real, to socialism, which he thought might be possibly applied in the remote future. But in spite of this and of his narrow philosophic utilitarianism, Mill is an orthodox economic writer, and is among those who have best understood the character of the science, its special method, and its points of contact with social and political questions.

Among contemporary English economists, J. E. Cairnes (died 1875) stands foremost, professor first at Dublin 'and then at University College, London. We must pass over those of less note, as Scrope, Eisdell, Hearn, Musgrave, Shadwell ; and numerous authors of merely special works, as Sargant, Baxter, Scratchley, Lewins, &c. Professor Cairnes was the author of several monographs which have been collected in two volumes, *Essays on Political Economy, Political Essays,* 1873 ; of a work on slavery in the United States (*The Slave Power,* 1862) ; of a most interesting work on method in economics mentioned above (p. 38), the *Character and Logical Method of Political Economy,* and a still more important work entitled, *Some Leading Principles of Political Economy newly expounded,* 1874. In this last work, after touching slightly on the more generally received theories, he occupies himself chiefly with giving new developments and greater exactness to the doctrines of supply and demand, value, cost of production, wages, international commerce, &c., correcting some inaccuracies of Mill's.

Professor W. Stanley Jevons, now of University College, London, has dealt particularly with circulation, exchange, commerce, value, money, credit, and crises. Among his writings is the *Theory of Political Economy* (1871, 2nd ed. 1879), in which he advocates the application of the calculus to economic investigations, and another work, very clear and good, on money, abounding in facts and very important technical illustrations : *Money and the Mechanism of Exchange*, London, 1875 (4th ed. 1878).

Professor Fawcett, of Cambridge, is the author of several writings ; on pauperism (1871), on the condition of working-men, on free trade (1878), and of an excellent *Manual of Political Economy*, London, 1863 (5th ed. 1876). This manual is a compendium of Mill's *Principles*, enriched by special development of questions relating to the precious metals, slavery, trades-unions, co-operative societies, local taxation, &c. Mrs. Fawcett, who assisted him in this work, gathered together its doctrines in a little book called *Political Economy for Beginners*, 1870 (3rd ed. 1874). A still more excellent compendium is that by Mr. and Mrs. Marshall, *The Economics of Industry*, London, 1879.

The late W. T. Thornton has written on population, on peasant proprietors, and more especially on labour and working-men's societies. His book *On Labour* (1869, one vol.) is an excellent work. It made a great impression on Mill, and induced him to abandon his theory of the wages fund, which has also been opposed by Lange, the American economist Walker, and Brentano. It is, however, still maintained by Fawcett, and with some modifications by Cairnes and Lampertico.

Credit and banking have been treated in several works by H. Dunning Macleod, a learned and acute, but somewhat paradoxical writer. His works contain many good observations on special questions, but are also full of dangerous errors and old sophisms under a new form. His doctrines are more briefly given in *Economics for Beginners*, London, 1878.

There have been other writers on banking subjects. The excellent work called *Lombard Street* (London, 1873) was written by Walter Bagehot (died 1877), who succeeded Wilson as editor of the *Economist*. To Mr. Göschen we owe original illustrations of the theory of the course of the exchange, *Theory of the Foreign Exchanges*, 8th ed., London, 1875.

Professor James E. Thorold Rogers has done good work in his history of agriculture and prices in England from 1255 to 1783, of which two volumes are already out, *History of Agriculture and Prices in England*, Vols. I. and II., London, 1866.

Mr. Cliffe Leslie is the author of learned and very interesting essays, and is especially noted for his works on systems of agriculture, and on financial reform. He represents the doctrines of the historical school, and in part also those of the so-called *professorial socialists* of Germany, though he avoids many of their exaggerations. Professor J. K. Ingram is also very favourable to the inductive method. He has lately (1878) reproduced with much clearness the objections made against the classical economists by A. Comte and the positivists.

§ 2. *France.*

Political Economy has never been popular in France, and is called *littérature ennuyeuse* even among cultivated people. It has been opposed by protectionists and socialists; the first being powerful in the sphere of Government, the second among the working-classes. But at intervals, in a transitory and exceptional way, it has made some slight progress in popular opinion. This has been especially the case since 1860, when the *movable scale* was abolished and a great treaty of commerce concluded with England. Here and there the science has been taught in the law schools.

Notwithstanding the important obstacles which have been mentioned, France can boast in the present century of a number of excellent economists. Since 1842 there has been regularly published the *Journal des Économistes*, which contains many good special writings. Every month, too, the leading French economists meet in the *Société des Économistes* to discuss questions of theory and application. The *Dictionnaire de l'Économie politique*, edited by Coquelin and Guillaumin (Paris, 1851–53, 2 vols. royal 8vo.), is an alphabetical encyclopædia of economic science. It certainly has many defects, and ought in great part to be rewritten to bring it into accordance with the subsequent progress of the science. But it is a scientific monument such as no other nation can boast of. Boccardo was stirred up by it to bestow on Italy a work of the same kind, with the help of the materials collected in it and elsewhere.

Among the innumerable authors of special works, of

whom many are now forgotten, we may mention the following. De Gerando (died 1842), rather an administrator than an economist, was the author of the classical work *De la Bienfaisance publique* (1839, 4 vols.). G. A. Blanqui (died 1854) was a professor and a brilliant though light writer, and the successor of Say at the Conservatoire des Arts et Métiers. L. R. Villerme, a physician, a philanthropist, and an economist, wrote a remarkable work on the Physical and Moral Condition of the Working Classes (1840, 2 vols.). He was, with Baron Charles Dupin, one of the first in France to give his attention to the abuses of the labour of women and children, a subject treated with much force by Jules Simon, Leroy-Beaulieu, Tallon, and others. Léon Faucher, the minister (died 1854), wrote some *Études sur l'Angleterre* (1845), which were a good deal read at one time. Charles Coquelin (died 1852) was the author of a brightly written volume on credit and banking (1848), not very profound, and now forgotten, other works having superseded it.

Charles Dunoyer and Frédéric Bastiat had a wider fame, and are still well known. Dunoyer (died 1862) is the author of a work of considerable originality entitled *De la liberté du travail*, &c. (Paris, 1845, 3 vols. 8vo.). In this book he treated diffusely of the conditions which give the greatest amount of energy to human labour in all its applications, and especially with regard to the so-called immaterial industries. Bastiat (died 1850) was a less profound, but a more popular and effective, writer. His style was powerful, and he was eminent as a critic and a publicist. His brief scientific career, prematurely cut off, was marked by two periods. During the first, fired by the success of

Cobden and the English league, he wished to become the apostle of free trade in France. He translated the best speeches of the English champions of
commercial liberty (*Cobden et la Ligue*, 1845), and confuted in his *Sophismes économiques* (1846-47) the arguments of the protectionists, reducing them by rigorous
logic *ad absurdum*. Later on he attacked socialism,
and showed in several little works, all very interesting,
its connection with the theories of protection. He was
less successful in the pure theory, his arguments in this
sphere being influenced by his alarm at the inter-
pretations which certain socialists put upon the doctrines
of Malthus and Ricardo. In his *Harmonies économiques*
(1850 ; 2nd ed. 1851) he expresses ideas about value,
population, and rent, which are neither original nor
exact, being founded to a great extent upon ambigu-
ities. Thus they lead to an economic optimism which
closes its eyes to the possibility of social perturbations and momentary conflicts between the interests of
the various productive classes, such as in reality often
necessitate the moderate intervention of the social power.
Among recent French economists, however, Michel
Chevalier stands first (died 1879). He was a former
Saint-Simonist and a brilliant writer, and was the
author of a *Cours d'économie politique* (Paris, 1842-50,
3 vols. 8vo. ; 2nd ed. 1855-66). In this work he expounded admirably the subjects of money and the means
of transport. In other writings he treated of the
probable depreciation of gold, the *protective system*, the
organization of labour, liberty of banking, &c. Chevalier
was a professor at the Collège de France, and took a
leading part in arranging the treaty of commerce with
England in 1860.

Louis Wolowski (died 1876), of Polish origin, was an opponent of Chevalier. He was professor at the Conservatoire des Arts et Métiers, and wrote chiefly on mortgage credit, commercial liberty, banks of issue, and monetary problems generally. His arguments with regard to banks of issue are sometimes too exclusive, and he holds that paper currency should be issued by a single government bank possessing a legal monopoly. In monetary questions he defends the double standard system with arguments which are partly original, and are at least comparatively valuable.

Hippolyte Passy wrote little but well on systems of cultivation (1853), and on the causes of inequalities of wealth. L. de Lavergne (died 1880), an agriculturist as well as an economist, described the agrarian conditions of England and France and the relations between agriculture and population. Louis Reybaud (died 1879), a novelist as well as an economist, began by studying modern socialism in some of its principal representatives. He then published several volumes on the *régime des manufactures*, in which, at the demand of the French Institute, he described the conditions of the various industries, silk, wool, cotton, iron, &c. Levasseur is known to fame chiefly by his two histories of the working-classes in France, before and since 1789. De Parieu has written on the subject of taxation in a very learned and excellent treatise, leaving nothing to be desired except greater originality and a better style. Subsequently he entered into money questions, and became the most decided and the soundest champion of the introduction into France of the single gold standard.

There are also many authors of treatises and compendiums of political economy, of which we may mention a few.   Courcelle-Seneuil, Mill's translator, besides some excellent works on *banking operations, industrial undertakings,* and *socialism,* wrote a *Traité théorique et pratique d'économie politique* (Paris, 1858-59, 2 vols. 8vo., 2nd ed. 1867) which is certainly one of the best treatises in the French language.   Joseph Garnier is the author of an elementary course of economic studies (*Traité d'économie politique,* 8th ed., Paris, 1880 ; also *Notes et petits Traités,* 2nd ed. 1858 ; *Traité de finances,* 3rd ed. 1872), a compilation which is not altogether very profound, and has grave defects, but contains many dates and interesting references.   Henri Baudrillart, an accurate writer, a philosopher and a journalist, has written an admirable compendium (*Manuel d'Économie politique,* 1857, 3rd ed. 1872) and other works in which he specially illustrates the relations between economics and morality.

In his *Lectures d'économie politique rationelle* (Paris, 1861, 1 vol. 18mo.), the Russian Colonel, Wolkoff, tried to spread in France the theories of the German von Thünen on rent and wages.   The work of the distinguished mathematician Cournot (died 1877), *Principes de la théorie des richesses* (Paris, 1863, 8vo.), is very good in many respects.   In this book and in that begun by Léon Walras, professor at Lausanne (*Eléments d'économie politique pure,* 1874), the writers propose the application of algebraic analysis to economic investigations.

We cannot enumerate all the authors of special works, among whom are Horace and Léon Say, M. Monjean, the Marquis d'Audiffret, P. Boiteau, A. Batbie, Frédéric Passy, R. Fontenay, P. Paillottet, J. J. Clamagéran, V. Modeste, G. du Puynode, A.

Clément, Paul Leroy-Beaulieu, A. de Foville, and many others. We have said enough to show that in the present century France may boast of excellent economists who are too often ignored by those of England and Germany.

§ 3. *Germany.*

It would be an arduous task to give even a brief account of the progress of economic science in Germany during this century. This progress has indeed been most remarkable, although denied by some, and exaggerated with easy-going complacency by others. A great deal of information about it has been collected in a learned work by Professor Cusumano with much diligence and accuracy. But his facts are not always lucidly expounded and co-ordinated, nor brought into their necessary connection with the development of the culture, the legislation, and the economic conditions of Germany.

V. Cusumano, *Le Scuole economiche della Germania in rapporto alla questione sociale.* Naples, 1875, 1 vol. 8vo.

Among those German economists who have been in the main faithful to the new scientific bent given to political economy by Adam Smith, and have expounded his doctrines with breadth, learning and moderation, the first place doubtless belongs to Karl Heinrich Rau (died 1870). He was a professor in the university of Heidelberg, and the author of a complete course of political economy. This work was divided by him into the three parts of national economy, economic politics, and the science of finance. It is an encyclopædia of economic doctrines, being rich in statistical and

bibliographical illustrations, and paying special attention
to the application of economics to the administration of
the State. Rau was gifted with qualities which enabled
him for many years to keep his work on a level with
the progress of the science. He had a solid mind, wide
culture, and an impartial judgment. His opinions
were moderate, his exposition orderly and clear; and
he had a keen perception of the relation between theory
and practice. His work was used as a text-book in the
principal universities of Germany, and till 1854 it met
with no serious competition. Indeed many works which
were written before and after it were forgotten or
neglected in consequence, several of them being of some
merit. Such, for example, were those by Zachariä (1832),
by Riedel (1838-42), by Schmitthenner (1839 et seq.),
by Kudler (1846), by von Schüz (1846), and some others.

K. H. Rau, *Lehrbuch der politischen Oekonomie*, 1st
vol., Leipzig, 1826 (8th ed. 1868), 2nd vol., 1828 (5th
ed. 1862), 3rd vol., 1832 et seq. (5th ed. 1864).

Greater originality and more acute ability distinguish
some of Rau's contemporaries who illustrated certain
branches of economic and financial science in extensive
monographs. The principal of these are Nebenius and
Hoffmann, statesmen and administrators; von Thünen,
a rich philanthropist; and Hermann, a man of science
and a professor.

Nebenius, to whom honour is due for the active
part which he took in the negotiations concerning the
Zollverein, is the author of a famous monograph on
public loans. Notwithstanding the progress since made
in the analysis of the economic consequences of national
indebtedness, this is still the most learned and complete
work on the subject.

Nebenius, *Der öffentliche Credit.* Carlsruhe, 1820, 8vo. (2nd ed., 1st vol., 1829).

Hoffmann, the excellent director of the Statistical Office at Berlin, was a no less acute thinker, besides having wide administrative experience; in some respects, however, he is too much influenced by prejudices and by his desire to defend Prussian institutions. Among his economic works the best are those on money (1838) and on taxes (1840). In the first he shows himself to be one of the most decided champions of the single gold standard system, the idea of which seemed quite absurd in that country and at that time.

Count Johann Heinrich von Thünen, an agriculturist and economist, was a self-taught writer, standing alone in his opinions. He treated the theories of the distribution of wealth, and more especially those of rent and wages, with a wholly abstract method, partly similiar to that of Ricardo. His analysis of the influence that the distance of the market exercises on methods of culture may be considered as a most useful complement of the doctrine of rent. But on the other hand his theory of *natural wages* is rendered impossible by the difficulty of fixing with mathematical exactness the relative importance of capital and labour in production.

J. H. v. Thünen, *Der isolirte Staat in Beziehung auf Landwirthschaft und National-Oekonomie,* 2nd ed. Rostock, 1842-63, 4 vols. 8vo.

A still wider influence on the progress of economic investigations was exercised by the *Researches* published in 1832 by Friedrich Benedict Wilhelm Hermann (died 1869). He was an able mathematician, a professor of political economy, and later on director of the Royal Statistical Office at Monaco. Hermann chiefly turned his

attention to determining the more general conceptions
of the science, which he did with great critical acumen,
profoundness of doctrine and exactness of method, far sur-
passing in his book the previous works of Lotz, Hufeland,
and many others.   His analysis of the theories of productiveness, capital, prices, rent, profits, and consumption,
has enriched the science with useful demonstrations
and important corrections which have been very valuable
to later economists.   The fame of this author, which
some of his countrymen have declared to be decreasing,
will certainly last longer than that of many of his
detractors.   His writings had an influence on the researches of Helferich, Roscher, Schäffle, Mangoldt, and
Schmoller, which was too great and beneficial to be soon
forgotten.

F. B. W. v. Hermann, *Staatswirthschaftliche Untersuchungen.*   Munich, 1832, 8vo.   (A 2nd edition, in
great part rewritten, was published after the death of
the author in 1870.)

The above writers may be considered the successors
of Adam Smith's school, the opinions of which they
corrected and otherwise modified in several respects.
Their modifications were most frequent in relation to
administrative matters, the German economists generally giving larger scope to the action of the State.
There was another school of economists who were
animated by hostility to what they called *English* or
cosmopolitan economics, in opposition to which they
wished to create a *national* or *German* political economy.

Several publicists, aptly called *romanticists* by Roscher,
took up these reactionary theories, which had arisen
during the wars with the first Napoleon.   They opposed
economic liberty in all its forms, and endeavoured to

idealise the happy economic conditions promoted by those feudal institutions which had disappeared with the Revolution. The first place among the champions of this school belongs to Friedrich Gentz, the friend of Metternich, the Swiss Karl Ludwig von Haller, and above all, to Adam Müller. Similar ideas have been professed more recently, but with some modification, by Kosegarten, Lavergne-Peguilhen, and some others.

We must not confound the reactionary economists with the so-called *social conservatives*. These occupy themselves especially with the condition of working men, for the improvement of whom they advocate State intervention, in opposition to the liberal school. Wagener, the author of a political conservative dictionary, is one of this school. Another is Professor V. A. Huber, the unwearying promoter of co-operative societies, and the author of a great number of writings tending to propagate them. Rodbertus (died 1876) was another, whose researches into the economic antiquities of Rome were marked by great acuteness. He was an opponent of the theory of rent, but not a very successful one. Finally, there was R. Meyer, a journalist and the author of a work which is remarkable for the abundance of facts which it contains about what he calls the struggle for the emancipation of the fourth estate.

R. Meyer, *Der Emanzipationskampf des vierten Standes*, 1874 et seq.

The protectionists form another group of opponents to the doctrines of Adam Smith. They had most influence in Southern Germany, where new industries which were only moderately flourishing demanded the help of duties. They tried to modify the liberal policy which had previously triumphed in Prussia as regards the *Zollverein*. Among German protectionists Friedrich List is the most eminent for his originality, his patriotism, and the excellence of some of his monographs. He expounded his doctrine in an unfinished work entitled *Das nationale System der politischen Oekonomie*, 1st vol. 8vo., Stuttgart, 1841. List's system proclaimed the temporary necessity of protectionism to help the growth of important industries in Germany, and thus to educate the nation at the cost of a momentary loss to consumers. His system has some point of contact with the ideas propounded under analogous conditions in the United States, before the time of List by Alexander Hamilton, and after his time by Carey. It met with acceptance among practical men, journalists, and up to a certain point among economists, and was not without influence on the theories latterly professed with greater breadth of view by the historic school.

The historic school can claim among contemporary writers the three illustrious professors, Bruno Hildebrand of Jena, Wilhelm Roscher of Leipzig, and Karl Knies of Heidelberg.

In an unfinished work, *Die Nationalökonomie der Gegenwart und Zukunft*, 1st vol., Frankfort on the Main, 1848, Bruno Hildebrand (died 1878) has given an extensive criticism of various economic systems, distinguishing what in his opinion is true in them from what is false. His censures of Smith are exaggerated, but in his objections to socialistic opinions he is nearly always just.

Still greater reputation attaches to the name of Roscher, the author of most excellent historical works, and some interesting monographs on the *corn trade, colonies, manufacturing industry, luxury,* &c. His greatest work is a course of political economy, not yet finished, which is one of the most remarkable economic treatises of our time.

W. Roscher, *System der Volkswirthschaft*, 1st vol., *Grundlagen der Nationalökonomie*, Stuttgart, 1854, 14th ed., 1879. 2nd vol., *National-Oekonomik des Ackerbaues*, &c., 1860 ; 8th ed. 1875.

This work is devoted to the exposition of general theories and their application to territorial industries. Fundamentally, Roscher is a moderate and sound follower of the doctrines of Adam Smith, Ricardo, Malthus, von Thünen, Hermann, and Mill. In his two volumes he has gathered together valuable materials from classical literature, from historical, geographical, and statistical works, and from books of travel, to illustrate the various phases of economic civilisation in nations, and to show that legislation ought to take these varieties of culture into account. Roscher was completely successful in his arguments with doctrinarians and idealists, who think that the results of their abstract speculations can be directly applied, without taking the circumstances of time and place into consideration. He fell into an error very like that into which the historic school in law had fallen, denying the existence of general economic laws, or at least underrating their importance. This led to the profession by many of his pupils of immoderate opinions which he himself had avoided, but which they deduced from his theories.

A no less profound writer than Roscher, inferior to him in historic learning, but his superior in legal knowledge, is Knies. He formulated with greater decision the canons of the historic school in a book called *Die politische Oekonomie vom Standpunkte der geschichtlichen*

o

Methode, Brunswick, 1853. The style of this work is not very clear. Later on he illustrated in some capital monographs certain of the principal questions in the doctrine of circulation, as those concerning railways (1853), and telegraphs (1857), finally, and more fully, those of money and credit, in the classical and still unfinished work entitled *Geld und Kredit* ; 1st part, *Das Geld*, Berlin, 1873 ; 2nd part, *Der Kredit*, 1876–79.

The progress of modern statistics has helped to moderate a little the exclusiveness of some of the partisans of the historic school and also the exaggerated belief in the deductive method. This progress was chiefly owing to Quetelet, Guerry, Dufau, and in Germany itself to the illustrious Engel, Wappäus, v. Oettingen, and several others. The short but profound and most excellent works of Rümelin are a model of the true method to be followed in economic investigations. They also bear witness to their author's lofty impartiality in his criticism of the works of foreign classical authors.

Gustav Rümelin, *Reden und Aufsätze*, Tübingen, 1875, 8vo.

A somewhat different line was taken by the followers of the so-called *liberal school*, called by its adversaries, not very appropriately, the *Manchester school* of Germany. Composed for the most part of journalists and publicists, this school was chiefly educated in economics by the easy works of Say and Bastiat. It turned its attention to legislative applications, and to bringing about the triumph of complete liberty in commerce and industry. The liberal economists formed the Society of Political Economy in Berlin under the presidency of Prince Smith (died 1874); they organised yearly congresses of economists to diffuse liberal ideas, and founded in 1863 a three-monthly review of political economy, *Vierteljahrsschrift für Volkswirthschaft und Culturgeschichte*. They also did a good work by their agitation for the reform of the old restrictive laws on the employment of labour, the limitation of interest, imprisonment for debt, working-men's dwellings, &c. They promoted the reform and unification of the systems of money, weights and measures, the organisation of banking, the abolition of protective duties, &c. Among others of the school, Schulze-Delitzsch has acquired a great reputation, not so much for his somewhat superficial learning, as for his successful efforts towards the creation of banks for the people, distributive and productive societies, and other forms of co-operative association. To the same group of economists belong Faucher, Braun, Wolff, Michaelis, and Wirth, the author of a *Course of Political Economy* which sums up the tendencies of the school. It is perhaps still better represented in the excellent dictionary of political economy edited by Rentzsch, *Handwörterbuch der Volkswirthschaftslehre*, Leipzig, 1865. Again, other writers of the school are distinguished for temperance of doctrine, and for their unquestionable competence in certain special questions. Ad. Soetbeer, Mill's translator—for many years secretary to the Chambers of Commerce at Hamburg, and now honorary professor at Göttingen—is the author of several writings on the subject of money and the precious metals, favouring a single gold standard. V. Böhmert, now Director of Statistics at Dresden, and editor of the excellent periodical, *Der Arbeiterfreund*, has written a very instructive book on the *participation of workmen in profits* (1878). A. Emminghaus is the author of many excellent monographs, among which is the *Economy of Manufactures* (1868) praised above. All the three last-mentioned authors avoided to a great extent the extreme opinions of many other partisans of the school, and their investigations were more profound.

A different standpoint is taken by other economists, among whom may be numbered most of the professors of economics in the German universities. Following in the steps of the first writers of the historical and statistical schools, they professed little faith in universal, or, as some say, natural, laws. They believed only in historical and relative laws, discovered by the inductive method, and deduced from simple psychological and abstract premisses. They doubted the omnipotence of the principle of liberty and individual self-government, and assigned a large sphere to the modifying action of the social power. Questions concerning the distribution of wealth attracted their special attention, and they endeavoured at least to help on the solution of the "social question." They are distinguished by their ability, their culture, their numbers, and their influence on the cultivated classes. Their doctrines, tending to a reconstruction of economic science, were given out in a large number of special works, and in the best economic reviews, such as the *Zeitschrift für die gesammte Staatswissenschaft*, published every three months since 1844, at Tübingen ; and the *Jahrbücher für Nationalökonomie*, which has been issued every month at Jena since 1863. Among the numerous polemical writings which express the opinions of these economists, those of Wagner, Schmoller, and von Scheel will suffice to give an idea of the new doctrines. The not very appropriate name of *professorial socialists* (Catheder-Socialisten) has been given to the followers of the school by their opponents, because they supported the principle of authority.

Ad. Wagner, *Rede über die sociale Frage*, Berlin, 1872.

H. v. Scheel, *Die Theorie der socialen Frage*, Jena, 1871.

G. Schmoller, *Ueber einige Grundfragen des Rechts und der Volkswirthschaft*, Jena, 1875.

Schmoller was answered from the liberal standpoint, and with many good observations of a partial nature, by the distinguished publicist,

H. v. Treitschke, *Der Socialismus und seine Gönner*, Berlin, 1875.

Friedrich Albrecht Lange (died 1876) shows still more divergent tendencies, and even agrees on many points with the true socialists. This can be seen from his book, *Die Arbeiterfrage* (3rd ed., Winterthur, 1875), which abounds in acute and important discussions.

The most important work of the new school is the *Course of Political Economy*, by Professor Adolf Wagner of Berlin, consisting in a new edition, prepared with the help of Nasse, of Rau's *Course*, which had become somewhat out of date. Next in importance is an original work of Wagner's, of which two volumes have been published. From these may be gathered the importance of the book, and its merits, both in the substance, the arrangement of material, and the manner of exposition. These so-called professorial socialists had no difficulty in overcoming the arguments of certain weak economists who wished to reproduce in Germany the doctrines of Bastiat, and of liberalism at any price. Consequently, they deceived themselves as to the originality and importance of their discoveries. They confounded economics with morals and law, under pretext of better harmonising their results. They did not distinguish theories, which are for the most part general, from applications, which are always contingent. They, and especially Brentano, exaggerated the importance of induction. For the gradual and peaceful evolution of political economy they wished to substitute a revolution, which they justified by an undeservedly severe condemnation of the defects and errors of the classical economists, and especially those of England and France. They started from the false supposition that the scientific progress of other nations at the present time is almost nothing in comparison with the acquisitions of the science in Germany.

To other economists, who cannot be enumerated here, we owe important monographs. Among those of which the merits have been most thoroughly tested are the works of Professors Hanssen and Helferich. Umpfenbach, Laspeyres, Dietzel, Lexis, and some other writers have not directly taken part in the fierce controversies between the so-called professorial socialists (Wagner, Engel, Schmoller, v. Scheel, Brentano, Held, Schönberg, &c.), and the so-called German Manchester school. Wagner himself and Nasse are specialists of the first class in matters of credit and banking.

Lorenz Stein, a professor in the University of Vienna, is entitled to special mention as the author of profound and original works, chiefly on the sciences of administration and finance. Though they are not free from defects, and are in general somewhat too abstract, they have several good qualities.

A. E. F. Schäffle, a journalist, professor, and for a short time Minister of Commerce at Vienna, published, at the same time with some good special works, a course of political economy. It is very remarkable for richness and variety of observation, for its original development of the conception which distinguishes general from particular economics, and for its other merits These are, however, rather thrown into the background by the inequality of the style, which is sometimes simple and popular, sometimes too abstract, and spoiled by philosophical mannerism.

A. E. F. Schäffle, *Das gesellschaftliche System der menschlichen Wirthschaft.* 3rd ed., Tübingen, 1873, 2 vols. 8vo.

A recent economic compendium by Professor H. Bischof, of Graz, will serve to give a conception of Schäffle's ideas, and of his manner of expounding and arranging the fundamental principles of the science.

H. Bischof, *Grundzüge eines Systemes der National-ökonomik.* Graz, 1874–6, 1 vol. 8vo.

In connection with this it will be well to mention a very recent sketch published by Professor Held, of Bonn, which, though rather more temperate and prudent, is in agreement with the principles of the professorial socialists.

Ad. Held, *Grundriss für Vorlesungen über National-ökonomie,* Bonn, 1876, 8vo. (2nd ed. 1878).

Professor H. v. Mangoldt (died 1868) was an acute thinker, with a well-balanced mind, full of sound, varied, and profound culture. He wrote a short but precise and correct compendium, and then published the first volume of a larger work, which is, most unfortunately, imperfect. It only comprehends the doctrines of production and distribution. Excepting the

author's erroneous ideas about rent, these works are
among the best, the most temperate and sober of all that
have been published in Germany.   He confounded *rent*
with *returns on monopolies*, an idea which is considered
an important discovery by several economists of merit
even in France (Boutron), and in Italy (Arrivabene,
Lampertico, and Toniolo).   In reality, it is an equivo-
cation not far removed from that which characterises
the ideas of Carey and Bastiat on the same subject.

  H. v. Mangoldt, *Grundriss der Volkswirthschaftslehre*,
Stuttgart, 1863, 8vo. (2nd ed., prepared by F. Kleinwächter, 1871); *Volkswirthschaftslehre*, 1st vol., Stuttgart, 1868, 8vo.

  The eminent position now occupied by Germany in
the progress of economic studies demands from the
economists of other countries a patient study of German
works.   Profound investigation, accurate historical and
statistical research, the number and merit of their
educational writings, their precise determination of
fundamental principles, their separation of economics
from the administrative and financial sciences, have
gained for them this position.   Works of great importance, and showing immense industry and careful-
ness, have been written by Mohl and Stein on *administration*, and by Rau, Malchus, Nebenius, Hoffmann,
Stein, Hock, Wagner, Vocke, and several others, on
finance.   But it cannot be denied that the German
economists have many grave defects.   They exaggerate
their own importance in comparison with the economists
of England, France, and Italy.   They are too subtle,
and sometimes even sophisticated or pedantic, in
doctrinal controversies.   Again, their style is usually
neither clear nor elegant.   We must, however, regard

as ridiculous the arrogant contempt for these economists which is professed by many who are not capable of understanding or appreciating their writings. Equally mistaken is the blind admiration of a few Italian writers who wish to reproduce exactly in their own country doctrines which require many corrections and additions.

§ 4. *The Netherlands, Belgium, and Switzerland.*

In the Netherlands there has been no abatement in the old enthusiasm for the study of economic questions, and especially of those relating to commerce, credit, and colonies. Eminent statesmen, like Thorbecke, were also distinguished economists. In the small but flourishing Universities of Leyden, Utrecht, and Gröningen, economics have been zealously taught by Tydemann, Vissering, Ackersdijk, later by v. Rees (died 1868), and at the present time by d'Aulnis dal Greven and by Tellegen. Popular compendiums like that of de Bruyn Kops have not been so numerous as careful monographs. These are often written by university students on the occasion of their examination for degrees, under the superintendence of professors who suggest themes and indicate the best sources. Among contemporary Dutch economists, besides those already mentioned, there are van Houten, Baert, van Voorthuysen, Verloren, Fokker, Buys, van Hall, &c. &c. Vissering, the Minister of Finance, an excellent writer, is the author of various essays and of a manual of applied political economy. This work is clear, well-arranged, and full of information concerning Dutch legislation. Professor Pierson, of Amsterdam, has published excellent monographs on the definition of wealth, on rent, wages, value, money, banking, the course of the exchanges, and colonies. He is also the author of a very good elementary economic treatise intended for the purpose of industrial and professional education.

S. Vissering, *Handboeck van practische Staathuishoud-kunde*. 4th ed. Amsterdam, 1878, 2 vols. 8vo.

N. G. Pierson, *Grondbeginselen der Staathuishoud-kunde*. 2nd part. Haarlem, 1875-76, 8vo.

But the best living economist of Holland is the illustrious president of the Bank of the Netherlands, a specialist of the highest order in matters relating to money and credit. He is the author of a history of ancient banks of deposit in his own country (1838); of some excellent monographs on the work of charitable institutions (1844), and on the monetary standard (1869); and more recently of a sober, profound, and accurate treatise illustrative of the theories of production, distribution, and international exchange.

W. C. Mees, *Overzicht van eenige Hoofdstukken der Staathuishoudkunde*. Amsterdam, 1866, one vol. 8vo.

A good example of the industry of the Dutch economists may be seen in the interesting articles contained in two monthly reviews, *De Economist*, and *De Gids*, the first of a special, the other of a general, character.

In Belgium, too, economic knowledge has been cultivated, though with less profundity. In the legal faculties (Ghent, Liége, Brussels, Louvain), and in other educational institutions, economics were taught, and often by men of distinction like Brasseur, Périn, De Molinari, and De Laveleye, the authors of works which are excellent in many respects. In an unfinished economic

Manual (Ghent, 1860–62, 2 vols.), Brasseur has developed, with much learning and clearness, but without much originality, the theories of production and circulation. Périn (*De la richesse dans les sociétés chrétiennes*, 2nd ed., Paris, 1868, three vols. 18mo.) treats of the relations between economics and religion. De Molinari, a brilliant writer and journalist, is competent in certain special questions, but on the subjects of credit and government intervention his opinions are somewhat eccentric (*Cours d'économie politique*, Paris, 1855–63, 2 vols. 8vo; *Questions d'économie politique*, Brussels, 1861, 2 vols. 8vo.). De Laveleye, a publicist and an elegant writer, is the author of articles and monographs which have a good deal of popularity. He is now professor at Liége, and of late he has inclined to the opinions of the so-called professorial socialists. His writings on free trade, on agriculture in Switzerland and in Belgium, on monetary questions, and especially the volume on *Primitive Property* (1874), are worth studying carefully. They contain information and observations which are very useful even to those who do not share the opinions of the author.

There are also other writers of interest in the same country. Jobard is an advocate of eccentric views on what is called industrial and literary property. Frère Orban, a statesman, is specially competent in banking matters, and recently defended the single monetary standard (1874), against Wolówski and De Laveleye. Vischers and Ducpétiaux are the authors of a number of interesting writings on questions relating to working men and to provident and charitable institutions. *L'Économiste belge*, edited by de Molinari, published in a collected form for several years the special works of learned Belgians which now appear in the *Revue de Belgique*.

Switzerland, and especially the French part of the country, is not wanting in economists, and there are professorships of economics in the faculties of law at the Polytechnic School of Zürich. At one time there were some excellent economists working on the economic part of the *Bibliothèque universelle*, now being published at Geneva. Among living authors of monographs specially relating to questions of the day, the writings of Feer-Herzog on money are particularly good. Naville is the author of a somewhat rigid and severe classical work, in which the defects of *legal charity* are pointed out. But the two most eminent economists of Switzerland are Sismondi and Cherbuliez.

G.-C.-L. Sismonde de Sismondi (died 1842) expounded Adam Smith's theories in his book, *De la richesse commerciale* (Geneva, 1803, 2 vols. 8vo). In another work, *Nouveaux principes d'économie politique* (Paris, 1819, 2nd ed. 1827, 2 vols. 8vo), he took a separate line. Alarmed at the dangers which accompany economic progress, and caring much for the well-being of the working classes, he attacked the division of labour, machinery, and competition. Without making any decided proposals, he framed the premisses from which socialism afterwards deduced pernicious consequences. In his *Études sur l'économie politique* (Paris, 1837–38, 2 vols. 8vo.) he gathered together some monographs on agriculture, manufactures, the balance between production and consumption, commerce, colonies, slavery, &c.

Superior to Sismondi both as a publicist and as an economist, though less popular, was the Genevese writer Antoine-Élise Cherbuliez (died 1869), the author of many economic writings, published in the *Journal des Économistes*, in the *Bibliothèque universelle*, in the *Dictionnaire de l'économie politique*, and separately. In his *Études sur les causes de la misère* (Paris, 1852, 12mo.), he urges that the wealthier classes should help to raise the others by economic and moral protection. But his most important work is the *Précis de la science économique* (Paris, 1862, 2 vols. 8vo), which is certainly the best treatise on economic science in the French language. The exactness of method, the profundity of investigation, the order and clearness of exposition displayed in this work are most admirable, as well as the clearness with which the pure science, the applied science, and administrative economics are kept distinct from one another. It is impossible to recommend the book enough to those who wish to study the economic sciences deeply.

§ 5. *Spain and Portugal.*

The instability of government, the administrative, economic, and financial disorder, the many obstacles to the diffusion of science in general, and the want of originality in the writers on social science, who nearly always imitate French books, suffice perhaps to explain the comparatively small importance of contemporary Spanish and Portuguese writers, particularly of those who wrote before 1848.

We may say of the Spanish compendiums that, though without striking defects, they show neither breadth nor profundity of doctrine, neither acuteness of criticism nor exactness of method. Among these may be cited the *Elementos* of Vallesantoro (1829), the *Tratado* (1831) of Espinosa de los Monteros, the *Principiós* of Pazo y Degalgado (1840), the *Compendia* of Gazquez Rubi (1856), the *Elementos* of Rubio y Dorado (1873), and these of Aller (1874). The book of this kind which is now most widely adopted in schools, and which is indeed not without merit, is the *Filosofia del interés personal*, (Madrid, 1865, 2nd ed. 1874) by Professor Mariano Carreras y Gonzales.

Larger treatises have been published by Florez Estrada, who has expounded, with occasional originality, the theories of Adam Smith, Malthus, and Ricardo. He is also the author of a work (*Curso de economia politica*, Paris, 1831, 2 vols. 8vo., 6th ed. 1848), which was translated into French, and was for some time popular both in Spain and other countries.

E. M. del Valle (*Curso de economia polit.*, Madrid, 1842) and A. Borrego (*Principios de economia polit.*, Madrid, 1844) are writers of rather less reputation. Prof. M. Colmeiro, better known as a writer on administrative law, and as the historian of economics in Spain, was at first an ardent protectionist. He is the author of a *Tratado elementar de economia. politica eclectica*, (Madrid, 1844–45, 2 vols.), which he afterwards summed up in his *Principios de econ. polit.* (Madrid, 1865, 2nd ed.), which was written after he had become favourable to free trade. B. Carballo y Wanguemert (died 1844) has expounded ideas which are wider and more in accordance with received theories in his *Curso de economia politica* (Madrid, 1855–56, 2 vols. 8vo). And lastly, Prof. S. D. Madrazo, of the University of Madrid, published a still longer work (*Lecciones de econ. polit.*, Madrid, 1874–76, 3 vols. 4to).

Among authors of special works may be noted the

numerous defenders of free trade, as, for example, Sanromà, Figuerola, Bona y Ureta, Ochoa, &c., who wrote
on that subject in the review *Gaceta economista* ; and a
large number of financial writers, as Canga y Arguelles,
the author of a brief summary (*Elementos de la ciencia
de hacienda*, 1833), and of a large dictionary (*Diccio-
nario de hacienda*, London, 1826–27, 5 vols.), Conde
(*Examen de la hacienda publica de España*, 1853), and
Lopez Narvaez, who wrote a somewhat superficial treatise,
Tratado de hacienda publica (1856) ; L. Maria Pastor
(died 1872), the author of some good treatises on taxation and on credit (*Filosofia del credito*, Madrid, 1858,
2nd ed.), and of an excellent history of public debt in
Spain (*Historia de la deuda publica española*, Madrid,
1863).

Still more recently a treatise by Piernas y Hurtado,
and by De Miranda y Eguia (*Manual de instituciones de
hacienda publica española*, 2nd ed., Madrid, 1875), has
appeared, containing much information on the history
and present organisation of Spanish finance, and another,
more brief, by F. Lozano y Montes (*Compendio de
hacienda publica*, Madrid, 1876).

Among the monographs concerning other points of
political economy, there is a most interesting history of
Spanish banks by R. Santillan (*Historia sobre los Bancos,
&c.*, Madrid, 1865, 2 vols. 4to.), and an essay on landed
property in Spain by De Cardenas (*Ensayo sobre la
historia de la propriedad territorial en España*, Madrid,
1873–75, 2 vols. 4to.). The superficialities of the Spanish
economists and their almost entire ignorance of any
other than Spanish and French books make the economic interest of their work centre upon such writings as
these, in which the economic institutions of their

country are historically described and criticised with special competence.

The state of things in Portugal was even less favourable to economic science than in Spain. After 1803 Rodriguez de Brito proposed that it should be taught in the faculty of law. But the proposal was not taken up, as public opinion was decidedly against it, having been for a long time under the influence of the restrictive system which had been inaugurated in the previous century by the Marchese di Pombal. We learn this fact from José Accursio das Neves, the author of some good pamphlets (*Variedades sobre objectos relativos as artes, commercio e manufacturas*, &c., 1814 et seq.).

The first Portuguese compendium of political economy, the greater part of which is taken from the works of Tracy and Storch, was written by José Ferreira-Borges (*Instituições de econ. polit.*, Lisbon, 1834). Others have appeared since, as the *Preleções* of Ag. Alb. da Silveira-Pinto (Oporto, 1838), the *Noções elementares* of. Ant. d'Oliveira-Marreca (Lisbon, 1838), and a very short French compendium by Pinheiro-Ferreira (*Précis d'un cours d'écon. polit.*, Paris, 1840, 12mo.).

A chair of economics having been founded at the University of Coimbra in 1836, it was given to Professor Adriano Pereira Forjaz de Sampajo. He published a compendium, the first edition (1839) being formed on the model of Say's *Catechism*, and the second (1841) on that of Rau's *Treatise*. It was much enlarged in later editions, and especially in the fifth. Though written with very little originality, and simply folllowing the French writers, it became the text-book of the University, and caused earlier compilations to be forgotten.

A. Pereira Forjaz de Sampajo, *Novos elementos de*

economia politica e estadistica (Coimbra, 1858-59, 3 vols. 8vo.)

Later on the public teaching of the science of finance was introduced, which occasioned the publication of two financial works. One was the *Estudos financeiros* of Mendonça Cortez, also a professor at Coimbra; the other the *Introducção a sciencia das finanças* of Carnido de Figueiredo (Coimbra, 1874).

Among the monographs we may record that by Morato Roma on *money* (*De la monnaie*, Lisbon, 1861), Serzedello's work on banks (*Os bancos*, &c., Lisbon, 1867), and that by the Visconte di Benalcanfor on the Vienna Exhibition (*Vienna e a Exposiçao*, Lisbon, 1874).

CHAPTER VII.

THE economic works published in Italy during the present century are not so interesting historically as those of the last century. But we may say without exaggeration that the science can boast of some distinguished Italian contemporaries, whose names demand at least a passing mention.

The progress of the science has necessarily been characterised by the political conditions of the various provinces of the peninsula. We may therefore conveniently divide our present account into four distinct periods.

§ 1.   1796-1830.

The progress of economic science during the first thirty years of the nineteenth century was kept back by various circumstances. These were :—The mistrust of government ; the deficiencies in public instruction ; the difficult relations existing between the various Italian States, and between them and other countries.

There were, however, excellent writers who struggled courageously with the difficulties of the time, and proved themselves competent to join in economic controversies. The important collection of the *Scrittori classici italiani di economia politica* was made by the diligent Baron Pietro Custodi, subsidised by the government of the Italian Republic, and later by that of the kingdom of Italy. It was published at Milan between 1802 and 1816, and contains a large number of works belonging to the second half of the previous century, and of earlier works which had been more or less forgotten.

After the fall of the kingdom of Italy several economic writings were printed from time to time in reviews and academic collections ; among which it will be enough to mention the following :—The *Biblioteca italiana* of Milan (from 1816 onwards) ; the *Conciliatore* (Milan, 1818–19), which was soon suppressed by Austrian policy ; the *Atti dell' Accademia dei Georgofili*, and the *Antologia* of Florence. The two last works vigorously defended the principles of economic liberty against the protectionist ideas taught in the schools and supported by Gioja.

Longer elementary treatises and compendiums, which were more or less in agreement with the theories of Adam Smith and Say, succeeded one another at intervals. The first to appear was a volume by the Neapolitan professor, Luca de Samuele Cagnazzi (1813). Then came the long and not very thoughtful works of Carlo Bosellini (died 1827), a native of Modena, and of Adeodato Ressi, of Romagna, a professor in the University of Pavia (died 1822). Better arranged are the scholastic works of two Sicilian professors, Ignazio Sanfilippo, of the University of Palermo, and Salvatore Scuderi, of the University of Catania, both protectionists.

The *Nuovo Prospetto delle Scienze economiche* (Series I.,

Teorie, Milan, 1815-1817, 6 vols. 4to.), by Melchiorre Gioja, of Piacenza, is superior to all the foregoing works. The illustrious author had proposed to himself to sum up in a treatise on economics, finance, and administration all that had been written and thought on these subjects. As it is, in the volumes which have appeared he has illustrated with much learning the principal doctrines of political economy. The judgment with which he compares the opinions of celebrated writers is not always just or impartial, and his method is not adapted to make the science attractive or to recommend its results. Again, he is often not successful in his arguments against Adam Smith and Say. And though he has cleared up certain special doctrines by original observations, we must set against this his mistaken apology for the restrictive system.

Although they have not published any general economic works, the following writers deserve special attention.

Luigi Molinari Valeriani (died 1828), a professor at Bologna, wrote some excellent works, though obscure and careless in style, in which he specially illustrated the theories of value, price, money, and the exchanges, and also showed the close relations which exist between economics and jurisprudence.

The Tuscan author Giovanni Fabbroni (died 1822) wrote interesting monographs, the most important being those defending liberty in the corn-trade. They were collected in two volumes (Florence, 1847-48).

Francesco Fuoco (died 1840), a Neapolitan, who had an eventful life, wrote some profound essays, *Saggi economici* (Pisa, 1825-27). At first they did not receive much attention, but later on they were praised in

Germany by Mohl, and they are really remarkable for the acute observations on certain abstract points of doctrine which they contain. Fuoco was one of the first to point out the importance of Ricardo's theory of land rent.

Paolo Balsamo (died 1816), a Sicilian, was a brave patriot, an agriculturist, and an economist. In the University of Palermo he taught the doctrines of Adam Smith, and attacked with constant pertinacity the anti-economic institutions which still existed in his country.

In Piedmont, Count Prospero Balbo (died 1837) proposed to found a chair of political economy in the University of Turin, but this was prevented by the events of 1821. Two other Piedmontese writers were Giuseppe Cridis and Francesco Gambini of Asti. In Lombardy and Venetia there were Racchetti, Ridolfi, de Carli, and de Welz of Como, the author of a paradoxical book called the *Magia del credito* (1824, two vols.). In Tuscany there were Targioni, Capponi, Ricci, Ridolfi, &c. In Romagna the works of Monsignor Poalo Vergani, Count Marco Fantuzzi, Abbot Nicola Maria Nicolai, and a number of *memorie* in the *Giornale arcadico* (1819 et seq.), are noteworthy. At Naples, Marulli, Winspeare, and Lodovico Bianchini, in some of his early writings, kept alive the interest in the science of Galiani and Genovesi. Finally, in Sicily, among numerous partial and occasional writings, Niccolò Palmeri's (died 1837) *Saggio delle cause e dei rimedi delle angustie attuali dell' economia agraria della Sicilia* (Palermo, 1826) is particularly interesting. In this essay the author attacks with much vigour the restrictive theories which then predominated in legislation and instruction.

§ 2. 1831–1848.

Although the political condition of Italy had not changed, or had changed very little, in the fifteen years which preceded 1848, some progress in the study of economics was made, chiefly at Milan and Naples.

At Milan the *Annali universali di statistica* were started in 1824 by Custodi, Gioja, and Romagnosi. After Gioja's death, Romagnosi (died 1835) became the moving spirit of the economic department of this periodical. His writings and conversation educated a number of men who have since rendered useful service to the social sciences. Among these may be cited Carlo Cattaneo, Cesare Correnti, and Giuseppe Sacchi, the last of whom directed the *Annali* until their cessation in 1871, warmly advocating the principles of free trade.

At Naples Lodovico Bianchini started a review called *Il Progresso* (1832–46, forty vols.), which contains numerous writings by young economists. The most distinguished of them are Carlo Mele, M. de Augustinis, Baron G. Durini, P. S. Mancini, and some others, all having liberal principles.

In other countries the reputation of Italian economists was kept up by several illustrious exiles; for example, the Neapolitan Chitti, and the still more able Mantuan Count, Giovanni Arrivabene, the Nestor of living Italian publicists. Pellegrino Rossi of Carrara, the distinguished criminalist, was invited to Paris to occupy the chair left vacant by G. B. Say. He gave there, not without opposition at first, lectures on economics, which were brilliant if not original, popularising the doctrines of Smith, Malthus, Ricardo, MacCulloch, and Senior.

In the *Congressi degli Scienziati* (1839–46) economic investigation made advances, overcoming not a few obstacles. In what were innocently called the *Sezioni di agronomia* and *tecnologia* questions were specially discussed relating to *food, agriculture, savings-banks, beneficient institutions, railways,* &c.

Among the economists of this period Romagnosi stands first. During the last unfortunate years of his life he occupied himself with economic investigations, dealing chiefly with general subjects, such as : the point of view, the arrangement, and the definition of economic science ; its relations with jurisprudence ; the conditions, advantages, and limits of economic liberty in many of its applications ; and the theory of population—about which he fell into grave errors.

The Milanese writer, Carlo Cattaneo, was inferior in doctrine to Romagnosi, but his style is far more powerful. In the *Politecnico*, which he edited, he treated with much discretion economic questions in their relation to practical needs. He had a special interest in questions connected with rural legislation and with free trade, which he ardently defended, combating, among other arguments, the specious sophisms of the German protectionist, Friedrich List.

In 1840 a young Neapolitan, Antonio Scialoja, of Procida, attempted, in a work entitled *Principii d' economia sociale*, to connect with a good philsophical basis the more general economic doctrines. He well deserved his appointment to the chair of Political Economy, which had been restored in 1846, at the University of Turin. Here he taught for a year, and would no doubt have written economic works later on, as was hoped, if the cares of State had not deprived him of sufficient strength and leisure.

But the fame of Romagnosi, Rossi, Cattaneo, and Scialoja must not make us forget other most meritorious writers on economics. Count Carlo Ilarione Petitti di Roreto (died 1850) treated with great profoundness the subjects of public poor-relief, the labour of women, and lotteries; he attempted also to cope with the new and hazardous theme of railways. Giovanetti, a lawyer of Novara, and, like Petitti, a contributor to the *Annali di statistica*, opposed the grist tax and the duties on the production of raw silk. Count G. B. Michelini wrote chiefly on forest legislation; and Count R. G. di Salmour illustrated with much learning the subject of *landed and agrarian credit* (1845).

In Lombardy Andrea Zambelli gave forth from the chair of Pavia, as in Venetia Cristoforo Negri did from that of Padua, the sound doctrines of the masters of the science. In the same province Baldassare Poli compared with much precision and clearness the principles of various schools; Pio Magenta wrote on charitable institutions from the administrative point of view; and Francesco Restelli treated of the influence of industrial and commercial associations on public prosperity, this subject having been suggested by the Lombardian Institute of Science. In the Venetian provinces we may note some writings by Bernardi, Casarini, and Zennari on public poor-relief, by Tolomei on the subjection of pasture-land, by Meguscher (a Tyrolese) on forests, and a few others.

In Tuscany the Accademia dei Georgofili kept up with frequent lectures the zeal for economic studies and the

Leopoldine traditions. In the Romagna too there was no lack of economists, especially among the writers in the *Giornale Arcadico*, which had for a long time a well-deserved reputation. It will be enough to mention Cardinal Luigi Morichini, who gave a very good account of the management of beneficent institutions in the city of Rome, with complete statistical information, and the Abbot Marco Mastrofini, whose theological-legal-economic book on *Usury* (1831), though intended to settle the ancient controversies, really served to excite their renewal. But the book was soon forgotten.

At Naples the vivacious and imaginative intellects of the publicists were exercised in economic and financial controversies, occasioned by various questions of the day, such as those relating to sulphur, to the shipping-trade between the provinces of the mainland and Sicily, free ports, duties on books, the Tavoliere di Puglia,[1] and the conversion of rent. Among the many writings published on these subjects there are several which present a general interest.

In Sicily the *Giornale dell' Ufficio di Statistica*, edited since 1848 by Francesco Ferrara, with the help of able coadjutors, became the centre of studies which prove that wider ideas and the doctrines of commercial liberty had gained ground there.

§ 3.   1849–1858.

The vicissitudes of 1848 and the political reaction which followed them in most parts of Italy brought together at Turin, among a number of other emigrants,

---

[1] The Tavoliere di Puglia is the name of some landed property of the State in the Neapolitan provinces.

several economists who wrote chiefly in *reviews*. *La Rivista contemporanea*, which appeared between 1853 and 1869, contained a good many writings on economic subjects.

The highest position among the Italian economists of this period was held by the Sicilian, Francesco Ferrara, a professor at the University of Turin from 1849 to 1858. He was a writer of remarkable ability and of great power in criticism, especially negative criticism. He was widely read in English and French works, and was indefatigable in impartial investigation as to the origin of the science. He also showed great diligence and sagacity in his editorship of the *Biblioteca dell'Economista*, which is a rich collection of general and special economic works, such as the literature of no other nation can boast of. His brilliant style, easy and incisive language, and passionate ardour in controversy gained a school of followers for him in a very few years. In this school were educated, directly or indirectly, the greater number of professors now teaching in Italy. Ferrara's influence was to a great extent most useful, and would have been more so if he had not helped to diffuse error at the same time with truth. He shared the paradoxical opinions of Carey and Bastiat with regard to value and rent, and he believed that all the problems of economic legislation were to be solved by the merely negative principle of *laisser-faire*, interpreted and applied in a manner far from agreeing with the ideas of Adam Smith.

There was no want of general treatises in this period, among which are those by Giacomo Savarese (1848), unfinished; one less known by Trinci (1858); the *Corso* of Trinchera (1852), a Neapolitan, formed on the model of Rossi's, and the *Discorsi* of Marescotti (1853–56).   Shorter compendiums were multiplied, such as those by Meneghini (1851), Rusconi (1852), the above-mentioned Trinchera (1855), and De Luca (1852); and, superior to all the others, the *Trattato teorico-pratico di economia politica*, by the young Genoese, Gerolamo Boccardo (Turin, 1853, three vols. 12mo., reprinted several times).   Boccardo is a disciple of Ferrara, an admirer of Bastiat, and a clear, simple, and pleasant writer of great diligence.   Some years after the appearance of the *Trattato* he published a voluminous *Dizionario* (1857 et seq.), comprehending all branches of economic doctrine.   It is formed on the model of Coquelin and Guillaumin's French dictionary.

In Lombardy a number of students of economic science published the *Crepuscolo*, a liberal review, which was suppressed in 1857.   It was contributed to by Correnti, Broglio, Allievi, de Cristoforis, Zanardelli, and some others.   Antonio Mora began some interesting writings on money, on public loans, and on mortgage credit, which were gathered together in the *Giornale delle Scienze politico-legali* (1850–53).   Stefano Jacini, of Casalbuttano, published an interesting book on *Proprietà fondiaria e la popolazione agricola in Lombardia* (Milan, 1854, 3rd ed. 1857).   On this excellent model were formed two new works by Salmour on landed and agrarian credit.

In Venetia, Valentino Pasini di Schio (died 1864), whose life and writings were described by Lampertico and Bonghi, showed profoundness and moderation of mind in some monographs which he wrote.   Political cares, however, and a premature death prevented his powers from bearing more abundant fruit.   The *Piano*

di Ristorazione economica delle Province Venete, by G.
B. Zannini (died 1866), was a bold protest against the
Austrian administration.

In Tuscany the Georgofili, Corbani from the chair of
Siena, and a few economists, among them the Bosellini
and Martinelli, in Emilia, most efficiently pursued
economic investigations. At the same time there was
a large number of economists in the southern provinces.
Scialoja, who did not occupy any post at the university,
being engaged in the duties of other public offices, gave
a brief but very remarkable example of his economic
knowledge in his vivacious little book, *Carestia e Governo*
(1853). Lodovico Bianchini was the author of two
works on economic and financial history, and of some
less successful attempts at treating the pure science.
His fame was almost greater in other countries than it
was in Italy, where it was injured by the interference
of the Bourbon Government.

Among the Sicilian economists the following are noteworthy :—the two emigrants, Cordova and Busacca,
learned and industrious writers, and distinguished later
on in high public offices ; Giovanni Bruno, a Professor
at the University of Palermo ; F. Maggiore Perni, and
Giulio Albergo. In his *Storia dell' economia pubblica in
Sicilia,* the completion of which was expected for many
years, the last-mentioned writer described works which
were little known in other parts of Italy.

§ 4.   1859–1880.

The political revival of Italy exercised no little
influence on economic progress. Professorships of
economic science were multiplied in the universities,
and were created in industrial and professional schools.

Complete liberty of discussion and of the press, and the agitation of urgent economic and financial questions— some of a complicated nature—gave rise to scientific investigations, and to official and parliamentary publications which show unmistakable signs of the growing national culture. But it cannot be denied that, notwithstanding the noticeable improvement of the last few years, Italy does not hold the honourable position that it has held in other times. There has been a want of originality in Italian writers and teachers (that is, among those who have devoted themselves wholly to economic science) and very imperfect knowledge of later economic progress, especially in England and Germany. The somewhat heterodox ideas diffused by Ferrara have prevailed widely, side by side with an optimism imbibed from the *Harmonies* of Bastiat. The first of living Italian economists is undoubtedly Angelo Messedaglia, a Veronese writer. His mind is remarkably acute, and his economic and statistical knowledge both profound and wide. In his mathematical acquirements he is also distinguished. As a writer he is precise, cautious, temperate, and effective. Since 1858 he has been eminent as a professor in the University of Padua. His works on *public loans* (1850), on *population* (1858 et seq.), and his other economic and statistical monographs are among the most striking publications of the day, and make us most anxious for the appearance of his works on *money* and *credit*.

The Bolognese, Marco Minghetti, a cultured and elegant writer, as well as an eloquent orator, published a most remarkable and excellent work, mentioned before, on the eve of his laborious and honourable career in the highest offices of the State. The title of this work was,

Economia pubblica e le sue attinenze colla morale e col diritto (1859). Later on he collected his minor writings in a little volume (1872).

Fedele Lampertico of Vicenza was a pupil and friend of Messedaglia, and one of the most diligent of the living Italian economists. His writings on the Isthmus of Suez, on Ortes, on mining legislation, and on the reports on paper-money, not to speak of minor writings, give undeniable proof of his great analytical subtlety, his wide and solid learning, and his thorough knowledge of the best Italian and foreign works. His *Economia dei Popoli e degli Stati* (vols. i.–v., Milan, 1874–80) is intended as a complete course of economic, financial, and administrative studies. It is a work of the highest order, containing the best results of German science, interpreted and modified to meet Italian views. What it wants is greater simplicity and homogeneousness of style, and more order and proportion in the subjects treated.

Besides Lampertico's *Corso* there are other treatises. Some, by de Rocchi, Bruno, Majorano, and others, are unfinished; others, by Reymond (1860–61), Marescotti (1861), Ponsiglioni (1870–72), G. E. Garelli (1875), and S. Pizperno, are good in parts, and wholly conscientious. The *Principii d' economia sociale*, by Professor Antonio Ciccone, is a long work, of which a second edition, considerably enlarged, has already appeared (1874, three vols. royal 8vo).

A brilliant exception to the other compendiums, which, as a rule, are not worth much, is the *Sunto d'Economia politica*, by Emilio Nazzani, a Pavian professor (2nd ed., Milan, 1875). This work is very remarkable for its exact scientific orthodoxy, and its wide and sound learning, not concealed by the modesty and simplicity of the style, which is also sober, clear, and elegant. No less could have been expected from the author of the *Saggio sulla rendita fondiaria* (Forli, 1872), and of the essays on *profits* (Milan, 1877), and on the *demand for labour* (1880), which are among the best monographs published in this period.

We have not space to name the large number of writers on special subjects in the different parts of Italy. There are a few authors, however, who deserve to be associated with those already mentioned.

In Piedmont, Liguria, and Sardinia there was a want of activity in the study of economics, which was cultivated in a merely accessory way by distinguished statesmen like Sclopis and Sella, or by able jurisconsults like Pescatore, the author of an excellent work on *taxes* (1867). Todde, Virgilio, Boselli, Pellarcioni, and Alessandro Garelli are noteworthy ; and more especially Vittorio Ellena, Maggiorino Ferraris, and Carlo F. Ferraris. Carlo Ferraris is an economist of acute and versatile mental powers, and of wise judgment. He is the author of an excellent monograph on *money and the forced currency* (1879), and of other remarkable essays on *economics, statistics*, and *administration* (1880).

At Genoa Gerolamo Boccardo, having brought together a great deal of new material by laborious study, is publishing a third series of the *Biblioteca dell' Economista*, to continue and complete the other two series. His editorship of the work is marked by great breadth of view and impartiality.

In Lombardy there are new names to be associated with those of the veterans of the science before mentioned, such as Arrivabene, Poli, Sacchi, and, again,

Cattaneo (died 1869), in whose later writings scientific calmness was sacrificed to his preoccupation with politics. Enrico Cernuschi, a Milanese, is the author of an ingenious and somewhat paradoxical work, the *Meccanica degli scambii*. He defends the double standard to an exaggerated extent, and is hostile to banknotes and cooperative societies. Enrico Fano is a distinguished specialist on the subjects of provident institutions and co-operation. Stefano Allocchio is the author of essays on free-trade and mortgage credit which have been praised. Among younger writers the following are distinguished: Romanelli, Buzzetti, Manfredi, Nicolini, Loria, the author of a powerful volume on *land-rent* (1880), and Pietro Rota of Bergamo (died 1875). Rota's *Principii di scienza bancaria* (2nd ed. 1873), and the *Storia delle banche* (1874), raised hopes, too soon cut off, of later works which would have been remarkable for subtility learning, and simplicity of style.

The Lombard economists are rivalled by those of Venetia, the disciples, directly or indirectly, of Messedaglia and Lampertico. The ablest of them is Luigi Luzzati, the zealous advocate of popular banks and other co-operative societies. Later on he was Minghetti's most active coadjutor in the Ministry of Agriculture and Commerce; and he showed his ability in the negotiation of commercial treaties. As a lecturer he was eloquent and influential; as a writer, simple, and averse to vague and exaggerated formulas. His writings are very useful, being mostly written with the intention of combating prejudices and paving the way for reforms. Considering his distinguished merits and his singleness of purpose, the most severe critic will pardon Luzzati a few inaccuracies and an occasional excess of emphasis.

Among Venetian economists there are, besides Alessandro Rossi, the following writers :—Emilio Morpurgo, an elegant writer of economic, statistical, and financial articles ; Elia Lattes, who has given a learned and able account of the early Venetian banks, and of mortgage credit ; Alberto Errera, the laborious compiler of books and articles on economic history and statistics ; Tullio Martelli, the historian of the *Internazionale ;* Stivanello ; Forti, the editor of the *Giornale degli Economisti* (which has now stopped) ; Salvioni, &c. ; and finally, Giuseppe Toniolo, the sober and accurate writer of memoirs on small industries, on method, on the moral element in economics, on wages, on participation in profits, and on rent.

In Central Italy and in Tuscany the good traditions of the science were kept up in teaching and writing ; in the former by Torrigiani, Montanari, Marescotti, Martinelli, Carpi, Piperno, and Pompilj ; and in the latter by Ridolfi, Corsi, Cini, Andreucci, Rubieri, Fontanelli, the two Sonnino, Franchetti, Protonotari, the careful director of the *Nuova Antologia,* and others.

In the southern provinces the writers on the social sciences, though sometimes a little vague and abstract, and even careless in style, are now as always zealous in the study of economics. There is a distinguished group of teachers who are free from the above defects, and who from time to time have given excellent proofs of profound and able investigation. The highest positions in this group are held by Scialoja (died 1877), Magliani, Baer, de Cesare, Racioppi, and the Sicilian Busacca. Among those whose powers have been less tested we may note the Neapolitans, Miraglia, Schiattarella, Lo Savio, Simoni, Fiorilli, Fortunato, and

more especially—on account of the line of study which
they followed—Antonio Salandra, a critic of great ability
and of varied and solid culture ; Cognetti de Martiis,
a learned contributor to the *Biblioteca dell' Economista*, an authority on the Neapolitan economists, and
well versed in monetary theories ; Tommaso Fornari,
who is preparing a learned and accurate historical work on
the Neapolitan economists ; and the Sicilians, Vito Cusumano and Giuseppe Ricca Salerno, who specially studied
the German economists.   Cusumano was the author of
some learned historical works, some of which have been
already mentioned.   Ricca wrote three excellent monographs on the *theory of capital* (1877), the *theory of
wages* (1878), and the *theory of public loans* (1879), besides many remarkable critical articles which appeared
in various reviews.

During the last seven years the more accurate study
which has been bestowed on foreign writers, particularly
by young men from the universities of Northern Italy,
has given an effectual impulse to scientific investigation.
The instructors of these younger economists were publicly denounced in 1874 by Ferrara, and branded as
Germanists, socialists, and corrupters of the Italian
youth.   This provoked a prompt and successful retort
from Luzzati, who, with the help of Lampertico and
Scialoja, convoked in Milan the first Congress of Economists (January, 1875).   The purpose of this gathering
was to make clear the intentions of those who do not
blindly believe that the science was born and died
with Adam Smith and his commentators.   It gave rise
to vivacious and not invariably courteous disputes,
diffusely stated in a large number of writings, which,
either from hasty compilation or from an incomplete

study of authorities, seldom led to serious or satisfactory results. Better results perhaps may come before long. But we must, in conclusion, express the hope that calm scientific discussion will no longer be disturbed by political wrangling, from which the economist should hold himself steadily aloof.

INDEX OF AUTHORS QUOTED IN
THE TEXT.

INDEX OF AUTHORS QUOTED IN THE TEXT.

ACCURSIO DAS NEVES, 208
Ackersdijk, 201
Agricola, Giulio, 114, 115
Albergo, 220
Alberti, 108
Albertus Magnus, 103
Alciato, 114
Aller, 206
Allievi, 219
Allocchio, 224
Anderson, 171
Andreucci, 225
Antonine of Florence, 106
Apollodoros of Lemnos, 90
Aquila, 115
Argelati, 133
Aristotle, 66, 89, 90, 91, 92, 93, 102, 104, 121
Arrivabene, 200, 214, 223
Asher, 164
Augustinus, De, 214

BABBAGE, 22
Baden Karl Friedrich von, 140
Baer, 225,
Baert, 162, 201
Bagehot, 162, 181
Balbo, 213
Balchen, 81
Ballerini, 140
Balsamo, 213
Bandini, 139
Barianno, 114
Bartolo di Sassoferrata, 104
Bastiat, 23, 183, 194, 200, 218, 219, 221
Batbie, 145, 186,
Baudeau, 148
Baudrillart, 24, 25, 73, 110, 186
Baxter, 179
Beccaria, 143, 155, 156, 157, 158, 159
Becher, 128
Belloni, 140

Benalcanfor, 209
Bentham, 69, 171
Berkeley, 136
Bernardi, 216
Bernardino da Busto, 114
Bernardin of Siena, 106
Beroaldo, 107
Bianchini, 79, 155, 213, 214, 220
Biedermann, 84, 119
Biel, 106
Bischof, 199
Blanqui, A. 75, 79, 80, 81, 162, 183
Blanqui, G. A., 183
Block, 26
Bluntschli, 82, 144
Boccardo, 46, 182, 219, 223
Bocchi, 133
Bodin, 110, 111, 117, 119, 121
Bodio, 26
Böhmert, von, 195
Boisguillebert, 137, 138
Boiteau, 186
Bona y Ureta, 207
Bonghi, 219
Borghini, 114
Borrego, 206
Boselli, 223
Bosellini, 211, 220
Botero, 111, 121
Boutron, 200
Brachelli, 27
Brasseur, 202, 203
Brater, 144
Braun, 195
Brentano, 45, 181, 198
Briganti, 155, 159
Bright, 176
Broedersen, 140
Broggia, 140
Broglio, 219
Bruno Alberto, d'Asti, 115
Bruno, Giordano, 112
Bruno, Giovanni, 73, 220, 222
Bruyn Kops, De, 201

Buchanan, 165
Budaeus, 114
Budelio, 115
Buoninsegni, 114
Buridan, 105, 115
Busacca, 220, 225
Buzzetti, 224
Buys, 201

CADET, 138
Cagnazzi, de Samuele, 211
Cairnes, 8, 38, 72, 179, 181
Calkoen, 97
Callicratidas, 90
Calvin, 113
Campanella, 132
Canga y Arguelles, 207
Capello, 159
Capponi, 218
Caraffa, 107
Carballo y Vanguemert, 79, 206
Cardenas, De, 207
Carey, 23, 43, 81, 192, 200, 218
Carli, 158, 159
Carli, De, 213
Carlisle, 118
Carnido de Figueiredo, 209
Carpi, 225
Carreras y Gonzales, 206
Casarini, 216
Cato, 97
Cattaneo, 214, 215, 216, 224
Cernuschi, 224
Cesare, De, 225
Chalmers, 179
Chares of Pharos, 90
Cherbuliez, 16, 19, 204
Chevalier, 162, 184
Child, 129, 150, 155
Chitti, 214
Cibrario, 99
Ciccone, 222
Cicero, 97
Cicogna, 158
Cini, 225
Cicé, 151
Clamageran, 134, 186
Clément, Antoine, 24, 187
Clément, Pierre, 125
Cliffe Leslie, 72, 181
Cobden, 176, 184
Cochut, 134
Cognetti de Martiis, 217, 226
Cohn, 125, 138
Colmeiro, 83, 118, 206
Colonna, Egidio, 104
Columella, 97
Comte, Charles, 172, 182
Concina, 120
Conde, 207
Condillac, 149
Condorcet, 149

Contzen, 99, 106
Copernicus, 115, 116
Coq, 22
Coquelin, 183
Coquelin et Guillaumin, 137, 144, 182, 219
Corbani, 220
Cordova, 220
Cornewall Lewis, 37, 42
Coronelli, 159
Correnti, 214, 219
Corsi, 225
Cossa, 89, 99, 129, 143
Costantini, 159
Courcelle-Seneuil, 19, 21, 49, 186
Cournot, 45, 186
Court, Jean De la, 132, 150
Court, Pierre De la, 132
Cousin, 162
Cridis, 213
Cristoforis, De, 219
Culpeper, 130
Custodi, 82, 114, 140, 156, 158, 211, 214
Cusumano, 103, 106, 187, 226

DAIRE, 134, 144
D'Alembert, 145
Dameth, 24
Dankwardt, 30
D'Audriffret, 186
D'Aulnis de Bourouill, 46
D'Aulnis dal Greven, 201
Davanzati, 114, 116
Delfico, 155
Del Valle, 206
Diderot, 145
Dietzel, 198
Dithmar, 136
Donati, 159
Donaudi delle Mallere, 159
Doni, 112
Doria, 139
Droz, 23, 68, 172
Ducpétiaux, 208
Dufau, 26, 37, 194
Dühring, 79, 81
Du Mesnil-Marigny, 86
Dunoyer, 183
Duns Scotus, 103
Dupont de Nemours, 148
Dupin, 183
Durini, 214
Dutot, 138
Duval, 127

EINERT, 30
Eisdell, 179
Ellena, 223
Emminghaus, 22, 149, 195

Endemann, 31, 102
Engel, 26, 194, 198
Errera, 225
Eschines, 92
Espinosa de los Monteros, 206

Fabbroni, 159, 212
Fabiano da Genova, 114
Fano, 224
Fantuzzi, 213
Faucher, Jules, 195
Faucher, Léon, 183
Fauveau, 45
Favre, 115
Fawcett, Henry, 16, 180
Fawcett, M. G., 16, 180
Feer-Herzog, 204
Ferrara, 17, 18, 23, 45, 57, 126, 140, 144, 154, 164, 217, 218, 219, 221, 226
Ferraris, Carlo, 32, 223
Ferraris, Maggiorino, 223
Ferreira-Borges, 208
Figuerola, 207
Filangieri, 149, 155
Fiorilli, 225,
Florez Estrada, 15, 79, 206
Folcker, 201
Fontanelli, 225
Fontenay, 186
Forbounais, 143, 155
Fornari, 127, 226
Forti, 225
Fortunato, 225
Foville, De, 187
Franchetti, 225
Frank, 112
Franklin, 173
Frère-Orban, 203 *
Front de Fontpertuis, 92
Fullarton, 177
Funk, 106
Fuoco, 212, 213

Gabaglio, 27
Gaetano (v. Tommaso da Vio), 113, 114
Galanti, 155
Galeani Napione, 111
Galiani, 126, 159, 213
Gambini, 213
Ganilh, 172
Garelli, Alessandro, 223
Garelli, Giusto Emanuele, 222
Garnier, Germano, 149, 164
Garnier, Joseph, 79, 144, 186
Gasser, 136
Gazquez, Rubi, 206
Gebhart, 103
Genovesi, 128, 143, 152, 154, 155, 156, 157, 159, 213
Gentz, 191

Gerando, De, 183
Gerson, 105
Giginta, 119
Gilbert, 118
Gioja, 14, 26, 211, 212, 214
Giovanetti, 216
Gladstone, 176
Glaser, 88, 93, 119
Godwin, 170
Gogel, 173
Goldschmidt, 31
Gorani, 140, 149
Goschen, 181
Gournay, 150
Graswinkel, 132
Gregory of Toulouse, 111
Grotius, 132
Grote, 215
Guerry, 26, 194
Guicciardini, 110
Guillaumin, 138

Hagen, 92
Hakluyt, 118
Hall, van, 201
Haller, 191
Hamilton, Alexander, 192
Hamilton, Sir William, 162
Hanssen, 198
Harrington, 131
Harris, 136
Haushofer, 22, 26
Hearn, 179
Held, 119, 198, 199
Helferich, 190, 198
Helfnich, 162
Henry of Ghent, 104
Herbert, 154
Hermann, 50, 72, 96, 188, 189, 190, 193
Herodotus, 89
Heymann, 134
Hildebrand, 46, 92, 192
Hieron, 90
Hippodamus of Miletus, 91
Hobbes, 129
Hock, 200
Hoffman, 188, 189, 200
Hogendorp, 173
Horn, 198
Hörnigk, von, 128
Houten, van, 201
Hoyta, von, 105
Huber, 191
Hufeland, 173, 190
Hugo, 49
Hume, 150, 155, 163
Hutcheson, 135, 163

Inama, 162
Ingram, 72, 181
Iselin, 149

JAKOB, 173
Jacini, 219
Jevons, 46, 136, 180
Jobard, 203
Jourdain. 102, 105
Joyce, 165
Justi, 142

KAUTZ, 57, 72, 79, 80, 84, 85
Kellner, 144
Kleinwächter, 200
Klock, 121, 128
Knapp, 26
Knies, 46, 110, 192, 198
Kolb, 27
Kosegarten, 191
Kraus, 172
Kübel, 87
Kudler, 188

LABOULAYE, 22
Lacroix, 129
Lampertico, 26, 72, 158, 159, 181, 200, 219, 222, 224, 226
Lange, 181, 197
Langenstein, von, 105
Laspeyres, 83, 132, 144, 162, 198
Latini, Brunetto, 103
Lattes, 225
Laveleye, De, 202, 203
Lavergne, 144, 162, 185
Lavergne-Peguilhen, 191
Law, 134, 138, 151
Le Hardy de Beaulieu, 203
Leroy-Beaulieu, 183, 187
Le Trosne, 118
Levasseur, 134, 185
Lewins, 179
Lexis, 26, 198
List, 81, 192, 215
Locke, 129, 133, 159
Longe, 181
Lopez Narvaez, 207
Loria, 224
Lo Savio, 225
Lotz, 79, 173, 190
Lozano y Montes, 207
Luca, De, 219
Lüder, 172
Lumbroso, 87
Luther, 113
Luzzati, 162, 224, 226

MACAULAY, 25
Machiavelli, 110
MacCulloch, 14, 15, 78, 128, 137, 162, 177, 215
Macleod, 181
Madrazo, 206,
Maffei, 140

Magenta, 216
Maggiore Perni, 220
Magliani, 225
Majorana, 222
Malchus, 200
Malestroit, 117
Malthus, 158, 170, 171, 177, 179, 193, 206, 215
Mancini, 214
Manfredi, 224
Mangoldt, 15, 43, 72, 190, 199, 200
Manin, 159
Manna, 82
Manzoni. 62
Marchesini, 159
Marescotti. 219, 222, 225
Mariana, 111
Marshall, Alfred. 180
Marshall, Mary P. 180
Martello, 225
Marlo (v. Winkelblech)
Martinelli, 220, 225
Marulli, 218
Mastier. 145
Mastrofini, 217
Mauvillon, 149
Medina, Giovanni di 119,
Mees, 202
Meguscher. 216
Melanchthon, 113
Mele, 214
Melon, 138
Mendonça Cortes, 209
Meneghini, 219
Mengotti, 159
Mercier de la Rivière, 148
Messedaglia, 15, 43, 47, 221, 222, 224
Meyer, 191
Michaelis, 195
Michelini, 216
Mill, James, 15, 171
Mill, John Stuart, 6, 8, 16, 19, 37, 171, 177, 178, 179, 180, 193, 195
Minghetti, 24, 30, 221, 224
Mirabeau, 148
Miraglia, 225
Miranda y Egreia, De, 207
Mocenigo, 159
Modeste, 186
Mohl, 78, 92, 200, 213
Molinari, De, 202, 203
Molster, 81
Mommsen, 25, 49
Monjean, 162, 186
Montanari, Augusto, 116, 225
Montanari, Geminiano, 138
Montchrétien, 126, 127
Montesquieu, 139
Mora, 219
Morato Roma, 209
More, Sir Thomas, 112
Morichini, 217
Morpurgo, 26, 225

Müller, 191
Mun, 126, 127, 128
Muratori, 160
Musgrave, 179

Nani, 159
Nasse, 117, 197, 198
Naville, 204
Nazzani, 15, 17, 72, 222
Nebenius. 188, 189, 200
Negri, 216
Neri. 98, 159
Newmarch, 177
Nicolai, 213
Nicolini, 224
Niebuhr, 49
Norman, 177
North, Sir Dudley, 129, 120

Obrecht, 121
Ochoa, 207
Oettingen, 26, 194
Oliveira-Marreca, 208
Oncken, A. 162, 162, 163
Onken, W. 93
Orèsme, 105, 115
Ortes, 158, 159. 222
Overstone, 177

Pagano, 155
Pagnini, 159
Paillottet, 186
Palmeri, 213
Palmieri, 155, 159
Paoletti, 149
Paradisi, 143
Parieu, De, 31, 115
Pascoli, 139
Pasini, 219
Passy, Frédéric, 186
Passy, Hippolyte, 185
Pastor, 207
Patrizzii, 107
Patterson, 136
Paul, 98
Pazo y Degalgado, 206
Pecchio, 82, 83, 140
Peckham, 118
Peel, Sir Robert, 176
Pellarcioni, 223
Pereira Forjaz de Sampajo, 208
Périn, 202, 203
Perni, 220
Perry, 79
Pescatore, 223
Petitti, 216
Petty, 129, 130, 150, 155
Phaleas of Chalcedon, 91
Philolaos of Thebes, 90
Pickford, 72

Piernas y Hurtado, 207
Pierson, 83, 201, 202
Pinheiro-Ferreira, 208
Piperno, 225
Pizperno, 222
Platina, 107
Plato, 90, 92, 93, 94, 112
Pliny, 66, 97
Poli, 216, 223
Pompili, 225
Ponsiglioni, 222
Pontano, 107
Prince-Smith, 194
Protonatari, 225
Proudhon, 28
Puffendorf, 135
Puynode, Du, 162, 186
Pythagoras, 90

Quesnay, 143, 144, 145, 146, 147, 148,
    150, 154, 164
Quetelet, 26, 194

Racchetti, 213
Racioppi, 155, 225
Rae, 179
Raleigh, 118
Rau. 14, 15, 17, 19, 50, 79, 88, 187, 188,
    197, 200, 208
Raynal, 149
Rees, van, 83, 201
Reid, 163
Rentzsch, 195
Ressi, 211
Restelli, 216
Reybaud, 185
Reymond, 18, 222
Ricardo, 45, 170, 171, 172, 177, .179,
    184, 189, 193, 206, 213, 215
Ricca Salerno, 162, 226
Ricci, 213
Ricci, Lodovico, 159, 160
Ridolfi, Cosimo, 213
Ridolfi, Angelo, 213
Ridolfi, Luigi, 225
Riedel, 188
Rivet, 30
Rocchi, De, 222
Rodbertus, 191
Rodriguez de Brito, 208
Rogers, 181
Rouz, De, 81
Romagnosi, 26, 30, 214, 215, 216
Romanelli, 224
Rondelet, 24
Roscher, 15, 17, 46, 47, 48, 49, 50, 76,
    83, 84, 88, 90, 105, 106, 116, 128, 161
    162, 190, 192, 193
Rosellis, De, 114
Rösler, 169
Rossi, Alessandro, 225

Rossi, Pellegrino, 9, 15, 16, 19, 30, 73, 214, 216, 219
Rota, 224
Rousseau, 149
Rubieri, 225
Rubio y Dorado, 206
Rümelin, 194
Rusconi, 219
Russell, 176

SACCHI, 214, 223
Salandra, 226
Salfi, 126
Salmour, 216
Salvioni, 225
Sanfilippo, 211
Sanromà 207
Santillan, 207
Santis, De, 126, 127
Sargaut, 179
Sartorius, 172
Saumaise, 132
Savarese, 218
Say, Jean Baptiste, 14, 15, 68, 69, 79, 149, 171, 194, 208, 211, 212, 214
Say, Léon, 186
Say, Horace, 172, 186
Scaruffi, 116
Schäffle, 190, 198, 199
Scheel, von, 98, 145, 196, 197, 198
Schiattarella, 47, 225
Schlettwein, 149
Schlözer, 172
Schmitthenner, 188
Schmoller, 190, 196, 197, 198
Schönberg, 198
Scratchley, 179
Schröder, 128
Schuhmacher, 45
Schulze-Delitzsch, 195
Schüz, von, 188
Schwarzkopf, 83
Scialoja 28, 215, 220, 225, 226
Sclopis, 223
Scola, 159
Scrope, 179
Scuderi, 211
Sella, 223
Seneca, 97
Senior, 8, 72, 178, 215
Sercambi, 105
Sergio, 143
Serra, 126, 127
Serzedello, 209
Settembrini, 140
Shadwell, 179
Silva Lisboa, Da, 173
Silveira-Pinto, 208
Simon, 183
Simoni, 225
Sismondi 173, 204
Skarzynski, 163
Smith, Adam, 75, 119, 128, 129, 135,

145, 149, 150,'155, 161—175, 179, 187, 190, 191, 193, 200, 206, 211, 212, 213, 215, 218, 226
Socrates, 91, 92
Soetbeer, 195
Sola, 115
Sonnenfels, 142, 155
Sonnino, 225
Soto, 119
Stafford, 117, 119
Stein, 82, 90, 198, 200
Stewart, Sir James, 143, 155
Stewart, Dugald, 162
Stivanello, 225
Storch, 173, 208
Struzzi, 129
Szecheny, 173

TALLON, 183
Targioni, 213
Telosio, 112
Tellegen, 201
Terrasson, 151
Tesauro, 115
Thales, 66
Thiers, 25, 134
Thorbecke, 201
Thornton, 180
Thucydides, 89
Thünen, von, 45, 186, 188, 189, 193
Tissot, 145
Todde, 223
Tolomei, 216
Tolomeo of Lucca, 104
Thomas Aquinas, St. 103, 104
Tommaso da Vio, 113,'114
Toniolo, 200, 225
Tooke, 177
Torcia, 155
Torrens, 177
Torrigiani, 225
Tracy, 14, 172, 208
Travers-Twiss, 79, 80
Treitschke, von, 197
Trinchera, 79, 86, 218, 219
Trinci, 218
Turbolo, 156
Turgot, 16, 144, 145, 150, 151, 152, 153, 154, 158, 164, 165, 166, 171
Tydemann, 98, 201

ULLOA, 155
Umpfenbach, 198
Usseli: , 132
Ustari', 155.

VALERIANI, Molinari, 30, 212
Vallesantoro 205
Varro, 97
Vasco, 159
Vauban, 137
Veegens, 182
Vergani, 213

Verloren, 201
Verri, 155, 157, 159
Vidari, 31
Villani, Giovanni, 103
Villani, Matteo, 103
Villeneuve-Bargemout, 79, 80
Villermé, 183
Virgilio, 223
Vischers, 203
Vissering, 201, 202
Vocke, 200
Voorthuysen, 201

Wagener, 191
Wagner, 26, 196, 197, 198, 200
Waitz, 31
Wakefield, 179
Walker, 181
Walras, 46, 186
Wappäus, 194
Welz, De, 213
West, 171

Whateley, 57, 72, 177
Whewell, 37, 45
Wilson, 177, 181
Winkelblech, 79
Winspeare, 213
Wirth, 79, 195
Witt, De, 133
Wolff, 195
Wolkoff, 186
Wolowski, 47, 105, 115, 185, 203
Woolsey, 32

Xenophon, 94, 97

Zachariae, 188
Zambelli, 216
Zanardelli, 219
Zannini, 220
Zanon, 159
Zennari, 216
Zwingli, 113

THE END.

LONDON :
R. CLAY, SONS, AND TAYLOR,
BREAD STREET HILL.

BEDFORD STREET, COVENT GARDEN, LONDON,
December, 1879.

*MACMILLAN & CO.'S CATALOGUE of WORKS
in MATHEMATICS and PHYSICAL SCIENCE;
including PURE and APPLIED MATHE-
MATICS; PHYSICS, ASTRONOMY, GEOLOGY,
CHEMISTRY, ZOOLOGY, BOTANY; and of
WORKS in MENTAL and MORAL PHILOSOPHY
and Allied Subjects.*

MATHEMATICS.

Airy.—Works by Sir G. B. AIRY, K.C.B., Astronomer Royal :—
ELEMENTARY TREATISE ON PARTIAL DIFFERENTIAL
EQUATIONS. Designed for the Use of Students in the Univer-
sities. With Diagrams. New Edition. Crown 8vo. 5s. 6d.
ON THE ALGEBRAICAL AND NUMERICAL THEORY OF
ERRORS OF OBSERVATIONS AND THE COMBINA-
TION OF OBSERVATIONS. Second Edition. Crown 8vo.
6s. 6d.
UNDULATORY THEORY OF OPTICS. Designed for the Use of
Students in the University. New Edition. Crown 8vo. 6s. 6d.
ON SOUND AND ATMOSPHERIC VIBRATIONS. With
the Mathematical Elements of Music. Designed for the Use of
Students of the University. Second Edition, revised and enlarged.
Crown 8vo. 9s.
A TREATISE ON MAGNETISM. Designed for the Use of
Students in the University. Crown 8vo. 9s. 6d.

Ball (R. S., A.M.).—EXPERIMENTAL MECHANICS. A
Course of Lectures delivered at the Royal College of Science for
Ireland. By ROBERT STAWELL BALL, A.M., Professor of Applied
Mathematics and Mechanics in the Royal College of Science for
Ireland (Science and Art Department). Royal 8vo. 16s.

" *We have not met with any book of the sort in English. It eluci-
dates instructively the methods of a teacher of the very highest
rank. We most cordially recommend it to all our readers.*"—
Mechanics' Magazine.

Merriman.—ELEMENTS OF THE METHOD OF LEAST SQUARES. By MANSFIELD MERRIMAN, Professor of Civil and Mechanical Engineering, Lehigh University, Bethlehem, Penn., U.S.A. Crown 8vo. 7s. 6d.

Morgan.—A COLLECTION OF PROBLEMS AND EXAMPLES IN MATHEMATICS. With Answers. By H. A. MORGAN, M.A., Sadlerian and Mathematical Lecturer of Jesus College, Cambridge. Crown 8vo. cloth. 6s. 6d.

Newton's Principia.—4to. cloth. 31s. 6d.

It is a sufficient guarantee of the reliability of this complete edition of Newton's Principia that it has been printed for and under the care of Professor Sir William Thomson and Professor Blackburn, of Glasgow University.

Parkinson.—A TREATISE ON OPTICS. By S. PARKINSON, D.D., F.R.S., Fellow and Tutor of St. John's College, Cambridge. Third Edition, revised and enlarged. Crown 8vo. cloth. 10s. 6d.

Phear.—ELEMENTARY HYDROSTATICS. With Numerous Examples. By J. B. PHEAR, M.A., Fellow and late Assistant Tutor of Clare Coll. Cambridge. Fourth Edition. Cr. 8vo. cloth. 5s. 6d.

Pirrie.—LESSONS ON RIGID DYNAMICS. By the Rev. G. PIRRIE, M.A., Fellow and Tutor of Queen's College, Cambridge. Crown 8vo. 6s.

Puckle.—AN ELEMENTARY TREATISE ON CONIC SECTIONS AND ALGEBRAIC GEOMETRY. With numerous Examples and Hints for their Solution. By G. HALE PUCKLE, M.A. Fouth Edition, enlarged. Crown 8vo. 7s. 6d.

Rayleigh.—THE THEORY OF SOUND. By LORD RAYLEIGH, F.R.S., formerly Fellow of Trinity College, Cambridge. 8vo. Vol. 1. 12s. 6d.; Vol. II. 12s. 6d. [Vol. III. *in preparation.*

Reuleaux.—THE KINEMATICS OF MACHINERY. Outlines of a Theory of Machines. By Professor F. REULEAUX. Translated and edited by A. B. W. KENNEDY, C.E., Professor of Civil and Mechanical Engineering, University College, London. With 450 Illustrations. Royal 8vo. 20s.

Routh.—Works by EDWARD JOHN ROUTH, M.A., F.R.S., late Fellow and Assistant Tutor of St. Peter's College, Cambridge; Examiner in the University of London :—

AN ELEMENTARY TREATISE ON THE DYNAMICS OF THE SYSTEM OF RIGID BODIES. With numerous Examples. Third Edition, enlarged. 8vo. 21s.

Routh —*continued.*

STABILITY OF A GIVEN STATE OF MOTION, PARTI-
CULARLY STEADY MOTION. The Adams' Prize Essay for
1877. 8vo. 8s. 6d.

Tait and Steele.—DYNAMICS OF A PARTICLE. With
numerous Examples. By Professor TAIT and Mr. STEELE. Fourth
Edition, revised. Crown 8vo. 12s.

Thomson.—PAPERS ON ELECTROSTATICS AND MAG-
NETISM. By Professor SIR WILLIAM THOMSON, F.R.S.
8vo. 18s.

Todhunter.—Works by I. TODHUNTER, M.A., F.R.S., of
St. John's College, Cambridge :—

*"Mr. Todhunter is chiefly known to students of mathematics as the
author of a series of admirable mathematical text-books, which
possess the rare qualities of being clear in style and absolutely free
from mistakes, typographical or other."*—Saturday Review.

A TREATISE ON SPHERICAL TRIGONOMETRY. New
Edition, enlarged. Crown 8vo. cloth. 4s. 6d.

PLANE CO-ORDINATE GEOMETRY, as applied to the Straight
Line and the Conic Sections. With numerous Examples. New
Edition. Crown 8vo. 7s. 6d.

A TREATISE ON THE DIFFERENTIAL CALCULUS.
With numerous Examples. New Edition. Crown 8vo. 10s. 6d.

A TREATISE ON THE INTEGRAL CALCULUS AND ITS
APPLICATIONS. With numerous Examples. New Edition,
revised and enlarged. Crown 8vo. cloth. 10s. 6d.

EXAMPLES OF ANALYTICAL GEOMETRY OF THREE
DIMENSIONS. New Edition, revised. Crown 8vo. cloth. 4s.

A TREATISE ON ANALYTICAL STATICS. With numerous
Examples. New Edition, revised and enlarged. Crown 8vo.
cloth. 10s. 6d.

A HISTORY OF THE MATHEMATICAL THEORY OF
PROBABILITY, from the Time of Pascal to that of Laplace.
8vo. 18s.

RESEARCHES IN THE CALCULUS OF VARIATIONS,
Principally on the Theory of Discontinuous Solutions: An Essay
to which the Adams' Prize was awarded in the University of
Cambridge in 1871. 8vo. 6s.

Todhunter—*continued.*

A HISTORY OF THE MATHEMATICAL THEORIES OF ATTRACTION, and the Figure of the Earth, from the time of Newton to that of Laplace. Two vols. 8vo. 24*s.*

AN ELEMENTARY TREATISE ON LAPLACE'S, LAME'S, AND BESSEL'S FUNCTIONS. Crown 8vo. 10*s.* 6*d.*

Wilson (W. P.).—A TREATISE ON DYNAMICS. By W. P. WILSON, M.A., Fellow of St. John's College, Cambridge, and Professor of Mathematics in Queen's College, Belfast. 8vo. 9*s.* 6*d.*

Wolstenholme.—MATHEMATICAL PROBLEMS, on Subjects included in the First and Second Divisions of the Schedule of Subjects for the Cambridge Mathematical Tripos Examination. Devised and arranged by JOSEPH WOLSTENHOLME, late Fellow of Christ's College, sometime Fellow of St. John's College, and Professor of Mathematics in the Royal Indian Engineering College. New Edition, greatly enlarged. 8vo. 18*s.*

Young.—SIMPLE PRACTICAL METHODS OF CALCULATING STRAINS ON GIRDERS, ARCHES, AND TRUSSES. With a Supplementary Essay on Economy in suspension Bridges. By E. W. YOUNG, Associate of King's College, London, and Member of the Institution of Civil Engineers. 8vo. 7*s.* 6*d.*

PHYSICAL SCIENCE.

Airy (G. B.).—POPULAR ASTRONOMY. With Illustrations. By Sir G. B. AIRY, K.C.B., Astronomer Royal. New Edition. fcap. 8vo. 4s. 6d.

Balfour.—A TREATISE ON COMPARATIVE EMBRYOLOGY. By F. M. BALFOUR, F.R.S. Illustrated. 8vo. [*Shortly*.

Bastian.—Works by H. CHARLTON BASTIAN, M.D., F.R.S., Professor of Pathological Anatomy in University College, London, &c. :—

THE BEGINNINGS OF LIFE : Being some Account of the Nature, Modes of Origin, and Transformations of Lower Organisms. In Two Volumes. With upwards of 100 Illustrations. Crown 8vo. 28s.

"*It is a book that cannot be ignored, and must inevitably lead to renewed discussions and repeated observations, and through these to the establishment of truth.*"—A. R. Wallace *in* Nature.

EVOLUTION AND THE ORIGIN OF LIFE. Crown 8vo. 6s. 6d.

"*Abounds in information of interest to the student of biological science.*"- -Daily News.

Blake.—ASTRONOMICAL MYTHS. Based on Flammarion's "The Heavens." By John F. BLAKE. With numerous Illustrations. Crown 8vo. 9s.

Blanford (H. F.).—RUDIMENTS OF PHYSICAL GEOGRAPHY FOR THE USE OF INDIAN SCHOOLS. By H. F. BLANFORD, F.G.S. With numerous Illustrations and Glossary of Technical Terms employed. New Edition. Globe 8vo. 2s. 6a.

Blanford (W. T.).—GEOLOGY AND ZOOLOGY OF ABYSSINIA. By W. T. BLANFORD. 8vo. 21s.

Bosanquet.—AN ELEMENTARY TREATISE ON MUSICAL INTERVALS AND TEMPERAMENT. With an Account of an Enharmonic Harmonium exhibited in the Loan Collection of Scientific Instruments, South Kensington, 1876 ; also of an Enharmonic Organ exhibited to the Musical Association of London, May, 1875. By R. H. Bosanquet, Fellow of St. John's College, Oxford. 8vo. 6s.

Clifford.—SEEING AND THINKING. By the late Professor W. K. CLIFFORD, F.R.S. With Diagrams. Crown 8vo. 3s. 6d. [*Nature Series.*

Coal: ITS HISTORY AND ITS USES. By Professors GREEN, MIALL, THORPE, RÜCKER, and MARSHALL, of the Yorkshire College, Leeds. With Illustrations. 8vo. 12s. 6d.

" *It furnishes a very comprehensive treatise on the whole subject of Coal from the geological, chemical, mechanical, and industrial points of view, concluding with a chapter on the important topic known as the ' Coal Question.'*"— Daily News.

Cooke (Josiah P., Jun.).—FIRST PRINCIPLES OF CHEMICAL PHILOSOPHY. By JOSIAH P. COOKE, Jun., Ervine Professor of Chemistry and Mineralogy in Harvard College. Third Edition, revised and corrected. Crown 8vo. 12s.

Cooke (M. C.).—HANDBOOK OF BRITISH FUNGI, with full descriptions of all the Species, and Illustrations of the Genera. By M. C. COOKE, M.A. Two vols. crown 8vo. 24s.

" *Will maintain its place as the standard English book, on the subject of which it treats, for many years to come.*"—Standard.

Crossley.—HANDBOOK OF DOUBLE STARS, WITH A CATALOGUE OF 1,200 DOUBLE STARS AND EXTENSIVE LISTS OF MEASURES FOR THE USE OF AMATEURS. By E. CROSSLEY, F.R.A.S., J. GLEDHILL, F.R.A.S., and J. M. WILSON, F.R.A.S. With Illustrations. 8vo. 21s.

Dawkins.—Works by W. BOYD DAWKINS, F.R.S., &c., Professor of Geology at Owens College, Manchester.

CAVE-HUNTING : Researches on the Evidence of Caves respecting the Early Inhabitants of Europe. With Coloured Plate and Woodcuts. 8vo. 21s.

" *The mass of information he has brought together, with the judicious use he has made of his materials, will be found to invest his book with much of new and singular value.*"—Saturday Review.

EARLY MAN IN BRITAIN, AND HIS PLACE IN THE TERTIARY PERIOD. With Illustrations. 8vo.   [*Shortly.*

Dawson (J. W.).—ACADIAN GEOLOGY. The Geologic Structure, Organic Remains, and Mineral Resources of Nova Scotia, New Brunswick, and Prince Edward Island. By JOHN WILLIAM DAWSON, M.A., LL.D., F.R.S., F.G.S., Principal and Vice-Chancellor of M'Gill College and University, Montreal, &c. With a Geological Map and numerous Illustrations. Third Edition, with Supplement. 8vo. 21s. Supplement, separately, 2s. 6d.

Fiske.—DARWINISM; AND OTHER ESSAYS. By JOHN FISKE, M.A., LL.D., formerly Lecturer on Philosophy in Harvard University. Crown 8vo. 7s. 6d.

Fleischer.—A SYSTEM OF VOLUMETRIC ANALYSIS. By Dr. E. FLEISCHER. Translated from the Second German Edition by M. M. Pattison Muir, with Notes and Additions. Illustrated. Crown 8vo. 7*s. 6d.*

Flückiger and Hanbury.—PHARMACOGRAPHIA. A History of the Principal Drugs of Vegetble Origin met with in Great Britain and India. By F. A. FLÜCKIGER, M.D., and D. HANBURY, F.R.S. Second Edition, revised. 8vo. 21*s.*

Forbes.—THE TRANSIT OF VENUS. By GEORGE FORBES, B.A., Professor of Natural Philosophy in the Andersonian University of Glasgow. With numerous Illustrations. Crown 8vo. 3*s. 6d.*

Foster and Balfour.—ELEMENTS OF EMBRYOLOGY By MICHAEL FOSTER, M.D., F.R.S., and F. M. BALFOUR, M.A., Fellow of Trinity College, Cambridge. With numerous Illustrations. Part I. Crown 8vo. 7*s. 6d.*

Galton.—Works by FRANCIS GALTON, F.R.S. :—
METEOROGRAPHICA, or Methods of Mapping the Weather. Illustrated by upwards of 600 Printed Lithographic Diagrams. 4to. 9*s.*
HEREDITARY GENIUS: An Inquiry into its Laws and Consequences. Demy 8vo. 12*s.*
The Times *calls it " a most able and most interesting book."*
ENGLISH MEN OF SCIENCE; THEIR NATURE AND NURTURE. 8vo. 8*s. 6d.*
" The book is certainly one of very great interest."—Nature.

Gamgee.—A TEXT-BOOK, SYSTEMATIC and PRACTICAL, OF THE PHYSIOLOGICAL CHEMISTRY OF THE ANIMAL BODY. By ARTHUR GAMGEE, M.D., F.R.S., Professor of Physiology in Owens College, Manchester. With Illustrations. 8vo. *[In the press.*

Geikie.—Works by ARCHIBALD GEIKIE, LL.D., F.R.S., Murchison Professor of Geology and Mineralogy at Edinburgh :—
ELEMENTARY LESSONS IN PHYSICAL GEOGRAPHY. With numerous Illustrations. Fcap. 8vo. 4*s. 6d.* Questions, 1*s. 6d.*
OUTLINES OF FIELD GEOLOGY. With Illustrations. Crown 8vo. 3*s. 6d.*
PRIMER OF GEOLOGY. Illustrated. 18mo. 1*s.*
PRIMER OF PHYSICAL GEOGRAPHY. Illustrated. 18mo. 1*s.*

Gordon.—AN ELEMENTARY BOOK ON HEAT. By J. E. H. GORDON, B.A., Gonville and Caius College, Cambridge. Crown 8vo. 2*s.*

Gray.—STRUCTURAL BOTANY ON THE BASIS OF MORPHOLOGY. By Professor ASA GRAY. With Illustrations. 8vo.   *[In the press.*

Guillemin.—THE FORCES OF NATURE : A Popular Introduction to the Study of Physical Phenomena. By AMÉDÉE GUILLEMIN. Translated from the French by MRS. NORMAN LOCKYER ; and Edited, with Additions and Notes, by J. NORMAN LOCKYER, F.R.S. Illustrated by Coloured Plates, and 455 Woodcuts. Third and cheaper Edition. Royal 8vo. 21*s.*

" Translator and Editor have done justice to their task. The text has all the force and flow of original writing, combining faithfulness to the author's meaning with purity and independence in regard to idiom ; while the historical precision and accuracy pervading the work throughout, speak of the watchful editorial supervision which has been given to every scientific detail. Nothing can well exceed the clearness and delicacy of the illustrative woodcuts. Altogether, the work may be said to have no parallel, either in point of fulness or attraction, as a popular manual of physical science."—Saturday Review.

THE APPLICATIONS OF PHYSICAL FORCES. By A. GUILLEMIN. Translated from the French by Mrs. LOCKYER, and Edited with Notes and Additions by J. N. LOCKYER, F.R.S. With Coloured Plates and numerous Illustrations. Cheaper Edition. Imperial 8vo. cloth, extra gilt. 36*s.*

Also in Eighteen Monthly Parts, price 1*s.* each. Part I. in November, 1878.

" A book which we can heartily recommend, both on account of the width and soundness of its contents, and also because of the excellence of its print, its illustrations, and external appearance."—Westminster Review.

Hanbury.—SCIENCE PAPERS : chiefly Pharmacological and Botanical. By DANIEL HANBURY, F.R.S. Edited, with Memoir, by J. INCE, F.L.S., and Portrait engraved by C. H. JEENS. 8vo. 14*s.*

Henslow.—THE THEORY OF EVOLUTION OF LIVING THINGS, and Application of the Principles of Evolution to Religion considered as Illustrative of the Wisdom and Beneficence of the Almighty. By the Rev. GEORGE HENSLOW, M.A., F.L.S. Crown 8vo. 6*s.*

Hooker.—Works by Sir J. D. HOOKER, K.C.S.I., C.B., F.R.S., M.D., D.C.L. :—

THE STUDENT'S FLORA OF THE BRITISH ISLANDS. Second Edition, revised and improved. Globe 8vo. 10*s.* 6*d.*

" Certainly the fullest and most accurate manual of the kind that has yet appeared. Dr. Hooker has shown his characteristic industry

Hooker—*continued.*

and ability in the care and skill which he has thrown into the characters of the plants. These are to a great extent original, and are really admirable for their combination of clearness, brevity, and completeness."—Pall Mall Gazette.

PRIMER OF BOTANY. With Illustrations. 18mo. 1s. New Edition, revised and corrected.

Hooker and Ball.—JOURNAL OF A TOUR IN MAROCCO AND THE GREAT ATLAS. By Sir J. D. HOOKER, K.C.S.I., C.B., F.R.S., &c., and JOHN BALL, F.R.S. With Appendices, including a Sketch of the Geology of Marocco. By G. MAW, F.L.S., F.G.S. With Map and Illustrations. 8vo. 21s.

" This is, without doubt, one of the most interesting and valuable books of travel published for many years."—Spectator.

Huxley and Martin.—A COURSE OF PRACTICAL INSTRUCTION IN ELEMENTARY BIOLOGY. By T. H. HUXLEY, LL.D., Sec. R.S., assisted by H. N. MARTIN, B.A., M.B., D.Sc., Fellow of Christ's College, Cambridge. Crown 8vo. 6s.

" This is the most thoroughly valuable book to teachers and students of biology which has ever appeared in the English tongue."— London Quarterly Review.

Huxley (Professor).—LAY SERMONS, ADDRESSES, AND REVIEWS. By T. H. HUXLEY, LL.D., F.R.S. New and Cheaper Edition. Crown 8vo. 7s. 6d.

Fourteen Discourses on the following subjects:—(1) *On the Advisableness of Improving Natural Knowledge:*—(2) *Emancipation— Black and White :*—(3) *A Liberal Education, and where to find it :*—(4) *Scientific Education:*—(5) *On the Educational Value of the Natural History Sciences:*—(6) *On the Study of Zoology:*— (7) *On the Physical Basis of Life:*—(8) *The Scientific Aspects of Positivism:*—(9) *On a Piece of Chalk:*—(10) *Geological Contemporaneity and Persistent Types of Life:*—(11) *Geological Reform:*— (12) *The Origin of Species:*—(13) *Criticisms on the " Origin of Species:"*—(14) *On Descartes' " Discourse touching the Method of using One's Reason rightly and of seeking Scientific Truth."*

ESSAYS SELECTED FROM "LAY SERMONS, ADDRESSES, AND REVIEWS." Second Edition. Crown 8vo. 1s.

CRITIQUES AND ADDRESSES. 8vo. 10s. 6d.

Contents :—1. *Administrative Nihilism.* 2. *The School Boards : what they can do, and what they may do.* 3. *On Medical Education.* 4. *Yeast.* 5. *On the Formation of Coal.* 6. *On Coral and Coral Reefs.* 7. *On the Methods and Results of Ethnology.* 8. *On some Fixed Points in British Ethnology.* 9. *Palæontology*

Huxley (Professor)—*continued.*

and the Doctrine of Evolution. 10. Biogenesis and Abiogenesis. 11. Mr. Darwin's Critics. 12. The Genealogy of Animals. 13. Bishop Berkeley on the Metaphysics of Sensation.

LESSONS IN ELEMENTARY PHYSIOLOGY. With numerous Illustrations. New Edition. Fcap. 8vo. 4s. 6d.

"*Pure gold throughout.*"—Guardian. "*Unquestionably the clearest and most complete elementary treatise on this subject that we possess in any language.*"—Westminster Review.

AMERICAN ADDRESSES : with a Lecture on the Study of Biology. 8vo. 6s. 6d.

PHYSIOGRAPHY : An Introduction to the Study of Nature. With Coloured Plates and numerous Woodcuts. New Edition. Crown 8vo. 7s. 6d.

"*It would be hardly possible to place a more useful or suggestive book in the hands of learners and teachers, or one that is better calculated to make physiography a favourite subject in the science schools.*"—Academy.

Jellet (John H., B.D.).—A TREATISE ON THE THEORY OF FRICTION. By JOHN H. JELLET, B.D., Senior Fellow of Trinity College, Dublin ; President of the Royal Irish Academy. 8vo. 8s. 6d.

Jones.—Works by FRANCIS JONES, F.R.S.E., F.C.S., Chemical Master in the Grammar School, Manchester.

THE OWENS COLLEGE JUNIOR COURSE OF PRACTICAL CHEMISTRY. With Preface by Professor ROSCOE. New Edition. 18mo. With Illustrations. 2s. 6d.

QUESTIONS ON CHEMISTRY. A Series of Problems and Exercises in Inorganic and Organic Chemistry. 18mo. 3s.

Kingsley.—GLAUCUS : OR, THE WONDERS OF THE SHORE. By CHARLES KINGSLEY, Canon of Westminster. New Edition, with numerous Coloured Plates. Crown 8vo. 6s.

Landauer.—BLOWPIPE ANALYSIS. By J. LANDAUER. Authorised English Edition, by JAMES TAYLOR and W. E. KAY, of the Owens College, Manchester. With Illustrations. Extra fcap. 8vo. 4s 6d.

Langdon.—THE APPLICATION OF ELECTRICITY TO RAILWAY WORKING. By W. E. LANGDON, Member of the Society of Telegraph Engineers. With numerous Illustrations. Extra fcap. 8vo. 4s. 6d.

"*There is no officer in the telegraph service who will not profit by the study of this book.*"—Mining Journal.

Lockyer (J. N.).—Works by J. NORMAN LOCKYER, F.R.S.—
ELEMENTARY LESSONS IN ASTRONOMY. With numerous Illustrations. New Edition. Fcap. 8vo. 5s. 6d.
" The book is full, clear, sound, and worthy of attention, not only as a popular exposition, but as a scientific 'Index.'" — Athenæum.
THE SPECTROSCOPE AND ITS APPLICATIONS. By J. NORMAN LOCKYER, F.R.S. With Coloured Plate and numerous Illustrations. Second Edition. Crown 8vo. 3s. 6d.
CONTRIBUTIONS TO SOLAR PHYSICS. By J. NORMAN LOCKYER, F.R.S. I. A Popular Account of Inquiries into the Physical Constitution of the Sun, with especial reference to Recent Spectroscopic Researches. II. Communications to the Royal Society of London and the French Academy of Sciences, with Notes. Illustrated by 7 Coloured Lithographic Plates and 175 Woodcuts. Royal 8vo. cloth, extra gilt, price 31s. 6d.
" The book may be taken as an authentic exposition of the present state of science in connection with the important subject of spectroscopic analysis. . . . Even the unscientific public may derive much information from it."—Daily News.
PRIMER OF ASTRONOMY. With Illustrations. 18mo. 1s.

Lockyer and Seabroke.—STAR-GAZING: PAST AND PRESENT. An Introduction to Instrumental Astronomy. By J. N. LOCKYER, F.R.S. Expanded from Shorthand Notes of a Course of Royal Institution Lectures with the assistance of G. M. SEABROKE, F.R.A.S. With numerous Illustrations. Royal 8vo. 21s.
" A book of great interest and utility to the astronomical student." --Athenæum.

Lubbock.—Works by SIR JOHN LUBBOCK, M.P., F.R.S., D.C.L.:
THE ORIGIN AND METAMORPHOSES OF INSECTS. With Numerous Illustrations. Second Edition. Crown 8vo. 3s. 6d.
"As a summary of the phenomena of insect metamorphoses his little book is of great value, and will be read with interest and profit by all students of natural history. The whole chapter on the origin of insects is most interesting and valuable. The illustrations are numerous and good."—Westminster Review.
ON BRITISH WILD FLOWERS CONSIDERED IN RELATION TO INSECTS. With Numerous Illustrations. Second Edition. Crown 8vo. 4s. 6d.
SCIENTIFIC LECTURES. With Illustrations. 8vo. 8s. 6d.
CONTENTS:—*Flowers and Insects—Plants and Insects—The Habits of Ants—Introduction to the Study of Prehistoric Archæology, &c.*

Macmillan (Rev. Hugh).—For other Works by the same Author, see THEOLOGICAL CATALOGUE.
HOLIDAYS ON HIGH LANDS; or, Rambles and Incidents in search of Alpine Plants. Globe 8vo. cloth. 6s.

Macmillan (Rev. Hugh)—*continued.*

FIRST FORMS OF VEGETATION. Second Edition, corrected and enlarged, with Coloured Frontispiece and numerous Illustrations. Globe 8vo. 6s.

The first edition of this book was published under the name of "Footnotes from the Page of Nature; or, First Forms of Vegetation. Probably the best popular guide to the study of mosses, lichens, and fungi ever written. Its practical value as a help to the student and collector cannot be exaggerated."—Manchester Examiner.

Mansfield (C. B.).—Works by the late C. B. MANSFIELD :—

A THEORY OF SALTS. A Treatise on the Constitution of Bipolar (two-membered) Chemical Compounds. Crown 8vo. 14s.

AËRIAL NAVIGATION. The Problem, with Hints for its Solution. Edited by R. B. MANSFIELD. With a Preface by J. M. LUDLOW. With Illustrations. Crown 8vo. 10s. 6d.

Mayer.—SOUND : a Series of Simple, Entertaining, and Inexpensive Experiments in the Phenomena of Sound, for the Use of Students of every age. By A. M. MAYER, Professor of Physics in the Stevens Institute of Technology, &c. With numerous Illustrations. Crown 8vo. 3s. 6d.

Mayer and Barnard.—LIGHT. A Series of Simple, Entertaining, and Useful Experiments in the Phenomena of Light, for the use of Students of every age. By A. M. MAYER and C. BARNARD. With Illustrations. Crown 8vo. 2s. 6d.

Miall.—STUDIES IN COMPARATIVE ANATOMY. No. 1, The Skull of the Crocodile. A Manual for Students. By L. C. MIALL, Professor of Biology in Yorkshire College. 8vo. 2s. 6d. No. 2, The Anatomy of the Indian Elephant. By L. C. MIALL and F. GREENWOOD. With Plates. 5s.

Miller.—THE ROMANCE OF ASTRONOMY. By R. KALLEY MILLER, M.A., Fellow and Assistant Tutor of St. Peter's College, Cambridge. Second Edition, revised and enlarged. Crown 8vo. 4s. 6d.

Mivart (St. George).—Works by ST. GEORGE MIVART, F.R.S. &c., Lecturer in Comparative Anatomy at St. Mary's Hospital:—

ON THE GENESIS OF SPECIES. Second Edition, to which notes have been added in reference and reply to Darwin's "Descent of Man." With numerous Illustrations. Crown 8vo. 9s.

"In no work in the English language has this great controversy been treated at once with the same broad and vigorous grasp of facts, and the same liberal and candid temper."—Saturday Review.

Mivart (St. George)—*continued.*
THE COMMON FROG. With Numerous Illustrations. Crown
8vo. 3*s.* 6*d.* (Nature Series.)
" *It is an able monogram of the Frog, and something more. It
throws valuable crosslights over wide portions of animated nature.
Would that such works were more plentiful.*"—Quarterly Journal
of Science.

Moseley.—NOTES BY A NATURALIST ON THE "CHAL-
LENGER," being an account of various observations made during
the voyage of H.M.S. "Challenger" round the world in the years
1872—76. By H. N. MOSELEY, M.A.. F.R.S., Member of the
Scientific Staff of the "Challenger." With Map, Coloured
Plates, and Woodcuts. 8vo. 21*s.*
" *This is certainly the most interesting and suggestive book, descriptive of a naturalist's travels, which has been published since Mr.
Darwin's 'Journal of Researches' appeared, now more than forty
years ago. That it is worthy to be placed alongside that delightful
record of the impressions, speculations, and reflections of a master
mind, is, we do not doubt, the highest praise which Mr. Moseley
would desire for his book, and we do not hesitate to say that such
praise is its desert.*"—Nature.

Muir.—PRACTICAL CHEMISTRY FOR MEDICAL STU-
DENTS. Specially arranged for the first M. B. Course. By
M. M. PATTISON MUIR, F.R.S.E. Fcap. 8vo. 1*s.* 6*d.*

Murphy.— HABIT AND INTELLIGENCE: a Series of
Essays on the Laws of Life and Mind. By JOSEPH JOHN
MURPHY. Second Edition, thoroughly revised and mostly re-
written. With Illustrations. 8vo. 16*s.*

Nature.—A WEEKLY ILLUSTRATED JOURNAL OF
SCIENCE. Published every Thursday. Price 6*d.* Monthly
Parts, 2*s.* and 2*s.* 6*d.* ; Half-yearly Volumes, 15*s.* Cases for binding
Vols. 1*s.* 6*d.*
" *This able and well-edited Journal, which posts up the science of
the day promptly, and promises to be of signal service to students*
*and savants. . . . . Scarcely any expressions that we can employ
would exaggerate our sense of the moral and theological value of
the work.*"—British Quarterly Review.

Newcomb.—POPULAR ASTRONOMY. By SIMON NEW-
COMB, LL.D., Professor U.S. Naval Observatory. With 112
Engravings and Five Maps of the Stars. 8vo. 18*s.*
" *As affording a thoroughly reliable foundation for more advanced
reading, Professor Newcomb's 'Popular Astronomy' is deserving
of strong recommendation.*"—Nature.

Oliver.—Works by DANIEL OLIVER, F.R.S., F.L.S., Professor of
Botany in University College, London, and Keeper of the Herbarium and Library of the Royal Gardens, Kew :—

Oliver—*continued.*
LESSONS IN ELEMENTARY BOTANY. With nearly Two
Hundred Illustrations. New Edition. Fcap. 8vo. 4s. 6d.
FIRST BOOK OF INDIAN BOTANY. With numerous
Illustrations. Extra fcap. 8vo. 6s. 6d.
"*It contains a well-digested summary of all essential knowledge
pertaining to Indian Botany, wrought out in accordance with the
best principles of scientific arrangement.*"—Allen's Indian Mail.

Pasteur.—STUDIES ON FERMENTATION. The Diseases
of Beer; their Causes and Means of Preventing them. By L.
PASTEUR. A Translation of "Études sur la Bière," With Notes,
Illustrations, &c. By F. FAULKNER and D. C. ROBB, B.A.
8vo. 21s.

Pennington.—NOTES ON THE BARROWS AND BONE
CAVES OF DERBYSHIRE. With an account of a Descent
into Elden Hole. By ROOKE PENNINGTON, B.A., LL.B.,
F.G.S. 8vo. 6s.

Penrose (F. C.)—ON A METHOD OF PREDICTING BY
GRAPHICAL CONSTRUCTION, OCCULTATIONS OF
STARS BY THE MOON, AND SOLAR ECLIPSES FOR
ANY GIVEN PLACE. Together with more rigorous methods
for the Accurate Calculation of Longitude. By F. C. PENROSE,
F.R.A.S. With Charts, Tables, &c. 4to. 12s.

Perry.—AN ELEMENTARY TREATISE ON STEAM. By
JOHN PERRY, B.E., Professor of Engineering, Imperial College of
Engineering, Yedo. With numerous Woodcuts, Numerical Examples, and Exercises. 18mo. 4s. 6d.
"*Mr. Perry has in this compact little volume brought together an
immense amount of information, new told, regarding steam and
its application, not the least of its merits being that it is suited to
the capacities alike of the tyro in engineering science or the better
grade of artisan.*"—Iron.

Pickering.—ELEMENTS OF PHYSICAL MANIPULATION.
By E. C. PICKERING, Thayer Professor of Physics in the Massa-
chusetts Institute of Technology. Part I., medium 8vo. 10s. 6d.
Part II., 10s. 6d.
"*When finished 'Physical Manipulation' will no doubt be considered the best and most complete text-book on the subject of
which it treats.*"—Nature.

Prestwich.—THE PAST AND FUTURE OF GEOLOGY.
An Inaugural Lecture, by J. PRESTWICH, M.A., F.R.S., &c.,
Professor of Geology, Oxford. 8vo. 2s.

Radcliffe.—PROTEUS: OR UNITY IN NATURE. By. C.
B. RADCLIFFE, M.D., Author of "Vital Motion as a mode of
Physical Motion. Second Edition. 8vo. 7s. 6d.

Rendu.—THE THEORY OF THE GLACIERS OF SAVOY. By M. LE CHANOINE RENDU. Translated by A. WELLS, Q.C., late President of the Alpine Club. To which are added, the Original Memoir and Supplementary Articles by Professors TAIT and RUS-KIN. Edited with Introductory remarks by GEORGE FORBES, B.A., Professor of Natural Philosophy in the Andersonian University, Glasgow. 8vo. 7s. 6d.

Roscoe.—Works by HENRY E. ROSCOE, F.R.S., Professor of Chemistry in Owens College, Manchester :—

LESSONS IN ELEMENTARY CHEMISTRY, INORGANIC AND ORGANIC. With numerous Illustrations and Chromo-litho of the Solar Spectrum, and of the Alkalis and Alkaline Earths. New Edition. Fcap. 8vo. 4s. 6d.

CHEMICAL PROBLEMS, adapted to the above by Professor THORPE. Fifth Edition, with Key. 2s.
"*We unhesitatingly pronounce it the best of all our elementary treatises on Chemistry.*"—Medical Times.

PRIMER OF CHEMISTRY. Illustrated. 18mo. 1s.

Roscoe and Schorlemmer.—A TREATISE ON IN-ORGANIC CHEMISTRY. With numerous Illustrations. By PROFESSORS ROSCOE and SCHORLEMMER.

Vol. I., The Non-metallic Elements. 8vo. 21s.

Vol. II., Part I. Metals. 8vo. 18s.

Vol. II., Part II. Metals. 8vo. 18s.

"*Regarded as a treatise on the Non-metallic Elements, there can be no doubt that this volume is incomparably the most satisfactory one of which we are in possession.*"—Spectator.

"*It would be difficult to praise the work too highly. All the merits which we noticed in the first volume are conspicuous in the second. The arrangement is clear and scientific; the facts gained by modern research are fairly represented and judiciously selected; and the style throughout is singularly lucid.*"—Lancet.

Rumford (Count).—THE LIFE AND COMPLETE WORKS OF BENJAMIN THOMPSON, COUNT RUMFORD. With Notices of his Daughter. By GEORGE ELLIS. With Portrait. Five Vols. 8vo. 4l. 14s. 6d.

Schorlemmer.—A MANUAL OF THE CHEMISTRY OF THE CARBON COMPOUNDS OR ORGANIC CHEMISTRY. By C. SCHORLEMMER, F.R.S., Lecturer in Organic Chemistry in Owens College, Manchester. 8vo. 14s.
"*It appears to us to be as complete a manual of the metamorphoses of carbon as could be at present produced, and it must prove eminently useful to the chemical student.*"—Athenæum.

B

Shann.—AN ELEMENTARY TREATISE ON HEAT, IN RELATION TO STEAM AND THE STEAM ENGINE. By G. SHANN, M.A. With Illustrations. Crown 8vo. 4s. 6d.

Smith.—HISTORIA FILICUM : An Exposition of the Nature, Number, and Organography of Ferns, and Review of the Principles upon which Genera are founded, and the Systems of Classification of the principal Authors, with a new General Arrangement, &c. By J. SMITH. A. L.S., ex-Curator of the Royal Botanic Garden, Kew. With Thirty Lithographic Plates by W. H. FITCH, F.L.S. Crown 8vo. 12s. 6d.
" No one anxious to work up a thorough knowledge of ferns can afford to do without it."—Gardener's Chronicle.

South Kensington Science Lectures.

Vol. I.—Containing Lectures by Captain ABNEY, F.RS., Professor STOKES, Professor KENNEDY, F. J. BRAMWELL, F.R.S., Professor G. FORBES, H. C. SORBY, F.R.S., J. T. BOTTOMLEY, F.R.S.E., S. H. VINES, B.Sc., and Professor CAREY FOSTER. Crown 8vo. 6s.   [Vol. II. *nearly ready*.

Vol. II.—Containing Lectures by W. SPOTTISWOODE, P.R.S., Prof. FORBES, H. W. CHISHOLM, Prof. T. F. PIGOT, W. FROUDE, F.R.S., Dr. SIEMENS, Prof. BARRETT, Dr. BURDEN-SANDERSON, Dr. LAUDER BRUNTON, F.R.S., Prof. McLEOD, Prof. ROSCOE, F.R.S., &c. Crown 8vo. 6s.

Spottiswoode.—POLARIZATION OF LIGHT. By W. SPOTTISWOODE, President of the Royal Society. With numerous Illustrations. Second Edition. Cr. 8vo. 3s. 6d. (Nature Series.)
" The illustrations are exceedingly well adapted to assist in making the text comprehensible."—Athenæum. *" A clear, trustworthy manual."*—Standard.

Stewart (B.).—Works by BALFOUR STEWART, F.R.S.,|Professor of Natural Philosophy in Owens College, Manchester :—

LESSONS IN ELEMENTARY PHYSICS. With numerous Illustrations and Chromoliths of the Spectra of the Sun, Stars, and Nebulæ. New Edition. Fcap. 8vo. 4s. 6d.
The Educational Times *calls this the beau-idéal of a scientific text-book, clear, accurate, and thorough."*

PRIMER OF PHYSICS. With Illustrations. New Edition, with Questions. 18mo. 1s.

Stewart and Tait.—THE UNSEEN UNIVERSE: or, Physical Speculations on a Future State. By BALFOUR STEWART, F.R.S., and P. G. TAIT, M.A. Sixth Edition. Crown 8vo. 6s.
" The book is one which well deserves the attention of thoughtful and religious readers. . . . It is a perfectly sober inquiry, on scientific grounds, into the possibilities of a future existence."—Guardian.

Stone.—ELEMENTARY LESSONS ON SOUND. By Dr. W. H. STONE, Lecturer on Physics at St. Thomas' Hospital. With Illustrations. Fcap. 8vo. 3s. 6d.

Tait.—LECTURES ON SOME RECENT ADVANCES IN PHYSICAL SCIENCE. By P. G. TAIT, M.A., Professor of Philosophy in the University of Edinburgh. Second edition, revised and enlarged, with the Lecture on Force delivered before the British Association. Crown 8vo. 9s.

Tanner.—FIRST PRINCIPLES OF AGRICULTURE. By HENRY TANNER, F.C.S., Professor of Agricultural Science, University College, Aberystwith, Examiner in the Principles of Agriculture under the Government Department of Science. 18mo. 1s.

Taylor.—SOUND AND MUSIC : A Non-Mathematical Treatise on the Physical Constitution of Musical Sounds and Harmony, including the Chief Acoustical Discoveries of Professor Helmholtz. By SEDLEY TAYLOR, M.A., late Fellow of Trinity College, Cambridge. Large crown 8vo. 8s. 6d.

"*In no previous scientific treatise do we remember so exhaustive and so richly illustrated a description of forms of vibration and of wave-moti n in fluids.*"—Musical Standard.

Thomson.—Works by SIR WYVILLE THOMSON, K.C.B., F.R.S. THE DEPTHS OF THE SEA : An Account of the General Results of the Dredging Cruises of H.M.SS. "Porcupine" and "Lightning" during the Summers of 1868-69 and 70, under the scientific direction of Dr. Carpenter, F.R.S., J. Gwyn Jeffreys, F.R.S., and Sir Wyville Thomson, F.R.S. With nearly 100 Illustrations and 8 coloured Maps and Plans. Second Edition. Royal 8vo. cloth, gilt. 31s. 6d.

The Athenæum *says : "The book is full of interesting matter, and is written by a master of the art of popular exposition. It is excellently illustrated, both coloured maps and woodcuts possessing high merit. Those who have already become interested in dredging operations will of course make a point of reading this work ; those who wish to be pleasantly introduced to the subject, and rightly to appreciate the news which arrives from time to time from the 'Challenger,' should not fail to seek instruction from it.*"

THE VOYAGE OF THE "CHALLENGER."—THE ATLANTIC. A Preliminary account of the Exploring Voyages of H.M.S. "Challenger," during the year 1873 and the early part of 1876. With numerous Illustrations, Coloured Maps & Charts, & Portrait of the Author, engraved by C. H. JEENS. 2 Vols. Medium 8vo. 42s.

The Times *says :—"It is right that the public should have some authoritative account of the general results of the expedition, and*

B 2

Thomson—*continued*.

that as many of the ascertained data as may be accepted with confidence should speedily find their place in the general body of scientific knowledge. No one can be more competent than the accomplished scientific chief of the expedition to satisfy the public in this respect. . . . The paper, printing, and especially the numerous illustrations, are of the highest quality. . . . We have rarely, if ever, seen more beautiful specimens of wood engraving than abound in this work. . . . Sir Wyville Thomson's style is particularly attractive; he is easy and graceful, but vigorous and exceedingly happy in the choice of language, and throughout the work there are touches which show that science has not banished sentiment from his bosom."

Thudichum and Dupré.—A TREATISE ON THE ORIGIN, NATURE, AND VARIETIES OF WINE. Being a Complete Manual of Viticulture and Œnology. By J. L. W. THUDICHUM, M.D., and AUGUST DUPRÉ, Ph.D., Lecturer on Chemistry at Westminster Hospital. Medium 8vo. cloth gilt. 25s.

"A treatise almost unique for its usefulness either to the wine-grower, the vendor, or the consumer of wine. The analyses of wine are the most complete we have yet seen, exhibiting at a glance the constituent principles of nearly all the wines known in this country." —Wine Trade Review.

Wallace (A. R.).—Works by ALFRED RUSSEL WALLACE. CONTRIBUTIONS TO THE THEORY OF NATURAL SELECTION. A Series of Essays. New Edition, with Corrections and Additions. Crown 8vo. 8s. 6d.

The Saturday Review *says: "He has combined an abundance of fresh and original facts with a liveliness and sagacity of reasoning which are not often displayed so effectively on so small a scale."*

THE GEOGRAPHICAL DISTRIBUTION OF ANIMALS, with a study of the Relations of Living and Extinct Faunas as Elucidating the Past Changes of the Earth's Surface. 2 vols. 8vo. with Maps, and numerous Illustrations by Zwecker, 42s.

The Times *says: "Altogether it is a wonderful and fascinating story, whatever objections may be taken to theories founded upon it. Mr. Wallace has not attempted to add to its interest by any adornments of style; he has given a simple and clear statement of intrinsically interesting facts, and what he considers to be legitimate inductions from them. Naturalists ought to be grateful to him for having undertaken so toilsome a task. The work, indeed, is a credit to all concerned—the author, the publishers, the artist—unfortunately now no more—of the attractive illustrations—last but by no means least, Mr. Stanford's map-designer."*

Wallace (A. R.)—*continued.*

TROPICAL NATURE : with other Essays. 8vo. 12*s.*

"*Nowhere amid the many descriptions of the tropics that have been given is to be found a summary of the past history and actual phenomena of the tropics which gives that which is distinctive of the phases of nature in them more clearly, shortly, and impressively.*"—Saturday Review.

Warington.—THE WEEK OF CREATION; OR, THE COSMOGONY OF GENESIS CONSIDERED IN ITS RELATION TO MODERN SCIENCE. By GEORGE WARINGTON, Author of "The Historic Character of the Pentateuch Vindicated." Crown 8vo. 4*s. 6d.*

Wilson.—RELIGIO CHEMICI. By the late GEORGE WILSON, M.D., F.R.S.E., Regius Professor of Technology in the University of Edinburgh. With a Vignette beautifully engraved after a design by Sir NOEL PATON. Crown 8vo. 8*s. 6d.*

Wilson (Daniel).—CALIBAN : a Critique on Shakespeare's "Tempest" and "Midsummer Night's Dream." By DANIEL WILSON, LL.D., Professor of History and English Literature in University College, Toronto. 8vo. 10*s. 6d.*

"*The whole volume is most rich in the eloquence of thought and imagination as well as of words. It is a choice contribution at once to science, theology, religion, and literature.*"—British Quarterly Review.

Wright.—METALS AND THEIR CHIEF INDUSTRIAL APPLICATIONS. By C. ALDER WRIGHT, D.Sc., &c., Lecturer on Chemistry in St. Mary's Hospital School. Extra fcap. 8vo. 3*s. 6d.*

Wurtz.—A HISTORY OF CHEMICAL THEORY, from the Age of Lavoisier down to the present time. By AD. WURTZ. Translated by HENRY WATTS, F.R.S. Crown 8vo. 6*s.*

"*The discourse, as a résumé of chemical theory and research, unites singular luminousness and grasp. A few judicious notes are added by the translator.*"—Pall Mall Gazette. "*The treatment of the subject is admirable, and the translator has evidently done his duty most efficiently.*"—Westminster Review.

SCIENCE PRIMERS FOR ELEMENTARY SCHOOLS.

Under the joint Editorship of Professors HUXLEY, ROSCOE, and BALFOUR STEWART.

Introductory. By Professor HUXLEY, F.R.S.   [*Nearly ready.*

Chemistry.—By H. E. ROSCOE, F.R.S., Professor of Chemistry in Owens College, Manchester. With numerous Illustrations. 18mo. 1*s.* New Edition. With Questions.

Physics.— By BALFOUR STEWART, F.R.S., Professor of Natural Philosophy in Owens College, Manchester. With numerous Illustrations. 18mo. 1*s.* New Edition. With Questions.

Physical Geography. — By ARCHIBALD GEIKIE, F.R.S., Murchison Professor of Geology and Mineralogy at Edinburgh. With numerous Illustrations. New Edition with Questions. 18mo. 1*s.*

Geology.—By Professor GEIKIE, F.R.S. With numerous Illustrations. New Edition. 18mo. cloth. 1*s.*

Physiology.—By MICHAEL FOSTER, M.D., F.R.S. Wit numerous Illustrations. New Edition. 18mo. 1*s.*

Astronomy.—By J. NORMAN LOCKYER, F.R.S. With numerous Illustrations. New Edition. 18mo. 1*s.*

Botany.—By Sir J. D. HOOKER, K.C.S.I., C.B., F.R.S. With numerous Illustrations. New Edition. 18mo. 1*s.*

Logic.—By Professor STANLEY JEVONS, F.R.S. New Edition. 18mo. 1*s.*

Political Economy.—By Professor STANLEY JEVONS, F.R.S. 18mo. 1*s.*

Others in preparation.   ·

ELEMENTARY SCIENCE CLASS-BOOKS.

Astronomy.—By the ASTRONOMER ROYAL. POPULAR ASTRONOMY. With Illustrations. By Sir G. B. AIRY, K.C.B., Astronomer Royal. New Edition. 18mo. 4*s.* 6*d.*

Astronomy.—ELEMENTARY LESSONS IN ASTRONOMY. With Coloured Diagram of the Spectra of the Sun, Stars, and Nebulæ, and numerous Illustrations. By J. NORMAN LOCKYER, F.R.S. New Edition. Fcap. 8vo. 5*s.* 6*d.*

Elementary Science Class-books—*continued.*

QUESTIONS ON LOCKYER'S ELEMENTARY LESSONS IN ASTRONOMY. For the Use of Schools. By JOHN FORBES ROBERTSON. 18mo, cloth limp. 1*s.* 6*d.*

Physiology.—LESSONS IN ELEMENTARY PHYSIOLOGY. With numerous Illustrations. By T. H. HUXLEY, F.R.S., Professor of Natural History in the Royal School of Mines. New Edition. Fcap. 8vo. 4*s.* 6*d.*

QUESTIONS ON HUXLEY'S PHYSIOLOGY FOR SCHOOLS. By T. ALCOCK, M.D. 18mo. 1*s.* 6*d.*

Botany.—LESSONS IN ELEMENTARY BOTANY. By D. OLIVER, F.R.S., F.L.S., Professor of Botany in University College, London. With nearly Two Hundred Illustrations. New Edition. Fcap. 8vo. 4*s.* 6*d.*

Chemistry.—LESSONS IN ELEMENTARY CHEMISTRY, INORGANIC AND ORGANIC. By HENRY E. ROSCOE, F.R.S., Professor of Chemistry in Owens College, Manchester. With numerous Illustrations and Chromo-Litho of the Solar Spectrum, and of the Alkalies and Alkaline Earths. New Edition. Fcap. 8vo. 4*s.* 6*d.*

A SERIES OF CHEMICAL PROBLEMS, prepared with Special Reference to the above, by T. E. THORPE, Ph.D., Professor of Chemistry in the Yorkshire College of Science, Leeds. Adapted for the preparation of Students for the Government, Science, and Society of Arts Examinations. With a Preface by Professor ROSCOE. New Edition, with Key. 18mo. 2*s.*

Practical Chemistry.—THE OWENS COLLEGE JUNIOR COURSE OF PRACTICAL CHEMISTRY. By FRANCIS JONES, F.R.S.E., F.C.S., Chemical Master in the Grammar School, Manchester. With Preface by Professor ROSCOE, and Illustrations. New Edition. 18mo. 2*s.* 6*d.*

Chemistry.—QUESTIONS ON. A Series of Problems and Exercises in Inorganic and Organic Chemistry. By F. JONES, F.R.S.E., F.C.S. 18mo. 3*s.*

Political Economy.—POLITICAL ECONOMY FOR BEGINNERS. By MILLICENT G. FAWCETT. New Edition. 18mo. 2*s.* 6*d.*

Logic.—ELEMENTARY LESSONS IN LOGIC ; Deductive and Inductive, with copious Questions and Examples, and a Vocabulary of Logical Terms. By W. STANLEY JEVONS, M.A., Professor of Political Economy in University College, London. New Edition. Fcap. 8vo. 3*s.* 6*d.*

Elementary Science Class-books—*continued.*

Physics.—LESSONS IN ELEMENTARY PHYSICS.   By BALFOUR STEWART, F.R.S., Professor of Natural Philosophy in Owens College, Manchester. With numerous Illustrations and Chromo-Litho of the Spectra of the Sun, Stars, and Nebulæ. New Edition. Fcap. 8vo. 4*s. 6d.*

Anatomy.—LESSONS IN ELEMENTARY ANATOMY. By ST. GEORGE MIVART, F.R.S., Lecturer in Comparative Anatomy at St. Mary's Hospital. With upwards of 400 Illustrations. Fcap. 8vo. 6*s. 6d.*

Mechanics.—AN ELEMENTARY TREATISE.   By A. B. W. KENNEDY, C.E , Professor of Applied Mechanics in University College, London. With Illustrations.   [*In preparation.*

Steam.—AN ELEMENTARY TREATISE. By JOHN PERRY, Professor of Engineering, Imperial College of Engineering, Yedo. With numerous Woodcuts and Numerical Examples and Exercises. 18mo. 4*s. 6d.*

Physical Geography. — ELEMENTARY LESSONS IN PHYSICAL GEOGRAPHY. By A. GEIKIE, F.R.S., Murchison Professor of Geology, &c., Edinburgh. With numerous Illustrations. Fcap. 8vo. 4*s. 6d.*
QUESTIONS ON THE SAME. 1*s. 6d.*

Geography.—CLASS-BOOK OF GEOGRAPHY. By C. B. CLARKE, M.A.. F.R.G.S. Fcap. 8vo. 2*s. 6d.*

Natural Philosophy.—NATURAL PHILOSOPHY FOR BEGINNERS. By I. TODHUNTER, M.A., F.R.S. Part I. The Properties of Solid and Fluid Bodies. 18mo. 3*s. 6d.* Part II. Sound, Light, and Heat. 18mo. 3*s. 6d.*

Sound.—AN ELEMENTARY TREATISE.   By Dr. W. H. STONE. With Illustrations. 18mo. 3*s. 6d.*

Others in Preparation.

MANUALS FOR STUDENTS.

Crown 8vo.

Dyer and Vines.—THE STRUCTURE OF PLANTS. By Professor THISELTON DYER, F.R.S., assisted by SYDNEY VINES, B.Sc., Fellow and Lecturer of Christ's College, Cambridge. With numerous Illustrations.   [*In preparation.*

Manuals for Students—*continued*.

Fawcett.—A MANUAL OF POLITICAL ECONOMY. By Professor FAWCETT, M.P. New Edition, revised and enlarged. Crown 8vo. 12*s*. 6*d*.

Fleischer.—A SYSTEM OF VOLUMETRIC ANALYSIS. Translated, with Notes and Additions, from the second German Edition, by M. M. PATTISON MUIR, F.R.S.E. With Illustrations. Crown 8vo. 7*s*. 6*d*.

Flower (W. H.).—AN INTRODUCTION TO THE OSTE-OLOGY OF THE MAMMALIA. Being the Substance of the Course of Lectures delivered at the Royal College of Surgeons of England in 1870. By Professor W. H. FLOWER, F.R.S., F.R.C.S. With numerous Illustrations. New Edition, enlarged. Crown 8vo. 10*s*. 6*d*.

Foster and Balfour.—THE ELEMENTS OF EMBRY-OLOGY. By MICHAEL FOSTER, M.D., F.R.S., and F. M. BALFOUR, M.A. Part I. crown 8vo. 7*s*. 6*d*.

Foster and Langley.—A COURSE OF ELEMENTARY PRACTICAL PHYSIOLOGY. By MICHAEL FOSTER, M.D., F.R.S., and J. N. LANGLEY, B.A. New Edition. Crown 8vo. 6*s*.

Hooker (Dr.)—THE STUDENT'S FLORA OF THE BRITISH ISLANDS. By Sir J. D. HOOKER, K.C.S.I., C.B., F.R.S., M.D., D.C.L. New Edition, revised. Globe 8vo. 10*s*. 6*d*.

Huxley.—PHYSIOGRAPHY. An Introduction to the Study of Nature. By Professor HUXLEY, F.R.S. With numerous Illustrations, and Coloured Plates. New Edition. Crown 8vo. 7*s*. 6*d*.

Huxley and Martin.—A COURSE OF PRACTICAL IN-STRUCTION IN ELEMENTARY BIOLOGY. By Professor HUXLEY, F.R.S., assisted by H. N. MARTIN, M.B., D.Sc. New Edition, revised. Crown 8vo. 6*s*.

Huxley and Parker.—ELEMENTARY BIOLOGY. PART II. By Professor HUXLEY, F.R.S., assisted by — PARKER. With Illustrations. [*In preparation.*

Jevons.—THE PRINCIPLES OF SCIENCE. A Treatise on Logic and Scientific Method. By Professor W. STANLEY JEVONS, LL.D., F.R.S., New and Revised Edition. Crown 8vo. 12*s*. 6*d*.

Manuals for Students—*continued.*

Oliver (Professor).—FIRST BOOK OF INDIAN BOTANY. By Professor DANIEL OLIVER, F.R.S., F.L.S., Keeper of the Herbarium and Library of the Royal Gardens, Kew. With numerous Illustrations. Extra fcap. 8vo. *6s. 6d.*

Parker and Bettany.—THE MORPHOLOGY OF THE SKULL. By Professor PARKER and G. T. BETTANY. Illustrated. Crown 8vo. *10s. 6d.*

Tait.—AN ELEMENTARY TREATISE ON HEAT. By Professor TAIT, F.R.S.E. Illustrated.   [*In the Press.*

Thomson.— ZOOLOGY. By Sir C. WYVILLE THOMSON, F.R.S. Illustrated.   [*In preparation.*

Tylor and Lankester.—ANTHROPOLOGY. By E. B. TYLOR, M.A., F.R.S., and Professor E. RAY LANKESTER, M.A., F.R.S. Illustrated.   [*In preparation.*

Other volumes of these Manuals will follow.

WORKS ON MENTAL AND MORAL PHILOSOPHY, AND ALLIED SUBJECTS.

Aristotle.—AN INTRODUCTION TO ARISTOTLE'S RHETORIC. With Analysis, Notes, and Appendices. By E. M. COPE, Trinity College, Cambridge. 8vo. 14*s.*

ARISTOTLE ON FALLACIES; OR, THE SOPHISTICI ELENCHI. With a Translation and Notes by EDWARD POSTE, M.A., Fellow of Oriel College, Oxford. 8vo. 8*s.* 6*d.*

Balfour.—A DEFENCE OF PHILOSOPHIC DOUBT: being an Essay on the Foundations of Belief. By A. J. BALFOUR, M.P. 8vo. 12*s.*

"*Mr. Balfour's criticism is exceedingly brilliant and suggestive.*"— Pall Mall Gazette.

"*An able and refreshing contribution to one of the burning questions of the age, and deserves to make its mark in the fierce battle now raging between science and theology.*"—Athenæum.

Birks.—Works by the Rev. T. R. BIRKS, Professor of Moral Philosophy, Cambridge :—
FIRST PRINCIPLES OF MORAL SCIENCE; or, a First Course of Lectures delivered in the University of Cambridge. Crown 8vo. 8*s.* 6*d.*

This work treats of three topics all preliminary to the direct exposition of Moral Philosophy. These are the Certainty and Dignity of Moral Science, its Spiritual Geography, or relation to other main subjects of human thought, and its Formative Principles, or some elementary truths on which its whole development must depend.

MODERN UTILITARIANISM; or, The Systems of Paley, Bentham, and Mill, Examined and Compared. Crown 8vo. 6*s.* 6*d.*

MODERN PHYSICAL FATALISM, AND THE DOCTRINE OF EVOLUTION; including an Examination of Herbert Spencer's First Principles. Crown 8vo. 6*s.*

SUPERNATURAL REVELATION; or, First Principles of Moral Theology. 8vo. 8*s.*

Boole. — AN INVESTIGATION OF THE LAWS OF THOUGHT, ON WHICH ARE FOUNDED THE MATHEMATICAL THEORIES OF LOGIC AND PROBABILITIES. By GEORGE BOOLE, LL.D., Professor of Mathematics in the Queen's University, Ireland, &c. 8vo. 14s.

Butler. — LECTURES ON THE HISTORY OF ANCIENT PHILOSOPHY. By W. ARCHER BUTLER, late Professor of Moral Philosophy in the University of Dublin. Edited from the Author's MSS., with Notes, by WILLIAM HEPWORTH THOMPSON, M.A., Master of Trinity College, and Regius Professor of Greek in the University of Cambridge. New and Cheaper Edition, revised by the Editor. 8vo. 12s.

Caird. — A CRITICAL ACCOUNT OF THE PHILOSOPHY OF KANT. With an Historical Introduction. By E. CAIRD, M.A., Professor of Moral Philosophy in the University of Glasgow. 8vo. 18s.

Calderwood. — Works by the Rev. HENRY CALDERWOOD, M.A., LL.D., Professor of Moral Philosophy in the University of Edinburgh :—

PHILOSOPHY OF THE INFINITE : A Treatise on Man's Knowledge of the Infinite Being, in answer to Sir W. Hamilton and Dr. Mansel. Cheaper Edition. 8vo. 7s. 6d.

"A book of great ability . . . . written in a clear stile, and may be easily understood by even those who are not versed in such discussions."—British Quarterly Review.

A HANDBOOK OF MORAL PHILOSOPHY. Sixth Edition. Crown 8vo. 6s.

"It is, we feel convinced, the best handbook on the subject, intellectually and morally, and does infinite credit to its author."—Standard. *"A compact and useful work, going over a great deal of ground in a manner adapted to suggest and facilitate further study. . . . His book will be an assistance to many students outside his own University of Edinburgh.* —Guardian.

THE RELATIONS OF MIND AND BRAIN. 8vo. 12s.

" It should be of real service as a clear exposition and a searching criticism of cerebral pyschology."—Westminster Review. *" Altogether his work is probably the best combination to be found at present in England of exposition and criticism on the subject of physiological psychology."*—The Academy.

Clifford. — LECTURES AND ESSAYS. By the late Professor W. K. CLIFFORD, F.R.S. Edited by LESLIE STEPHEN and FREDERICK POLLOCK, with Introduction by F. POLLOCK. Two Portraits. 2 vols. 8vo. 25s.

Clifford—*continued.*

" *The* Times *of October 22nd says :—"Many a friend of the author on first taking up these volumes and remembering his versatile genius and his keen enjoyment of all realms of intellectual activity must have trembled, lest they should be found to consist of fragmentary pieces of work, too disconnected to do justice to his powers of consecutive reading, and too varied to have any effect as a whole. Fortunately these fears are groundless. . . . It is not only in subject that the various papers are closely related. There is also a singular consistency of view and of method throughout. . . . It is in the social and metaphysical subjects that the richness of his intellect shows itself, most forcibly in the rarity and originality of the ideas which he presents to us. To appreciate this variety it is necessary to read the book itself, for it treats in some form or other of all the subjects of deepest interest in this age of questioning.*"

Fiske.—OUTLINES OF COSMIC PHILOSOPHY, BASED ON THE DOCTRINE OF EVOLUTION, WITH CRITICISMS ON THE POSITIVE PHILOSOPHY. By JOHN FISKE, M.A., LL.B., formerly Lecturer on Philosophy at Harvard University. 2 vols. 8vo. 25*s.*
" *The work constitutes a very effective encyclopædia of the evolutionary philosophy, and is well worth the study of all who wish to see at once the entire scope and purport of the scientific dogmatism of the day.*"—Saturday Review.

Harper.—THE METAPHYSICS OF THE SCHOOL. By the Rev. THOMAS HARPER (S.J.). In 5 vols. 8vo.
[*Vol I. in November.*

Herbert.—THE REALISTIC ASSUMPTIONS OF MODERN SCIENCE EXAMINED. By T. M. HERBERT, M.A., late Professor of Philosophy, &c., in the Lancashire Independent College, Manchester. 8vo. 14*s.*

" *Mr. Herbert's work appears to us one of real ability and importance. The author has shown himself well trained in philosophical literature, and possessed of high critical and speculative powers.*"— Mind.

Jardine.—THE ELEMENTS OF THE PSYCHOLOGY OF COGNITION. By ROBERT JARDINE, B.D., D.Sc., Principal of the General Assembly's College, Calcutta, and Fellow of the University of Calcutta. Crown 8vo. 6*s.* 6*d.*

Jevons.—Works by W. STANLEY JEVONS, LL.D., M.A., F.R.S., Professor of Political Economy, University College, London.

Jevons—*continued.*

THE PRINCIPLES OF SCIENCE. A Treatise on Logic and Scientific Method. New and Cheaper Edition, revised. Crown 8vo. 12s. 6d.

"*No one in future can be said to have any true knowledge of what has been done in the way of logical and scientific method in England without having carefully studied Professor Jevons' book.*"—Spectator.

THE SUBSTITUTION OF SIMILARS, the True Principle of Reasoning. Derived from a Modification of Aristotle's Dictum. Fcap. 8vo. 2s. 6d.

ELEMENTARY LESSONS IN LOGIC, DEDUCTIVE AND INDUCTIVE. With Questions, Examples, and Vocabulary of Logical Terms. New Edition. Fcap. 8vo. 3s. 6d.

PRIMER OF LOGIC. New Edition. 18mo. 1s.

Maccoll.—THE GREEK SCEPTICS, from Pyrrho to Sextus. An Essay which obtained the Hare Prize in the year 1868. By NORMAN MACCOLL, B.A., Scholar of Downing College, Cambridge. Crown 8vo. 3s. 6d.

M'Cosh.—Works by JAMES M'COSH, LL.D., President of Princeton College, New Jersey, U.S.

"*He certainly shows himself skilful in that application of logic to psychology, in that inductive science of the human mind which is the fine side of English philosophy. His philosophy as a whole is worthy of attention.*"—Revue de Deux Mondes.

THE METHOD OF THE DIVINE GOVERNMENT, Physical and Moral. Tenth Edition. 8vo. 10s. 6d.

"*This work is distinguished from other similar ones by its being based upon a thorough study of physical science, and an accurate knowledge of its present condition, and by its entering in a deeper and more unfettered manner than its predecessors upon the discussion of the appropriate psychological, ethical, and theological questions. The author keeps aloof at once from the à priori idealism and dreaminess of German speculation since Schelling, and from the onesidedness and narrowness of the empiricism and positivism which have so prevailed in England.*"—Dr. Ulrici, in "Zeitschrift für Philosophie."

THE INTUITIONS OF THE MIND. A New Edition. 8vo. cloth. 10s. 6d.

"*The undertaking to adjust the claims of the sensational and intuitional philosophies, and of the à posteriori and à priori methods, is accomplished in this work with a great amount of success.*"—Westminster Review. "*I value it for its large acquaintance with English Philosophy, which has not led him to neglect the great German works. I admire the moderation and clearness, as well as comprehensiveness, of the author's views.*"—Dr. Dörner, of Berlin.

M'Cosh—*continued.*

AN EXAMINATION OF MR. J. S. MILL'S PHILOSOPHY:
Being a Defence of Fundamental Truth. Second edition, with
additions. 10s. 6d.

*"Such a work greatly needed to be done, and the author was the man
to do it. This volume is important, not merely in reference to the
views of Mr. Mill, but of the whole school of writers, past and
present, British and Continental, he so ably represents."*—Princeton
Review.

THE LAWS OF DISCURSIVE THOUGHT : Being a Text-
book of Formal Logic. Crown 8vo. 5s.
*"The amount of summarized information which it contains is very
great; and it is the only work on the very important subject with
which it deals. Never was such a work so much needed as in
the present day."*—London Quarterly Review.

CHRISTIANITY AND POSITIVISM : A Series of Lectures to
the Times on Natural Theology and Apologetics. Crown 8vo.
7s. 6d.

THE SCOTTISH PHILOSOPHY FROM HUTCHESON TO
HAMILTON, Biographical, Critical, Expository. Royal 8vo. 16s.

Masson.—RECENT BRITISH PHILOSOPHY : A Review
with Criticisms ; including some Comments on Mr. Mill's Answer
to Sir William Hamilton. By DAVID MASSON, M.A., Professor
of Rhetoric and English Literature in the University of Edinburgh.
Third Edition, with an Additional Chapter. Crown 8vo. 6s

*"We can nowhere point to a work which gives so clear an exposi-
tion of the course of philosophical speculation in Britain during
the past century, or which indicates so instructively the mutual influences of philosophic and scientific thought."*—Fortnightly Review.

Maudsley.—Works by H. MAUDSLEY, M.D., Professor of Medical
Jurisprudence in University College, London.

THE PHYSIOLOGY OF MIND ; being the First Part of a Third
Edition, Revised, Enlarged, and in great part Re-written, of "The
Physiology and Pathology of Mind." Crown 8vo. 10s. 6d.

THE PATHOLOGY OF MIND. Revised, Enlarged, and in great
part Re-written. 8vo. 18s.

BODY AND MIND : an Inquiry into their Connexion and Mutual
Influence, specially with reference to Mental Disorders. An
Enlarged and Revised edition. To which are added, Psychological
Essays. Crown 8vo. 6s. 6d.

Maurice.—Works by the Rev. FREDERICK DENISON MAURICE, M.A., Professor of Moral Philosophy in the University of Cambridge. (For other Works by the same Author, see THEOLOGICAL CATALOGUE.)

SOCIAL MORALITY. Twenty-one Lectures delivered in the University of Cambridge. New and Cheaper Edition. Crown 8vo. 10s. 6d.

" *Whilst reading it we are charmed by the freedom from exclusiveness and prejudice, the large charity, the loftiness of thought, the eagerness to recognize and appreciate whatever there is of real worth extant in the world, which animates it from one end to the other. We gain new thoughts and new ways of viewing things, even more, perhaps, from being brought for a time under the influence of so noble and spiritual a mind.*"—Athenæum.

THE CONSCIENCE : Lectures on Casuistry, delivered in the University of Cambridge. New and Cheaper Edition. Crown 8vo. 5s.

The Saturday Review *says : "We rise from them with detestation of all that is selfish and mean, and with a living impression that there is such a thing as goodness after all."*

MORAL AND METAPHYSICAL PHILOSOPHY. Vol. I. Ancient Philosophy from the First to the Thirteenth Centuries ; Vol. II. the Fourteenth Century and the French Revolution, with a glimpse into the Nineteenth Century. New Edition and Preface. 2 Vols. 8vo. 25s.

Morgan.—ANCIENT SOCIETY : or Researches in the Lines of Human Progress, from Savagery, through Barbarism to Civilisation. By LEWIS H. MORGAN, Member of the National Academy of Sciences. 8vo. 16s.

Murphy.—THE SCIENTIFIC BASES OF FAITH. By JOSEPH JOHN MURPHY, Author of " Habit and Intelligence." 8vo. 14s.

" *The book is not without substantial value ; the writer continues the work of the best apologists of the last century, it may be with less force and clearness, but still with commendable persuasiveness and tact ; and with an intelligent feeling for the changed conditions of the problem.*"—Academy.

Paradoxical Philosophy.—A Sequel to "The Unseen Universe." Crown 8vo. 7s. 6d.

Picton.—THE MYSTERY OF MATTER AND OTHER ESSAYS. By J. ALLANSON PICTON, Author of " New Theories and the Old Faith." Cheaper issue with New Preface. Crown 8vo. 6s.

Picton—*continued.*

CONTENTS :— *The Mystery of Matter—The Philosophy of Igno-rance—The Antithesis of Faith and Sight—The Essential Nature of Religion—Christian Pantheism.*

Sidgwick.—THE METHODS OF ETHICS. By HENRY SIDGWICK, M.A., Prælector in Moral and Political Philosophy in Trinity College, Cambridge. Second Edition, revised throughout with important additions. 8vo. 14s.

A SUPPLEMENT to the First Edition, containing all the important additions and alterations in the Second. 8vo. 2s.

"*This excellent and very welcome volume. . . . . Leaving to meta-physicians any further discussion that may be needed respecting the already over-discussed problem of the origin of the moral faculty, he takes it for granted as readily as the geometrician takes space for granted, or the physicist the existence of matter. But he takes little else for granted, and defining ethics as 'the science of conduct,' he carefully examines, not the various ethical systems that have been propounded by Aristotle and Aristotle's followers downwards, but the principles upon which, so far as they confine themselves to the strict province of ethics, they are based.*"—Athenæum.

Thornton.—OLD-FASHIONED ETHICS, AND COMMON-SENSE METAPHYSICS, with some of their Applications. By WILLIAM THOMAS THORNTON, Author of "A Treatise on Labour." 8vo. 10s. 6d.

The present volume deals with problems which are agitating the minds of all thoughtful men. The following are the Contents:— I. Ante-Utilitarianism. II. History's Scientific Pretensions. III. David Hume as a Metaphysician. IV. Huxleyism. V. Recent Phase of Scientific Atheism. VI. Limits of Demonstrable Theism.

Thring (E., M.A.).—THOUGHTS ON LIFE-SCIENCE. By EDWARD THRING, M.A. (Benjamin Place), Head Master of Uppingham School. New Edition, enlarged and revised. Crown 8vo. 7s. 6d.

Venn.—THE LOGIC OF CHANCE: An Essay on the Founda-tions and Province of the Theory of Probability, with especial reference to its logical bearings, and its application to Moral and Social Science. By JOHN VENN, M.A., Fellow and Lecturer of Gonville and Caius College, Cambridge. Second Edition, re-written and greatly enlarged. Crown 8vo. 10s. 6d.

" *One of the most thoughtful and philosophical treatises on any sub-ject connected with logic and evidence which has been produced in this or any other country for many years.*"—Mill's Logic, vol. ii. p. 77. Seventh Edition.

C

Published every Thursday, price 6d.; Monthly Parts 2s. and 2s. 6d., Half-Yearly Volumes, 15s.

NATURE:

AN ILLUSTRATED JOURNAL OF SCIENCE.

NATURE expounds in a popular and yet authentic manner, the GRAND RESULTS OF SCIENTIFIC RESEARCH, discussing the most recent scientific discoveries, and pointing out the bearing of Science upon civilisation and progress, and its claims to a more general recognition, as well as to a higher place in the educational system of the country.

It contains original articles on all subjects within the domain of Science ; Reviews setting forth the nature and value of recent Scientific Works ; Correspondence Columns, forming a medium of Scientific discussion and of intercommunication among the most distinguished men of Science, Serial Columns, giving the gist of the most important papers appearing in Scientific Journals, both Home and Foreign ; Transactions of the principal Scientific Societies and Academies of the World, Notes, &c.

In Schools where Science is included in the regular course of studies, this paper will be most acceptable, as it tells what is doing in Science all over the world, is popular without lowering the standard of Science, and by it a vast amount of information is brought within a small compass, and students are directed to the best sources for what they need. The various questions connected with Science teaching in schools are also fully discussed, and the best methods of teaching are indicated.

www.ingramcontent.com/pod-product-compliance
Lightning Source LLC
Chambersburg PA
CBHW020513270326
41926CB00008B/854